INSIGHT **CITY GUIDE**

ST PETERSBURG

D0168194

APA PUBLICATIONS

Part of the Langenscheidt Publishing Group

✵ INSIGHT GUIDE
ᔆᵀPETERSBURG

Editor
Jason Mitchell
Writer and Updater
Shura Collinson
Art Director
Klaus Geisler
Picture Editor
Hilary Genin
Cartography Editor
Zoë Goodwin
Editorial Director
Brian Bell

Distribution

UK & Ireland
GeoCenter International Ltd
Meridian House, Churchill Way West
Basingstoke, Hampshire RG21 6YR
Fax: (44) 1256-817988

United States
Langenscheidt Publishers, Inc.
36–36 33rd Street 4th Floor
Long Island City, NY 11106
Fax: (1) 718 784-0640

Australia
Universal Publishers
1 Waterloo Road
Macquarie Park, NSW 2113
Fax: (61) 2 9888 9074

New Zealand
Hema Maps New Zealand Ltd (HNZ)
Unit D, 24 Ra ORA Drive
East Tamaki, Auckland
Fax: (64) 9 273 6479

Worldwide
Apa Publications GmbH & Co.
Verlag KG (Singapore branch)
38 Joo Koon Road, Singapore 628990
Tel: (65) 6865-1600. Fax: (65) 6861-6438

Printing

Insight Print Services (Pte) Ltd
38 Joo Koon Road, Singapore 628990
Tel: (65) 6865-1600. Fax: (65) 6861-6438

©2007 Apa Publications GmbH & Co.
Verlag KG (Singapore branch)
All Rights Reserved

First Edition 1991
Fifth Edition 2005, updated 2007

ABOUT THIS BOOK

The first Insight Guide pioneered the use of creative and full-color photography in guidebooks in 1970. Since then, we have expanded our range to cater for our readers' need not only for reliable information about their chosen destination but also for a real understanding of that destination. Now, when the internet can supply inexhaustible (but not always reliable) facts, our books marry text and pictures to provide that much more elusive quality: knowledge. To achieve this, they rely heavily on the authority of locally based writers and photographers.

How to use this book

The book is carefully structured both to convey an understanding of the city and its culture and to guide readers through its sights and activities:

◆ The Best Of St Petersburg section at the front of the guide helps you to prioritise what you want to see.

◆ To understand St Petersburg, you need to know something of its past. The city's history and culture are described in authoritative essays written by specialists with an intimate knowledge of its evolution and present-day challenges.

◆ The Places section provides a full run-down of the attractions worth seeing. The main sights are coordinated by number with full-colour maps.

◆ A list of recommended restaurants is included at the end of each Places chapter and plotted on the pull-out map provided with the guide.

◆ Photographs are chosen not only to illustrate geography and buildings but also to convey the moods of the city and the life of its people.

VYBORGSKAYA STORONA

Piskaryovskoe memorialnoe kladbishche

Botkinskaya ulitsa

Lebedeva

Akademika

Finlyandsky vokzal

Pl. Lenina

Ploshchad Lenina

Klinicheskaya

Bol. Sampsonievsky prosp.

-vskaya

Kutuzova

Mikhailova

ulitsa

Komsomola

Arsenalnaya naberezhnaya

Liteyny most

Kondratyevsky prosp.

Arsenalnaya ulitsa

Sverdlovskaya

naberezhnaya

Orlovskaya

ulitsa

Ordovskaya

Smolnovo

Smolny sobor

Ploshchad Rastrelli

Smolny Institut

naberezhnaya

Robespyera

Shpalernaya ulitsa

page 180

Tavrichesky dvorets

Tavrichesky pereulok

Stavropolskaya

ulitsa

Diktatury

ploshchad Proletarskoy Diktatury

Smolny prosp.

Bolshoy Okhtinsky most

prospekt

shpalernaya ul.

naberezhnaya

Zakhareyvskaya ulitsa

Furshtadtskaya

Tchaikovskovo

Tverskaya

ulitsa

Potyomkinskaya

TAVRICHESKY SAD

Kirochnaya

Chernyshevskaya

Kirochnaya ulitsa

Suvorovsky ulitsa

Kavalergardskaya

prospekt

Tulskaya ul.

Sinopskaya

prospekt

Mohova ul.

Pestelya

Manezhnaya

ulitsa Ryleeva

Artillersky ulitsa

Radishcheva

Memorialny muzey AV Suvorova

Paradnaya ulitsa

Saperny pereulok

Vilensky pereulok

9-ya

8-ya

7-ya

prospekt

Moiseyenko

zamok

Kordenny

Litenny

Baskov pereulok

Nekrasova

Mayakovskovo

10-ya

Sovetskaya

6-ya

Grechesky prospekt

5-ya

4-ya

3-ya

Sovetskaya

Suvorovsky

Starorusskaya

Kirillovskaya

Novgorodskaya ulitsa

Kr. Tekstilshchika

Muzey Akhmatovoy

Dvoretz Sheremetyevykh

Zhukovskovo

Vosstaniya

ulitsa

Degtyarny

Mayakovskaya

Stremyannaya ul.

Ploshchad Vosstaniya

Pl. Vosstaniya

2-ya

Mytninskaya

Diagnaya

prospekt

Bakunina

naberezhnaya

Kremchevskaya

Khersonsky Proezd

Sinopskaya

page 120

Zanevsky prospekt

Beloselsky-Belozersky dvorets

Anchkov most

Vladimirskaya

Vladimirsky sobor

Kuznechny rynok

Muzey Dostoevskovo

Vosstaniya

Goncharnaya

Stary

Pushkinskaya

Ligovsky prosp.

page 108

Moskovsky vokzal

Poltavskaya ulitsa

Mirgorodskaya

Nevsky

Telezhnaya

Poltavskaya

Konnaya

Perekupnoy

Nikolskovo

prospekt

Moskva Hotel

pl. Aleksandra Nevskovo

ploshchad Aleksandra Nevskovo

Aleksandra Nevskova most

Neva

Malookhtinsky prospekt

Lavrsky

Troitsky sobor

NIKOLSKOE KLADBISHCHE

Aleksandro-Nevskaya lavra

Shlisselburgsky most

Obukhovsky Oborony

uli. Dostoevskovo

Kolomenskaya

Ligovsky pr.

Transportny pereulo

Zasonova

Borovaya

Razyezhnaya

ul. Pech.

Grigoryeva

Konst.

Svechnoi

pereulok

Konstantinogradskaya ulitsa

Obvodnovo

Kanala

Glinovaya

Profressora Kachalova

ulitsa

Ligovsky

Konst.

Kolomenskaya

Chernyakhovskovo

Romenskaya

ulitsa

Atamanskaya

ulitsa

Menzhinskaya ulitsa

ul. Tyushina

Romenskaya

Atamansky most

Naberezhnaya

prospekt

Borovaya

Tambovskaya

Dnepropetrovskaya

Atamansky J most

Glukho Dzerskaya Shossa

Mirgorodskaya

naberezhnaya

Obvodnovo Kanala

Peterhof	page 192
Excursions from St Petersburg	page 198
Novgorod	page 206

bune, *Bloomberg News*, the *Art Newspaper* and other publications in Europe and America. **Claire Bigg** wrote the guided tours through the Hermitage and Russian Museums, as well as the Shopping chapter.

This edition builds on previous editions produced by **Clare Griffiths** and **Wilhelm Klein**. Previous contributors, some of whose text survives in this book, include the celebrated Russian poet **Yevgeny Yevtushenko**. **Igor Zakharov** wrote about the city's colourful history and about parks and palaces in the suburbs, while **N. Zorkaya**, a leading Russian film critic, and drama critic **Andrei Karaulov** contributed to the essay on theatre and cinema. **Rowlinson Carter** wrote the essay on religion, with additional text by **Robin Minney**, and the chapter on food and drink was revised by **Iain Law**.

Lidiya Ginzburg, who wrote the moving "Notes of a Blockade Survivor", passed away in 1990. The chapter on the "People of Peter" was written by **Fyodor Dmitriev**. The cultural aspects of this book were covered by various writers including **Elvira Kim** and **Olga Kalinina**, while **Leonid Ivanov** contributed to the Places section.

Additional assistance was provided by **Siân Lezard**, **Cathy Muscat, Dorothy Stannard** and **Sylvia Suddes**. **Helen Peters** indexed the text, while **Shura Collinson** kept it all up to date.

CONTACTING THE EDITORS

We would appreciate it if readers would alert us to errors or outdated information by writing to:

Insight Guides, P.O. Box 7910, London SE1 1WE, England. Fax: (44) 20 7403-0290. insight@apaguide.co.uk

www.insightguides.com
In North America:
www.insighttravelguides.com

◆ The Travel Tips listings section provides a point of reference for information on transport, accommodation, cultural attractions, shopping and other activities. There is also an A–Z directory of practical information and a useful language guide. Information may be located quickly by using the index printed on the back cover flap.

◆ A detailed street atlas is included at the back of the book, complete with a full index.

The contributors

This new edition was edited by **Jason Mitchell**, an American-born, London-based editor who is fluent in Russian. The principal writer for this edition, **John Varoli**, an American-born journalist, has lived in Russia since 1992, and writes for the *New York Times*, *International Herald Tri-*

Maps

Travel Tips

THE BEST OF ST PETERSBURG

Setting priorities, saving money, unique attractions...
here, at a glance, are our recommendations, plus some
tips and tricks even old spies don't know about

UNMISSABLE MASTERPIECES

You couldn't see all of Petersburg's art if you tried, but
these are three unique pieces not to be missed.

- One of his several masterpieces at the Hermitage, **Rembrant's** highly evocative work *Return of the Prodigal Son* was painted shortly before the artist's death *(see page 102)*.
- The **Egyptian Sphinxes** along the quay of Vasilievsky Island are made of pink granite and date back to the 15th century BC. They were bought from Egypt by Nicholas I in 1831 *(see page 174)*.
- **Leonardo da Vinci** is well represented in the Hermitage: the *Madonna Litta* is his most famous masterpiece on display *(see page 102)*.

ABOVE: There is no shortage of food markets in St Petersburg. Much of the produce is grown at the country retreats that many residents maintain outside the city.
BELOW RIGHT: Many grand old recipes are still served up in the city's finest restaurants and are delivered in style.

ABOVE: St Petersburg's arts scene is steeped in tradition, and some of the world's finest dancers have graced its stages.

FINE DINING, RUSSIAN STYLE

- **Demyanova Ukha** is one of the city's best places for fish. It's a local haunt and the atmosphere is relaxed *(see page 163)*.
- **Russkaya Rybalka** serves fine fish that you can catch yourself from the restaurant's pond. It's located on Krestovsky Island and is popular with President Putin *(see page 163)*.
- **Bliny Domik** has hands-down the best bliny in town *(see page 135)*.
- **Count Suvorov** is one of the few places serving exotic tsarist-era Russian dishes, such as bear meat. Many of the recipes were rescued from local archives *(see page 135)*.
- **Restoran** has a sleek and stylish setting with finely cooked traditional Russian fare *(see page 177)*.

ABOVE: There are fewer finer places to people-watch than Palace Square. Admission, of course, is free and you may well overhear whispers of any political changes ringing in the air.
BELOW: This golden statue from Peterhof is a prime example of the vast collection of outdoor sculpture on display in St Petersburg. In addition to palace grounds, the Summer Garden is the best place to stroll amongst statues.

FREE ACTIVITIES

- It is essential that you show respect – remain silent, cover your legs and your head if you're female, and don't cross your arms or put your hands in your pockets. Having kept to these rules you don't need a penny to attend a service at one of the city's many beautiful churches such as Smolny Cathedral and Church on the Spilled Blood.
- There is no expense involved in simply watching an auction at the **House of Furs** – a place where much money trades hands *(see page 185)*.
- Prices are slightly more reasonable at **Gostiny dvor**, though you'll only find the wealthiest of Russians

shopping here. Still, the atmosphere is free *(see page 114)*.
- If you feel the need to leave the city behind, the **Kirov Islands** (Stone, Yelagin and Krestovsky islands) are a picturesque archipelago with many parks and old mansions *(see pages 159–62)*.
- The **Summer Garden** is filled with sculptures, fountains, pavilions and summer houses – an open air museum surrounded by beautiful gardens *(see page 92)*.

ECHOES OF AUTHORS

- **The Bronze Horseman** on Decembrists' Square commemorates so much – Catherine the Great's ego, for a start. She used the statue to align herself with the city's founder, Peter the Great. And much like the Decembrists, whose short-lived rebellion took place here, Pushkin saw the upraised horse as a symbol of oppression. His *Bronze Horseman* has made this one immortal *(see pages 83–4)*.
- The price of books in **Dom Knigi** will shock you. Such affordability reveals the passion of many Russians for the written word and leaves no room for

excuses: take home a copy of Pushkin in the original *(see page 111)*.
- **Dostoevsky** died over the Griboedova Canal, but not before penning the *Brothers Karamazov* here. The museum commemorates his life and work and screens film adaptations of his novels *(see page 119)*.
- **Nikolai Gogol** lived at No. 17 Nevsky prospekt when he wrote *The Government Inspector*, *Taras Bulba*, the beginning of *Dead Souls* and his short story entitled *Nevsky prospekt (see page 109)*.
- **Pushkin** uttered his last words over the Moika Canal after he sustained a mortal wound from a duel. His house has now become the Pushkin House Museum. Here he wrote *The Captain's Daughter* and *The Bronze Horseman (see page 112)*.

CHURCHES

- Hidden away, some may say, in the city's southern suburbs – **Chesma Church**, though rather small, was grand enough for Catherine. The great empress stopped here to rest en route to her country residence *(see page 186–7)*.

- One of Russia's grandest monastic ensembles, **Alexander Nevksy Monastery** lies at the far, far end of Nevsky prospekt. One of the most sacred

places in all of Russia, its Trinity Cathedral is topped by three azure domes *(see page 120)*.

- In a different style altogether is the neo-classical gem of **Kazan Cathedral**. Its imposing Corinthian colonnade dominates Nevsky prospekt and serves as a popular meeting place. Under the Soviets, the church contained the Museum of Religion, a statement by the authorities of their intent to consign religion to the past *(see pages 110–1)*.

- The golden spire of **Peter and Paul Cathedral** is visible throughout the city. It was the city's first church and the final resting place of the tsars *(see page 146–7)*.

- The most fantastic church in St Petersburg and an echo of Moscow's St Basil's, the canalside **Church of the Spilled Blood** pays tribute to Russia's murdered tsar Alexander II with a gaudy assembly of folk styles *(see pages 111–2)*.

- The 100kg/220lbs of gold on top of **St Isaac's Catheral** shine above the city. More costly decorative indulgences await inside *(see page 127–8)*.

- Where once there was a smouldering tar yard now stands the elegant **Smolny Cathedral** – a masterpiece of baroque architecture *(see pages 122–3)*.

- It's a long journey to **Kizhi**, but amazing wooden churches await. Their intricate assemblies were accomplished without nails or modern tools *(see pages 208–9)*.

ABOVE: Park Pobedy in the southern suburbs is full of monumental sculpture built to commemorate the victory over Germany in the Great Patriotic War (World War II).
LEFT: Not to be missed is the heavy smell of incense burning in the orthodox churches throughout the city. Respect of their traditions is strictly enforced, but the experience is open to everyone, regardless of their faith.

GONE BUT NOT FORGOTTEN

- At **Tikvinskoe kladbishche** lie the last embers of many an artistic genius, including the immortal composers Tchaikovsky, Rimsky-Korsakov and Mussorgsky. Also buried here is the novelist Dostoevsky *(see page 121)*.

- Why Dostoevsky did not make it into the **Literatorskiye Mostki** is uncertain, as it is devoted mostly to writers. Here lie the novelist Ivan Turgenev (1818–83), Dimitry Mendeleyev (1834–1907, poet and father of the Periodic Table), the psychologist Ivan Pavlov (1849–1936), the "father of Russian Marxism" Georgi Plekhanov (1856–1918), plus Lenin's mother and extended family *(see page 121)*.

- A much more sombre affair, **Piskaryovskoe memorialnoe kladbishche** commemorates the 670,000 victims of the city's blockade during World War II. Exhibitions include the diary of a schoolgirl who suffered the blockade and how residents used a cocktail of innovation and deception to survive the German onslaught *(see page 181)*.

- The tsars' family crypt by another name, the **Peter and Paul Cathdral** inside the fortress of the same name contains the remains of every Russian tsar from Peter the Great to Alexander III *(see pages 146–7)*.

- Near Chernaya rechka metro station, a monument to the **death of Pushkin** marks the site of the duel which ended the life of Russia's national poet *(see page 160)*.

REMNANTS OF REVOLUTION

- On **ploschad Lenina**, just outside Finland Station, a statue marks the arrival of Lenin from Finland in 1917. Before leading the Bolshevik Revolution he stood on an armoured car in this square and issued a call to arms to his comrades *(see page 178–9).*
- The **House of Soviets** in Moscow Square was built with as much pomp as possible. This Monument to Lenin was erected on his 100th anniversary *(see page 187).*
- Bloody Sunday, 9 January 1905 was the date the tsarist regime began to crumble. A peaceful demonstration set out from **January 9th Park** in the southern suburbs of the city only to be met by troops at Narva Gate *(see pages 184–5).*
- At the location of their execution, the **Decembrists' Monument** marks the end of a short-lived rebellion that inspired the Bolshevik Revolution *(see page 151).*
- If you start to feel nostalgic about the good old Soviet days, just take a quick walk past the **Kresty Prison** – made infamous during Soviet times for the number of political prisoners held within *(see page 180).*

ABOVE: The Astoria hotel is just one of St Petersburg's hotels quickly learning to provide the luxury Western business travellers expect.
RIGHT: The sign of one of St Petersburg's oldest breweries. But don't think there's a tradition of beer drinking here; it's only recently that the beverage has been deemed a respectable tipple.

LUXURY HOTELS

- Russia's first five-star hotel, the **Grand Hotel Europe** boasts seven restaurants and a guest list that has included Bill Clinton and Paul McCartney *(see page 222).*
- Open since 1912, the **Astoria Hotel** has housed everyone from Bolsheviks to ballet stars in its elegant rooms. Its Davidov restaurant is one of the city's most popular watering holes *(see page 221).*
- Though it's the city's most modern hotel, the **Grand Hotel Emerald** is decorated like a tsarist palace and has its own Russian banya *(see page 222).*
- The **Corinthia Nevskij Palace**, commonly called the Nevsky, is the hotel of choice for upscale business travellers. The fantastic service is topped by the rooftop Landskrona restaurant – one of the city's best places to eat *(see page 222).*
- A retreat from the hustle and bustle, the **Baltic Star Hotel** is located on the Gulf of Finland on the grounds of the Konstantin Palace *(see page 225).*

ON THE CHEAP

The days when a wealthy westerner could easily buy out the contents of a Russian corner shop for less than a week's wages are long gone. Now it's the Russian oligarchs and Western businessmen who get to play the big spender – the former by buying English football clubs, the latter by indulging in the city's nightclub scene. However, there are still ways for the thrifty to enjoy a visit to St Petersburg for less.

- Taxis are a big expense if you're not careful. During daylight hours many residents choose to take private cars, waved down on the street, instead of official taxis. Of course this is less safe, but still common practice. If you're not comfortable with this, try to avoid flagging down a taxi near your hotel. Go down the block a bit and your fare will drop exponentially.
- Avoid any services, souvenirs on sale, cafes and restaurants at or near a luxury hotel. They are exorbitantly overpriced. You can find just as good quality on the high street.
- If you are visiting with family or friends, it can be significantly cheaper to rent a private apartment instead of a hotel room.
- If you plan on calling home, buy an Internet telephone card to make international calls. You'll save a fortune.

A CITY REBORN

Vladimir Putin, a native son, has restored
St Petersburg to the centre of Russian
power, suggesting that the city's future
could be as golden as its illustrious past

After enjoying more than 200 years as the capital of the world's greatest empire – in terms of geography if not influence – St Petersburg suffered grievously for most of the 20th century. Repeated wars, revolutions and political neglect sank the city into provincial obscurity. Today, peace, history – the city recently smartened itself up for its 300th anniversary – and a St Petersburg native, Vladimir Putin, as president of Russia have given the city a chance to reclaim some of its glamour. It may not be Russia's capital today, but its increasing influence means that it is nipping at Moscow's heels.

The city triumphantly entered the new millennium. On 31 December, 1999, political power in the Kremlin passed into Putin's hands, and since then he has made little effort to hide his favouritism toward the city. He has placed people from his home town in key positions in government ministries. Russia's most powerful corporations are increasingly led by men who call the city home. More and more frequently, when meeting visiting foreign heads of state, Putin chooses St Petersburg as the backdrop.

Who can blame him? Here is a city that reflects its European heritage and hints none too subtly at aspirations of empire. The stark Soviet buildings that line Moscow's streets and remind people of rationing, corruption and an ideology at constant odds with the West are hidden away in the suburbs of St Petersburg. In Peter, as the locals call it, one could be forgiven for forgetting that workers of the world once tried to unite in this city's main square. Here, history is everywhere, but *that* history – too recent and perhaps too painful – has faded into the background. Here it is much more evident that Peter the Great, followed by Catherine the Great, saw Russia as a European country in line with the Enlightenment – a grand empire forming the eastern border of Europe.

Some of Russia's greatest cultural achievements are associated with St Petersburg. Dostoevsky, Gogol and Pushkin spent much of their lives here – the last killed in a duel just outside the city. The grand architecture and tranquil canals inspired composers such as Rimsky-Korsokov and Tchaikovsky. And the palaces are not just beautiful state houses,

---

PRECEDING PAGES: preparing for a parade; snow falls at Peterhof.
LEFT: St Petersburg has inspired artists and writers since its creation.

but were once the homes of tsars, whose lives still capture the imagination of most visitors.

Inevitably, the rivalry between Moscow and St Petersburg has always been intense, and power shifts between the two as each generation redefines its priorities. It's no coincidence that the Peter and Paul Cathedral is the resting place for all the tsars from Peter the Great until Nicholas II, whereas Soviet dignitaries are buried in the shadow of Moscow's Kremlin. But now it can again be said that St Petersburg rules Russia.

And Putin rules St Petersburg. After he forced out the city's governor, Vladimir Yakovlev, in 2003, the post went to a Putin protégé, Valentina Matvienko. Such political compromises may have their price, but the rewards are apparent in any of the costly restoration projects funded by the government to celebrate the city's millennium. If, as political pundits now speculate, Putin is succeeded by a protegé of his in 2008, the fortunes of St Petersburg could remain golden for the next decade.

Such a golden future is desperately needed. Billions of dollars of federal money are required to rebuild the city's infrastructure after decades of neglect by Soviet authorities who favoured Moscow's industrial landscape. The refined architecture of St Petersburg was seen as far too bourgeois. Although redevelopment work has begun – such as a $1 billion ring road around the city – most projects will take more than a decade to complete. And such restoration projects in the past have often been halted when only half-complete because of a shift in the political winds.

Many of the grand palaces are shining again already. The tricentenary in 2003 was a celebration of one of Europe's largest, youngest and most significant cities. Although well over a decade has passed since the end of the Cold War, many misconceptions about Russia and St Petersburg persist in America and Europe. First-time visitors often come with concern and even trepidation, but almost all leave with the joy of finding an unexpected treasure. Certainly there are social and economic problems here, but they rarely impinge upon a tourist's stay.

Today Russians and foreigners (many of whom are joining the booming real estate market by taking up residence in the city's old communal flats) are flocking to the city in search of better jobs. In tandem with the city's increased political clout, St Petersburg's cultural institutions, such as the Hermitage Museum and the Mariinsky Theatre, have once again risen to international pre-eminence. The city is also one of Russia's main centres of the computer industry (and a notorious home for hackers), as well as a base to renewed heavy engineering and high-tech sectors that are attracting a good deal of interest from expanding Asian markets.

The history of St Petersburg has been one of continued struggle, destruction and rebirth. Perhaps it is this constant tumult that has made the city an inspiration to some of the world's greatest cultural, scientific and political innovators. ❑

RIGHT: with more than 2 million visitors every year, the Hermitage Museum is easily St Petersburg's most popular attraction.

A WINDOW ON THE WEST

Examine St Petersburg's past and you can discern Russia's revolutionary spirit as well as its serious flaws. A part-time capital conceived by the Eurocentric Peter the Great as a shop window to the West, the city has endured a turbulent history, signalled by its changes of name to Petrograd, then Leningrad, then back to St Petersburg

Peter the Great conceived St Petersburg as a crucial link with western Europe. Russia is for the most part a dissipated land – an endless expanse. Suddenly, three centuries ago, it was given this uncharacteristic city of stone. It would be mistaken, therefore, to think of St Petersburg, then or now, as being synonymous with Russia. Yet the rest of the country would not be as it is without the pervasive influence of St Petersburg.

Nevsky's times

The Neva has long been Russia's outlet into the Baltic. A thousand years before St Petersburg was founded, Lake Nevo (Ladoga) was the northern border of the territories of the Ilmen Slavs, the tribe that lived on the banks of the River Volkhov, Lake Ilmen and the rivers that flowed into it.

The Volkhov, which connected Ilmen and Ladoga, was the main route from the Varangians, also known as Vikings, to the Greeks in Byzantium; the route that started on the Neva and ended in the mouth of the Dnieper, on the coast of the Black Sea. Along this route Vikings, Slavs and Finns co-existed in trade and politics.

The Vikings gave rise to a unified Russian state in the 9th and 10th centuries, with centres in Kiev in the south, and Novgorod (*see page 205*) in the north.

With time, the ruling Viking elite became assimilated into the culture of the Eastern

Slavs, who by the 13th century found themselves at war with their Scandinavian neighbours. Birger, the earl of Sweden, was routed by Alexander, the prince of Novgorod, known as Alexander Nevsky ("of the Neva"). But the conflict would continue in some form for the next seven centuries.

Villages in the delta

The Swedes built the Landscrona fort on the Neva in 1300. The Russians destroyed it and built, in 1323, a fort of their own – Oreshek. After Moscow annexed Novgorod in 1471–78, the fort, which stood further inland on the Neva, became part of its northern

LEFT: Lenin issues a call to arms.
RIGHT: Alexander Nevsky, the ancient hero of Rus.

TREZZINI'S LEGACY

Though many architects have contributed to St Petersburg's architectural heritage, only Domenico Trezzini could claim he began it. He was commissioned in 1703 to work on the Kronshtadt fortress and spent the next 30 years working in the city. Not only did he construct the first Winter Palace, the Peter and Paul Fortress and the Twelve Colleges; he also planned the city's road design.

defensive chain. By the 16th century, there were several dozen villages in the delta of the Neva.

Undaunted by early defeats, Peter proceeded to renovate old fortifications, replenish the armed forces and create an artillery force almost from scratch.

In November 1702, Noteburg (Oreshek) fell to the Russians after a 30-hour assault. Peter gave the fort a new name – Schlüsselburg (Key Castle). On 1 May 1703, the Russians took Niensants. They now controlled the entire length of the Neva. But these forts were clearly not enough.

In the search for a new and more reliable stronghold, the Tsar explored the isles in the Neva. A site was chosen in the delta, on the small Hare Island.

After Russia, under Ivan the Terrible, lost the war of Livonia (1558–83), the northern forts were claimed by Sweden. On the site where Landscrona once stood, the Swedes built a new fort – Niensants.

War with Sweden

By the end of the 17th century the Swedes controlled the majority of the Baltic Sea region. In 1700 war against Sweden was declared by Russia. The goal of Peter the Great's Northern War was to reclaim the historic lands of the "fathers and grandfathers", the old Russian forts and most importantly, their important outlets to the Baltic.

The founding of the city

On 16 May 1703, Peter founded the new fort, which he named Saint Peter Burgh. That autumn, over 120 cannons were installed on its bastions. In November, it received its first guest – a peaceful merchant sailing from the Netherlands. Meanwhile, the Swedes still threatened the fortress from land and sea. But not for long: several years before the end of the Northern War, the Russians seized all lands to the north and west of the fortress within at least a 100-km (60-mile) radius. From the sea, the mouth of the Neva was protected by Fort Kronshlot on Kotlin Island (later to become the sea fortress Kronshtadt).

The early years

Thousands of workers were sent to St Petersburg from various Russian towns. But the city needed trained tradesmen. Peter issued a decree concerning the "eternal settlement" of masons, bricklayers, carpenters, metalworkers, joiners, tailors and bookkeepers in St Petersburg. These workers were given houses and vegetable plots. The offer attracted roughly 1,500 of them to the city every year.

In the beginning, construction was headed by the first governor of St Petersburg, Alexander Menshikov, and the city's first architect, Domenico Trezzini, from Switzer-

A CITY BUILT ON BONES

As there was no suitable building land, the first migrants to the city dragged earth from far-off places to the city bastions carrying it in old sacks, bark matting and even the hems of their coarse hemp clothes. Fever and disease claimed a great many lives. When a person died, he was wrapped in the matting in which he had just dragged earth, and was buried in the earth he had himself brought.

idences. Menshikov ordered a magnificent three-storey stone palace with a large garden on Vasilievsky Island. The Summer Palace was built on the left bank of the Neva for Peter

land. In 1710, building work began on the Church of Isaac Dalmatsky. That same year, the Alexander Nevsky Monastery was founded. The opening cut in the woods between the Admiralty and the monastery was called Great Perspective, but would later become Nevsky Prospekt.

In 1712, Trezzini started work on the stone Peter and Paul Cathedral inside the fortress. As the cathedral rose from the ground, the fortress around it assumed its name. Next came the construction of elaborate private res-

himself. The verdant Summer Garden surrounded the palace.

The capital of the north

St Petersburg became the Russian capital in 1712. Several months later, the Senate too moved there. Russia celebrated victories not only on the field of battle, it also carried out fundamental internal reforms which ushered in a new era of development.

Construction was booming. Peter himself presided over construction work on the Vyborg Side, Vasilievsky Island and at Peterhof and Oranienbaum (his summer palaces and parks). In 1714, almost 10 million bricks

LEFT: Schlüsselburg, where the city originated.
ABOVE: Ivan III and the Tartars at the court.

Peter the Great

Peter was born in the Moscow Kremlin in 1672. His mother, Natalya Naryshkina, was Tsar Alexei's second wife. At the age of 10, he was proclaimed tsar along with his sickly elder half-brother, Ivan. But his ambitious and wilful half-sister Sophia led the *streltsy*, the palace guard, against the Naryshkin faction at court. The coup became a bloodbath.

The boy Peter was spared, but many of his relatives and courtiers were hacked to death before his eyes. It is hard to

imagine the impression this made on the prince, but by all accounts Peter showed no emotion as he watched the butchery.

Sophia became regent and Peter, still co-tsar, was sent into semi-exile to Preobrazhenskoye, a hunting lodge near Moscow. Peter was left largely to his own devices. Guided by his insatiable curiosity, he set up a "toy regiment" with his young playmates. This game of soldiers soon became deadly serious: Preobrazhenskoye was transformed into a barracks where Peter drilled and trained a small army of teenage men-at-arms, fully equipped with artillery, dark-green uniforms and tricorn

hats. From these experiments grew the Preobrazhensky regiment – for 200 years the most elite unit in the Russian army.

Preobrazhenskoye also happened to be near the "foreign suburb" – home of Western merchants and specialists. Peter spent days in this Little Europe, and saw that the foreigners had all sorts of knowledge that was new to him. One of these foreigners taught Peter to sail a Western-style boat on the River Moskva. Now the three passions of his life were in place: a fascination with the West, a gift for waging war and a desire to build a navy.

When he came of age, Peter ended the regency and confined Sophia to Moscow's Novodevichy monastery. He then ruled with Ivan until the latter's death in 1696.

As soon as he was sole tsar, Peter did something so unprecedented that it was perceived by many of his subjects as a downright blasphemy. He went abroad.

No Russian tsar had ever left the country, but for more than a year Peter travelled Western Europe. This was no diplomatic process. Peter's aims were practical: he went to lectures on anatomy, made shoes, visited cannon foundries, but chiefly spent his days working as an apprentice in the shipyards of Holland and England under the incognito of Peter Mikhailov.

Peter returned from the West inspired to build a modern navy. He wrested the province of Karelia from Swedish control, and on this marshy desolate piece of land, at the mouth of the River Neva, built his seaport. Peter sent hundreds of young Russians west to learn the technologies and skills which Russia lacked. He also invited Western specialists to Russia and insisted Russians adopt Western dress and manners, hence the tax on beards.

By the time Peter died in 1725, at the age of 53, Russia had indeed changed irreversibly. No lesser personality could have shaken Russia out of its age-old slumber. Peter's successors could not turn the clock back, and some, notably Catherine the Great, made it their business to carry on the work of this remarkable man. ❏

LEFT: the bronze head of Peter the Great.

were produced for the city. Yet more building material was needed, and Peter banned construction in stone all over the country with the sole exception of St Petersburg. Masons and other "artists of the building trade" were sent to work on the new capital by force.

Many foreigners were also invited. Each of them was given a shop with 10 Russian apprentices. This turned St Petersburg into a unique training centre for builders, who were shown the most advanced methods and absorbed the latest word in their trade.

The Northern War ended in victory for the Russians in 1721. It had lasted for over two decades and cost Russia the lives of 40,000

connecting Central Asia and Western Europe. But exports and the transit of oriental goods were not the only factors of the economic boom in Russia. The country now had a well-developed industrial base. The number of manufacturing enterprises grew more than tenfold during Peter's reign and most of these innovative and previously unheard-of factories were concentrated in St Petersburg.

The scale of reform, which Peter implemented with utter ruthlessness, bred a new ideology, created new economic and political needs and promoted the dynamic development of education, science and culture – primarily in the new capital.

soldiers and at least 70,000 civilians. But the country did not pay this terrible price in vain: the gap between the Middle Ages and the new times was bridged. Russia emerged as a developed and mighty European power.

Industrial development

With St Petersburg providing access to the Baltic Region, Russia gained the right to join the circle of northern countries. Peter's Persian War (1722) strengthened Russia's presence on the Caspian Sea, with its trade routes

In 1711, the first print shop was opened in St Petersburg, producing the country's first newspaper, *Vedomosti*. Peter's library was moved to St Petersburg from Moscow, and it was opened to the public (although only noble classes were permitted to enter). Next door, a collection of rarities was on display – the first museum in town, now the Kunstkammer *(see page 169)*.

The volume of printed matter grew by 20 times in Peter's lifetime. Ninety percent of this output was secular literature concerning navigation, ship-building, mathematics and medicine, as well as calendars, manuals and translations from foreign languages.

ABOVE: Peter III, victim of Catherine the Great's ambition.
RIGHT: a plan of St Petersburg, early 1800s.

Many hitherto unknown things came to Russia: new uniforms and new firearms for the regular army regiments, huge naval vessels, libraries, a public theatre, museums and the Academy of Sciences, parks and park sculpture, fountains, canals and "exemplary houses". In the avenues of St Petersburg there were new clothes, new manners and a new style for daily intercourse, amusements and festivities.

From the graveyard of its first builders, St Petersburg grew into a beautiful city. But in the autumn of 1728 Moscow became the capital once again, and the Imperial Court moved back there. St Petersburg began to decline and

its many unfinished buildings started collapsing alongside the unfinished ships. Peter's city seemed consigned to history's scrapyard.

Anna and Elizabeth

In 1732 Empress Anna made St Petersburg the capital again but life in the city, which had once been so creative, now became parasitic as the gentry developed more elaborate ways of living off the state. The city became truly Frenchified when, in 1741, the palace guardsmen removed the regent Anna Leopoldovna, and placed Peter's energetic, fun-loving daughter, Elizabeth, on the throne. With her light feminine touch, Elizabeth wiped clean

CATHERINE THE GRIM

Subjected to the insults of her husband Peter and his ruling aunt, Elizabeth, Catherine once even attempted to commit suicide by stabbing herself, but the knife caught in her corset.

the window into Europe. The new rights and liberties gained by the nobility were instantly transformed into palaces and country estates, no less magnificent than the Imperial ones.

The St Petersburg Academy of Sciences, which had been founded by Peter but which had then stood idle for some time, resumed its activities. The Academy of Arts was founded. The vast potential of the so-called "simple" Russian was seen in Russia's first academician, the illustrious Mikhail Lomonosov, who, in true Renaissance style, combined the talents of a scientist, poet and artist.

The rise of the gentry

The gentry was expanding its influence, particularly its right to own estates and serfs, and concentrated on ridding itself of the rigidly prescribed duty (in accordance with Peter's decree) of state service. The gentry won the day: *On Bestowing Liberty to the Gentry of Russia*, the manifesto signed by Elizabeth's successor, Peter III, finally freed them of state duties. This essentially turned the gentry into a class of parasites, which controlled the entire might of the empire's military-bureaucratic machine. Their position grew stronger with each new military success: the war for the Black Sea with Turkey in 1735–39, the war for Finland with Sweden in 1741–43, the Seven-Year War with Prussia in 1756–63.

By the middle of the 18th century the population of St Petersburg reached the 100,000 mark (fewer than 40 percent were women). There were 2,000 aristocrats, as many merchants, and entire quarters filled with foreigners – Englishmen lived on the Neva behind St Isaac's Church, Germans and Frenchmen on Vasilievsky Island and Italians between Sadovaya, Nevsky and the Fontanka.

LEFT: a portrait of Catherine the Great.
RIGHT: she travelled throughout the country in style.

A centre of art and science

St Petersburg became the country's financial capital, home to wealthy clients and the imperial court. This offered a unique opportunity for architects, artists, actors and scientists to prosper. The court orchestra appeared in 1729 and many aristocrats kept orchestras and choirs of their own. In the 1730s, an opera and ballet theatre was put together in the imperial palace.

Catherine the Great

Peter III was deposed by his young German wife Catherine. In the coup that brought her to power, Catherine showed the skills she was to exhibit throughout her life: a politician's instincts, a lack of sentimentality, an appetite for personal glory, and a habit of making her lovers her closest advisers and political allies.

Catherine's reign began in the spirit of the Enlightenment. As a Westerner herself, she was aware of the backwardness of her adopted land and, like Peter, she was determined to impose change for the better. She liberalised the penal code, introduced plans for primary education, reformed local government, founded hospitals and orphanages and expressed the view (in her correspondence with Voltaire as well as to her advisers) that

PUGACHEV'S REBELLION

A turning-point in Catherine's reign was a peasant revolt of such scope and fury that it nearly tore the Russian state apart. The leader of the revolt was a Cossack deserter Emelian Pugachev.

In 1773 he appeared on the southern fringe of the Russian empire making the unlikely claim that he was Peter III – Catherine's murdered husband. Enough people chose to believe him – mostly outlaws, disaffected Cossacks and Old Believers, Moslem Kalmuks and Tatars – for him to raise a ragbag army. Once he was organised, serfs flocked to him in their thousands: for what did they have to lose?

Pugachev captured the city of Kazan and put it to the torch. The serfs of Nizhny Novgorod rose up and laid waste to the entire region. As Pugachev's confidence grew, so did his ferocity. His shabby juggernaut rolled on, murdering and raping as it went.

A loyal army, hurriedly recalled from the war with the Turks, headed Pugachev off when he marched on Moscow. Pugachev turned south, and this retreat damaged his prestige. He was betrayed by his own lieutenants and handed over to Catherine's forces, who paraded him through the desolate provinces in a cage. He was put to a cruel death in Moscow.

rulers were called to serve the state. She invited the leading architects of the day to Russia, and it was during her reign that St Petersburg first acquired its cool, classical character. These are some of the achievements that merit her title: "the Great".

Catherine also possessed an imperial acquisitiveness which would have made Peter proud. In her reign the Crimea was conquered, and Russia thus gained a port on the Black Sea at last. And at her behest, the vast riches of Siberia – the furs, the forests and the minerals – were exploited.

After quelling the Pugachev Rebellion *(see page 25)*, Catherine's rule slowly took on a darker hue. Her early intentions to abolish serfdom were quickly abandoned, and in fact by the end of her reign the serfs were more numerous and more tightly bound than ever – they had completely become the human property of the landowners.

Catherine's youthful plans and mature achievements were diminished still further after her death in 1796. Her son, the new Tsar Paul I, hated his mother with such a passion that he set about undoing her legacy the moment he came to the throne. He introduced a Prussian-style military dictatorship, and heaped scorn on his mother's memory and accomplishments.

LOVERS OF CATHERINE THE GREAT

Catherine was no great beauty, but she possessed an ability – part womanly instinct, part cold calculation – to inspire loyalty as well as passion in the men who wooed her. There were many such men in the course of her life, and for this her enemies dubbed her "the Messalina of the North". Among the first was Grigory Orlov, a leader of the coup that brought Catherine to power and the murderer of her demented husband. But before that, while Peter III was Emperor, she secretly had a son by Orlov. The infant was smuggled from the Winter Palace in the pelt of a beaver – *bobr* in Russian. In memory of this, the boy was named Alexei Bobritsky, and his descendants are still one of the proudest families in Russia today.

Before Orlov, there had been an assignation with Stanislaus Poniatowski, a Polish count. When Catherine tired of him she installed him as King of Poland, a typically Catherinesque conjunction of political and emotional convenience. But the great romance of her life came when she was 51. This was Grigory Potemkin, a shaggy, one-eyed giant of a man who conquered the Crimea for the love of his Empress. Catherine, for her part, was glad to surrender to so grand and untamed a personality. He was not her last love – she continued to take lovers into her sixties – but he was the one she always came back to, like a prodigal wife.

The new century

Emperor Pavel's time on the throne was one of the shortest but most controversial and colourful reigns in Russian history. Pavel was both an extraordinary visionary and pedantic reactionary.

During his short reign, he made spasmodic attempts to restore the austere might of Peter's time and to transform the gentry into a mechanically exact, powerful apparatus, which could successfully face a revolution comparable to the one that had taken place in France.

But the gentry responded with yet another conspiracy: no sooner had the emperor moved

march of the Russian army, and the taking of Paris boosted Russia's international prestige.

Growing national sentiment marked the new construction in St Petersburg. Helmets, shields and javelins became ubiquitous ornaments on the walls of palaces and administrative buildings. They are repeated on the facades of private mansions. Laurel wreaths and military symbols

to his new, impenetrable Mikhailovsky Castle than he was assassinated on 3 March 1801. His son, Alexander, ascended the throne. Russia's 19th century had begun as it was to continue: in bloodshed and turmoil.

Mirror of the tsars' might

The 1812 war, in which a 14,000-strong volunteer corps from St Petersburg took part, unleashed an unprecedented wave of patriotism. The victory over Napoleon, the triumphant

LEFT: view of the Strelka when it was the city's port.
ABOVE AND RIGHT: Napoleon occupies Moscow in 1812 before Alexander I drove the French forces away.

were incorporated into iron grilles. St Petersburg would allow no one to forget that it was an empire's capital, the seat of the all-powerful tsar.

But with this wealth came problems. There was no other place in the empire where social contrasts were felt so acutely. In the golden epoch of aristocratic culture, the apex of glamour and splendour, protests thundered in St Petersburg, voices which condemned the evils of serfdom and monarchy, voices which brought fuel to the call for revolution.

The Decembrists

Emperor Alexander died in 1825. Those wanting change played upon the indecision in the highest corridors of power concerning the nomination of a successor to the throne. On 14 December 1825, the Decembrists fired the first shot against tsarism in Senatskaya Square behind the statue of the Bronze Horseman.

They lost. The leaders were executed on the wall of the Peter and Paul Fortress on 13 July 1826. That year, the Emperor Nicholas created the ominous Third Department of his Chancellery; the gendarmes in its employment started their campaign of terror which struck against freedom of thought in Russia.

The total domination of the empire's military-bureaucratic machine, whose only purpose was to perpetuate serfdom, should have stopped the

country's economic, political and cultural development. Yet it did not, in large part because the country's defence needs, as in the time of Peter the Great, demanded that the country strive to keep up with other European powers. So, St Petersburg continued as the modern industrial centre of a backward, feudal Russia. Its enterprises were frequently equipped to state-of-the-art levels and manned by well-trained worker cadres supervised by professional engineers.

In 1828, the St Petersburg Technological Institute opened its doors, followed by the Civilian Engineers' School in 1832. The Academy of Sciences opened new branches. The Pulkovo Observatory (located near today's

A DEADLY WINTER

Of the 450,000 French troops who crossed the Niemen into Russia in 1812, barely 100,000 completed the long march home.

Pulkovo international airport) was opened in 1839. In 1842 there came another important scientific event – the foundation of the Depot of Standard Measures and Weights (where the famed Dmitry Mendeleev, the father of the periodic table, worked later). During these years, Alexander Pushkin, Mikhail Lermontov, Nikolai Gogol and Mikhail Glinka all lived and worked in St Petersburg.

St Petersburg's magazines – especially *Sovremennik* and *Otechestvennye Zapiski* – printed heated articles by the new generation of revolutionaries. Literary criticism, a legal form of expression, was used to criticise the social order. As new revolutionary ideas spread, underground circles appeared and the Tsar took action to suppress all criticism.

By 1855, the losses in the Crimean War against the European powers showed Russia could not keep up. Shortly before the fall of Sevastopol, the largest Russian fortress on the Black Sea, Nicholas I died in his Peterhof residence.

Times of terror

A new stage of the struggle for liberty started in the 1850s and the 1860s. The government of Alexander II proceeded with reforms, which opened the way for capitalist development in Russia yet preserved the foundations of absolutist rule. Serfdom was abolished, administrative management reorganised, self-management was allowed at grass-roots level and a judicial reform was carried out.

Yet society wanted more: the government lost popularity and appeared more and more conservative. *Narodniki* (populists) tried to provoke a peasant uprising through terrorism. In April 1866, Dmitry Karakozov, a student, attempted to shoot the Tsar near the wrought-iron fence of the Summer Garden. He failed in his assassination attempt, but there was now no stopping the march of the revolutionary terrorists.

In February 1880, Stepan Khalturin placed a bomb in the Tsar's apartment in the Winter Palace. The emperor again, miraculously, escaped death. One year later, however, on 1 March 1881, the death sentence passed on the Tsar by the populists was carried out.

On the embankment of Ekaterininsky kanal (now Griboyedov kanal), he was mortally wounded in a bomb attack; the blast also killed his assassin, Ignaty Grinetsky. From now on, all tsars and their high-ranking officials became targets and the government found itself constantly at war with organised revolutionaries. Six years later, on 1 March 1887, conspirators preparing to assassinate Alexander III were arrested and executed. Among them was Alexander Ulianov – Lenin's elder brother.

On 9 January (Bloody Sunday), a peaceful worker's demonstration was met by gunfire.

The first barricades appeared that same day. The first Russian Revolution had begun. It lasted for two years and covered the entire country, but gained nothing.

Reaction and police terror set in. By 1913, the volume of industrial production had increased tenfold over the previous 50 years; the city's 1,000 factories and plants employed half a million people. St Petersburg produced 15 percent of the national industrial output. The capital had almost 600 banks; 40 percent of the capital invested there belonged to monopolies. The long fuse of disparity waited for a spark.

Lenin himself first emerged as an activist in St Petersburg in 1895, when he presided over the creation of the Union for the Struggle to Liberate the Working Class, which later evolved into the proletariat's revolutionary party.

The Revolution begins

The defeat suffered by Russia in the war against Japan (1904–05) accelerated the Revolution. On 2 January 1905, the workers of St Petersburg's Putilovsky Works went on strike. This grew into a general strike by 8 January.

LEFT: the last tsar, Nicholas II.
ABOVE: the new leader, comrade Lenin.

Art flourishes

Spiritual life in the capital was also full of contradictions and tension. The Russian Museum was opened in 1897. Its creative approach to the country's artistic heritage brought artists to the attention of the general public. Traditional painting by Ilya Repin and Valentin Serov was still quite popular. The radical left-wingers rallied around the "Youth Union" and its stars – Kasimir Malevich and Vasily Kandinsky.

Plays by Anton Chekhov, Maxim Gorky and Leonid Andreev enjoyed immense popularity. The stage of the Mariinsky Theatre was graced by Fyodor Shaliapin and Leonid Sobinov, Anna Pavlova and Matilda Kseshinskaya.

Russian music was enriched by the works of Alexander Glazunov, Alexander Scriabin and Sergei Rachmaninov. The search for new forms in modern architecture, and the development of the St Petersburg architectural tradition by the neoclassicists (which continued even after the Revolution) brought new architectural solutions, and these served to determine the image and layout of the city for the following decades.

World War I

World War I became history's great accelerator. St Petersburg was in the centre of things (it was then given the more Russian name of Petrograd to avoid the German sounding

radical leftist Soviets of Workers, Soldiers and Peasants Deputies, ruled the country.

The Bolshevik coup

Lenin returned to the city in April 1917, and immediately called the workers and peasants to struggle for a socialist revolution. The conditions for this revolution were ripe by autumn. On 24 October (6 November, according to the modern, Gregorian calendar), an armed struggle for power began. The Bolsheviks ordered soldiers and workers from the Red Guard to take control of bridges, the telegraph system, railway stations and the central power station.

Peterburg). The ruling circles were losing their hold on power, workers and the other have-nots lived in want and the bourgeoisie got rich on manufacturing supplies for the military. The war took more and more lives, fuelling both pacifist and revolutionary sentiment among the workers.

In 1916, the revolutionary movement in Petrograd became a tangible threat to tsarism. In 1917, Russia was caught in a nationwide crisis, which led to a democratic revolution in February when Emperor Nicholas II abdicated. But a single, effective government could not be created, and two entities, the moderate Provisional Government and the

The next morning Lenin, who headed the uprising from the Bolshevik headquarters in the Smolny Institute and Leon Trotsky, the head of the Petrosoviet, ordered the State Bank and the central telephone exchange to be seized.

A single shot from the revolutionary battleship Aurora on the evening of 25 October signaled the beginning of the attack on the Winter Palace, where the Provisional Government was in conference.

The palace was taken, and the majority of delegates to the Second Congress of Soviets, which convened in Smolny, adopted Lenin's Decree on Peace and Decree on Land. This congress also elected the new Executive

Council and the council that was to govern the country – the Council of People's Commissars, chaired by Lenin.

In January 1918, the Bolshevik commissars dispersed the Constituent Assembly. This was Russia's first truly democratically elected body, but it worked for only one day, largely because the Bolsheviks did not have a majority there. The new state system was then legalised through force by the Third Congress of Soviets at the end of January.

From 6–8 March 1918, the Seventh Congress of the Communist Party convened in Petrograd. Lenin addressed the congress no fewer than 18 times. He managed to come out on top of the reign of terror that drove most educated and propertied classes from the city.

Where there were 2½ million people in February 1917, only 740,000 remained in the city in 1920. Many elements of society were either deported by the communists or fled into exile abroad, and the city remained inhabited by an uncontrollable rabble.

The Soviets, however, acted quickly to rein in the chaos. In January 1924, after Lenin's death, Petrograd was renamed Leningrad. As if to show its displeasure, Mother Nature wreaked havoc on the city that year, with the waters of the Neva river pouring forth one of the most devastating floods in the city's history. Still,

heated debate: the Brest peace with Germany, Austria-Hungary, Bulgaria and Turkey, which was concluded on 3 March, was approved. This was the last party congress to take place in Petrograd – on 10 March the government and all central authorities moved to Moscow, which once again became the capital of Russia.

Soviet times

The city of three revolutions, Petrograd remained at the front edge of the revolutionary struggle. The communists soon began a slowly the city's cultural and economic life began to flourish once again as a new generation arose to replace those who had left.

Stalin's brutal regime

Stalin, unlike most of the top-ranking Bolsheviks, was not a middle-class intellectual. He was the son of a Georgian cobbler, and made his name in the revolutionary underground by leading "expropriations" – bank robberies – in the Caucasus. He played a very minor role in the October Revolution, but had since established himself as a good organiser.

At the time of Lenin's death, Stalin occupied the key post of general secretary, con-

LEFT: Gorky and a group of literary friends.
ABOVE: the 1917 October Revolution.

trolling appointments within the party. It was through this office that he levered himself into power, out-manoeuvring factions led by high-profile leaders such as Trotsky.

Once swathed in Lenin's mantle, Stalin, drawing on massive support among rank and file Party members launched the first Five-Year Plan, a massive programme of state-led industrialisation intended to transform the Soviet Union into a modern power.

The parallel collectivisation of agriculture aimed to harness the country's productivity and bring it under state control. But the mass of peasants refused to be herded into collective farms; many killed their cows and sheep rather than hand them over. Stalin's response was brutal. He effectively declared war on the countryside. Millions were branded as *kulaks* (peasant exploiters) and herded into the burgeoning gulags; millions more died in artificially engineered famines, particularly in the Ukraine. Stalin said he was "liquidating the *kulaks* as a class".

The Great Terror

These measures were backed up by a purge of indescribable horror. The secret police, now renamed the NKVD, swept through the country, their task to arrest "enemies of the people". It was as if the vicious, pathological personality

THE SIEGE OF LENINGRAD

The scale of Russian casualties during World War II – estimates of military and civilian dead range from 20 million to 28 million (compared with around 6 million Germans) – is often forgotten. But the 900-day *blokada* of Leningrad, in which at least 670,000 Russians died, mostly from starvation and disease, shows the scale of sacrifice.

Less than three months after the Nazi invasion of Russia in June 1941, German troops had outflanked the Red Army and encircled Leningrad. There was no escape for the 2½ million adults and 400,000 children. By early 1942, in the middle of an exceptionally cold winter, the city had no heating, no water supply, hardly any electricity, and food rations had fallen to 125 grams (4.4 ounces) of bread a day. Art treasures were hidden in the basements of the Hermitage and St Isaac's Cathedral.

Some food and supplies reached Leningrad by sled in winter and barge in summer across Lake Ladoga, enabling the arms factories to go on working. The lake was also an escape route for several hundred thousand inhabitants who braved enemy artillery to cross it to the mainland.

The blockade was partially broken in January 1943 but it was not until January 1944 that the Germans were fully routed. Over half a million victims of the siege are buried in mass graves in Piskarevsky Cemetery *(see page 181)*.

of Stalin had been magnified and unleashed against the entire nation. In blind terror, arrestees denounced everybody they could think of, thereby providing new crops of pseudo-enemies to be harvested. Others denounced neighbours and workmates out of sheer ideological zeal.

The Great Terror of the 1930s was a silent slaughter of millions upon millions of people; later entire nationalities such as the Chechens were deported.

And through it all, in the country's factories and schools, happy workers and their children sang the Stalinist anthem: "I know no other country where a man can breathe so free..."

Times of war and suffering

In the winter of 1939–40 when the Soviet Union invaded Finland, Leningrad became a frontline town. In March 1940, a peace treaty was signed with Finland, in accordance with which the border was relocated to over 100 km (62 miles) from Leningrad.

On 22 June 1941, Germany invaded the USSR, starting what is known in Russia as the Great Patriotic War. On 18 July 1941, the first Nazi bombs fell on Leningrad. On 8 September the 900-day blockade of Leningrad began (*see panel on opposite page and pages 36–7*).

The Cold War era

After the war, the people of Leningrad worked hard to quickly repair and restore the city. By 1948, the city's industry had reached the pre-war level, which increased 2½ times by 1955.

Much of that production, however, was armaments to fight a new war, the Cold War against Western Europe and America. Besides churning out ships, tanks and rockets, the city was home to dozens of scientific research centres, mostly working for defence needs.

Industrial production grew rapidly, but the lot of the ordinary worker remained abysmal. Until the mid-1960s, most of the city's population were living in cramped communal flats, which were (and still are) some of the most wretched slums in Europe. The Soviet housing boom in the late 1960s, it was said, only took the people out of the gutter and onto the pavement. Workers were given small apartments,

where one family lived in 30 sq metres (323 sq ft), about one-third the West European average.

The only consolation was that, locked behind the Iron Curtain, Russians knew little of Western standards, and so, on the whole, remained content with what they had.

Cultural thaw

Nikita Khrushchev's great achievement as president was to denounce Stalin's Terror. He declared the nightmare to be over, and it is a measure of his success that when he was subsequently deposed he was not killed.

In the cultural thaw that accompanied "de-Stalinisation" Russians had a tiny intoxicat-

ing taste of freedom: to read, to speak, to criticise. It was not much – and as the tanks on the streets of Budapest in 1956 proved, it had very definite limits – but it was never entirely forgotten.

Nikita Khrushchev is fondly remembered in Russia for other reasons too. He increased state pensions, was fanatical about planting maize (during the Khrushchev years, Soviet shops overflowed with cornflakes and popcorn), and he launched a massive and much-needed housing programme: the five-storey apartment blocks which abound in the suburbs of most Soviet cities are known in his memory as *khrushchevki*.

LEFT: the devastation after an air raid in 1941.
RIGHT: Stalin, initiator of a reign of terror.

But Khrushchev made some terrible blunders: he helped bring the world to the brink of nuclear war by provoking the Cuban missile crisis; he quarrelled with China and so divided the world communist movement; he clowned around on the world stage, thumping tables at the UN with his shoe. It was to put a stop to these alarming and embarrassing escapades that he was removed by a conspiracy of cautious, faceless Party men.

The grip tightens

One of these Communist careerists – Leonid Brezhnev – replaced him. Brezhnev's tenure represented a return to a mild form of Stalin-

indolence and absenteeism. Consumer goods were scarce, and became practically non-existent by the end of the 1970s. People queued for hours to buy frozen chicken, or left work and rushed to a shop where, it was rumoured, there had been a shoe delivery. The black market became endemic, and was in fact the only efficient part of the economy.

This decrepitude was covered in a thick blanket of lies. Brave individuals who spoke out were silenced, or worse, declared insane as psychiatry became a weapon of the KGB. Christians were oppressed; Jews were persecuted, but refused permission to leave for Israel or the USA; the people were paralysed by cynicism.

ism. A monstrously bloated cult of personality grew up around this unappealing man, who unblushingly awarded himself high honours, including even the Lenin Prize for Literature. On the international stage, Brezhnev acted out policies perceived as being monumentally wrong for his country. In 1968, he crushed the Prague Spring, Czechoslovakia's experiment with liberal socialism; and in 1979 he sent Soviet forces into Afghanistan, committing his country to an unwinnable war.

Under Khrushchev and Brezhnev the USSR became deeply embroiled in the Cold War. The arms race against America drained a Soviet economy crippled by the age-old sicknesses of

The dawn of *perestroika*

This was the situation inherited by Mikhail Gorbachev in 1985. Gorbachev believed passionately in the communist ideal, but saw that the whole system was in need of a drastic overhaul; this project was given the slogan *perestroika*, restructuring (or "retuning", as of a sound but neglected piano). He knew he needed the genuine support of the people, and decided that the way to win it was to be honest about the country's problems. This part of the plan was called *glasnost*, usually rendered "openness", though a more accurate translation would be "frankness", because the Russian word implies owning up to what is already clear.

Perestroika was not intended to make the USSR more Western. Still less was it meant to dismantle the communist system altogether. It was all done under the banner of a "return to Leninist principles". At the same time, Gorbachev was careful to endear himself to the West: he put an end to some of the grossest (and most obvious) human rights abuses of his predecessors.

For example, he released the dissident physicist Andrei Sakharov from internal exile *(see page 87)*. He allowed the satellite states to pursue *glasnost* locally, even though several of them, such as Czechoslovakia and the GDR, were deeply opposed to the policy. He talked seriously about disarmament (with hindsight it appears he had little choice, considering the state of the Russian economy), and he cleverly made all of these concessions look as though he was simply doing the world a favour Also, he used his considerable personal charm to win American support (and with it dollars) for his reforms.

But Gorbachev had sown the seeds of his eventual downfall. The spotlight he turned on the Soviet system only revealed that it was rotten beyond repair. The limited debate under *glasnost* soon broadened into a discussion of the legitimacy of the entire regime. The peoples of Eastern Europe, who had always viewed communism as the oppressors' tool, turned on their Communist leaders. In 1989, the Soviet sphere in Europe fell apart in a series of popular revolts that swept from Berlin to Bucharest. Gorbachev just let it happen.

The USSR tottered on for two further years, but an attempted coup against Gorbachev in the summer of 1991 was the regime's death rattle. Gorbachev was sidelined: president of a geopolitical entity that was about to disappear. Power devolved to the popular new president, Boris Yeltsin.

Capitalism arrives

The new man in the Kremlin was master of a much-reduced domain. Russia was suddenly a smaller state than it had been at any time since Catherine the Great and was free of the responsibilities of Empire and the ideological constraints of communism. Yeltsin threw open the doors and invited capitalism in. Within a year Russia had all the trappings of a free market economy: a stock market, hyperinflation, robber millionaires, homelessness, food in the shops and mafia cartels.

The market economy was never given the chance to stabilise. Yeltsin constantly changed tack, throwing out the government and its policies by presidential decree.

When the reactionary parliament opposed him he sent tanks into Moscow and shelled their stronghold; he used similar strong-arm tactics, on a much bloodier scale, against the

separatist republic of Chechnya. In his second term, as his democratic credentials wore thin, he looked less like a Westernising reformer in the tradition of Peter the Great (which is how he saw himself), and more like a sad repeat of Leonid Brezhnev: unaware, drinking to excess, and helpless.

On the final day of the 20th century, in a move that surprised the world, Boris Yeltsin resigned from office and named Prime Minister Vladimir Putin as acting president. A former KGB officer, Putin rode a wave of patriotic fervour after the renewal of the military campaign in Chechnya and on 26 March 2000 he won the race to lead his country. ❑

LEFT: the ideological fathers of the USSR.
RIGHT: the dolls that embraced capitalism.

NOTES OF A BLOCKADE SURVIVOR

**These vivid recollections of the 1941–43
siege of the city are those of the writer and
historian Lidiya Ginzburg (1902–90)**

There was no peace, ever. Even at night. The fight for warmth continued even in one's sleep. It wasn't that people hadn't means to keep warm – they certainly piled enough warm things over themselves before going to bed. But this made the body struggle – all these heavy things were quite a load; what is worse, they slipped and constantly fell off. In order to hold the entire pile in place, one had to make insignificant yet tiring muscular efforts. One had to train oneself to sleep without moving. One could not afford to throw one's arms wide, or to lift one's knees beneath the blanket, or to turn and hide one's face in the pillow. This meant that the body never got a complete rest.

People fought for their lives in their own apartments just as polar explorers do in emergencies. In the morning they woke in a sack or in a cave constructed from every conceivable material they could pile up. People woke at four, at five. They may get warm during the night, yet all around cold tormented them all day.

Still, people waited with impatience – not even for morning, because morning (light) came much later – no, they waited for a suitable reason to get up. At 6am the stores and bakeries opened. This does not mean that everyone went to the baker's at six in the morning; on the contrary, many tried to stave off the moment for as long as they could. In a way, it was the best moment: all the bread of the day is still ahead, yet it is not the reality of the day.

Hungry impatience eventually got the upper hand over fear of cold. It pushed people out of their little caves, warmed with their own breath, into the coldness of the rooms. It was easy to get up, much easier than in the life where scrambled eggs were waiting for you.

The day started with a visit to the kitchen or the service staircase, where firewood had to be prepared for the temporary stove. Night was only just starting to disperse, and the walls of the building opposite did not yet carry even a hint of their colour; they loomed darkly through the broken glass of the staircase window. So one had to work by touch, driving the axe at an angle to the wood, and then striking. Hands were the greatest problem. Fingers tended to close and remain in some chance position. The hand lost its ability to grasp. It could only be used as a paw, a stump or a stick-like tool. People groped in the dark as they collected splinters from the stone floor of the landing, lifting them between two stumps, and placing them in a basket.

Next water was brought from the frozen cellar. Ice covered the steps of the laundry, so people slid down on their haunches. On the return trip, they went up with a full bucket, searching for dents in the icy surface to put the bucket in – a mountaineering exercise. The resistance of each thing had to be negotiated with one's will and one's body, without tools or devices.

One rested on the lower steps with full buckets. Far away, a ceiling with an alabaster knob… head thrown backwards, people measured the rise of the staircase, through which they were about to carry the water using sheer willpower.

The day was full of waiting spaces. The largest was the space separating one from dinner. The best place for dinner was a departmental canteen, where porridge tasted more like porridge. People would run, spurred on by the cold, through the insultingly beautiful city, snow crackling underfoot. Alongside, other people would run (or crawl) with bags, with covered dishes suspended from the ends of their stick-like arms. People would run in the cold, conquering space that had suddenly become material. In the canteen, it is so cold that the fingers that froze in the street will not open; people hold spoons between the thumb (the only digit that works) and the frozen stump.

Dinner itself is another hassle with space; the spaces of dinner are small yet agonisingly condensed with queues of people. A queue before the door, a queue before the inspector, a queue for an empty seat at the table. Dinner is something fleeting and ephemeral (a plate of soup, and so many grammes of porridge).

Then there was a period of successive air raids, which came one after another. On the way to dinner one had to hide in cellars or continue through the noise of the anti-aircraft guns and the whistles of the militia. People hated the militiamen, who saved them from the bombs, but kept them away from dinner.

Some people left home at eleven in the morning and sometimes came back at six or seven in the evening. It was absolutely dark at home. The stove was lit and, in its smoky light, the soup from the canteen was poured into a pot. Bread was cut into 40-gramme pieces. Then the person who came from the outside world, the world with dinner, moved closer to the stove and warmed frozen hands.

Until the day's supply of splinters burned out, nothing could tear that person away from this exquisite pleasure. In the room behind, cold was raging and darkness reigned. It was only near the small door of the stove that the life-giving circle of light and warmth shone. The only thing one could warm were one's palms. The palms absorbed the flames. It was

sheer ecstasy, which was invariably spoiled by its swift end.

It was waiting for the end and the realisation of the ebbing of our vital forces which spoiled any joy. The blockade made this formula self-evident. What takes place is the displacement of suffering with suffering, the mindless sense of purpose of the doomed. This explains how people survive in an isolated cell, a forced-labour camp, or in the lowermost depths of humiliation. This is something that the more fortunate people find difficult to understand: it is only people in comfortable cottages who blow their brains out without apparent reason. ❏

LEFT AND RIGHT: vegetables growing in front of St Isaac's Cathedral during the Blockade, whose victims are commemorated at Piskarevsky Cemetery.

Decisive Dates

1703 St Petersburg is founded by Peter the Great who commissions the construction of the Peter and Paul Fortress. A year later the Admiralty shipyard is built. Work on the Summer Gardens begins.

1710 Alexander Nevsky Lavra is founded.

1712 St Petersburg becomes Russia's capital.

1714 The Kunstkamera, Russia's first museum, is founded and the city's first stone buildings are built.

1715 Russia's first Naval Academy is founded.

1718 Peter the Great executes his son, Tsarevich Alexei, in the Peter and Paul Fortress – by now a prison for enemies of the government.

1721 Peace is made with Sweden, ending the long Northern War that had stretched over two decades. Peter takes the title emperor.

1724 The Academy of Sciences is founded. The remains of St Alexander Nevsky are moved from Vladimir to the Alexander Nevsky Monastery.

1725 Peter the Great dies, and his second wife, Catherine I, ascends the throne. The population of St Petersburg is about 40,000.

1728 Peter II, Peter the Great's son, becomes emperor and moves the capital back to Moscow.

1732 Under Empress Anna, Peter the Great's niece, St Petersburg becomes capital again.

1736–7 Fire destroys the centre of the city.

1741 Elizabeth Petrovna, Peter the Great's daughter, seizes power after deposing the child emperor, Ivan VI, who ruled for less than a year.

1750 The city's population reaches about 100,000.

1754 Francesco Bartolomeo Rastrelli begins building the Winter Palace.

1757 The Academy of Arts is founded.

1761 Elizabeth dies, Peter III becomes emperor.

1762 Peter is deposed by his wife, Catherine II (Catherine the Great).

1767 Catherine begins buying art collections, laying the foundation of the Hermitage museum.

1777 The city is hit by flooding.

1782 The Bronze Horseman monument is unveiled.

1785 The Marble Palace is built by Catherine II for her lover Prince Orlov and she purchases Diderot's library for her collection.

1789 Catherine II builds the Tauride Palace for her lover, Prince Potemkin.

1795 The Imperial Public Library is founded.

1796–7 When Catherine dies, her son Pavel begins his short rule. Construction work on the Mikhailovsky Castle begins.

1799 Pavel is assassinated in Mikhailovsky Castle, and Alexander I, later known as Alexander the Great, becomes emperor.

1811 The Kazan Cathedral is completed.

1812 Napoleon invades Russia.

1816 Russia's first stock exchange opens on the Spit of Vasilievsky Island.

1823 The Admiralty building is completed.

1824 Flooding in the city.

1825 Alexander I dies, and the Decembrists rise up when Nicholas I ascends the throne.

1826 Five of the Decembrist leaders are executed at the Arsenal (now the Artillery Museum).

1832 The Alexander Column is erected.

1834 The Senate and Synod buildings, designed by Carlo Rossi, are finished.

1837 Russia's leading poet, Alexander Pushkin, is killed in a duel. The first Russian railway opens between St Petersburg and Tsarskoe Selo. The Winter Palace burns down, and is rebuilt nearly a year later.

1850 The Annunciation Bridge, now Lt. Schmidt Bridge, opens as the city's first permanent bridge.

1851 The Moscow to St Petersburg railway opens.

1853 The city's population is over half a million. Nicholas I dies. Alexander II ascends the throne.

1858 St Isaac's Cathedral is finished.

1860 The Mariinsky Theatre is opened, and the State Bank of Russia is founded.

1861 Serfdom is abolished.

1863 A central water supply system is opened.
1869 Mendeleev, a professor at St Petersburg university, creates the periodic table.
1879 The first street lights appear.
1881 Alexander II is assassinated. The Church on the Spilled Blood is built on the site of his death.
1885 The St Petersburg sea port moves from the Spit of Vasilievsky Island to its current location in the southeast.
1890 Tchaikovsky's *Sleeping Beauty* premieres at the Mariinsky. The city's population reaches 1 million.
1894 Alexander III dies. Nicholas II becomes tsar.
1898 The Russian Museum opens.
1903 The Trinity Bridge spans the Neva, spurring a building boom on the Petrograd side.
1905 Hundreds of peaceful workers and their families are shot by government troops at Palace Square on Bloody Sunday. A general strike begins, leading to a full uprising across the empire.
1906 As part of the government's concessions, the State Duma, the Russian parliament, convenes for the first time in the Tauride Palace.
1907 The Church on the Spilled Blood is finished.
1910 The city's population exceeds 2 million.
1914 World War I. The city is renamed Petrograd.
1917 Tsar Nicholas II abdicates in what is called the February Revolution. The Bolsheviks seize power in October. The city's population reaches 2½ million.
1918 The Bolsheviks dissolve the democratically elected Constituent Assembly, called just after the Bolshevik seizure of power, to choose a new post-tsarist government. The Red Terror begins as anti-communist forces march on Petrograd. The capital is moved to Moscow.
1919 Petrograd is under siege by the White Army. The population flees as food supplies are cut off.
1920 Only 700,000 people remain in the city, which is totally paralysed by the communist terror.
1921 The sailors of the Kronstadt naval base rise up against the Bolsheviks. All are massacred.
1924 Lenin dies; the city is renamed Leningrad. The third worst flood in the city's history strikes.
1929 Communist authorities begin pulling down churches as part of their anti-religion campaign.
1934 Sergei Kirov is assassinated in his office in Smolny, setting off the Great Terror.
1939 The city population reaches 3.2 million.
1941 In June the Nazis invade Russia, and in September the Siege of Leningrad begins.
1944 The 900-day Siege is lifted on 27 January. Nearly 700,000 deaths plus mass emigration reduce the city's

population to 500,000.
1955 The city's underground railway opens.
1964 The Peterhof Palace opens to the public after restoration of damage caused by the war.
1979 Construction begins on the flood protection barrier in the Gulf of Finland.
1988 Fire rips through the library of the Academy of Sciences, destroying thousands of rare books.
1989 UNESCO makes the city a World Heritage Site. The population reaches 5 million.
1991 Anatoly Sobchak becomes the city's first mayor.
1996 Vladimir Yakovlev becomes city governor.
1998 The remains of Tsar Nicholas II, his family and servants are interred in the Peter and Paul Cathedral. Financial crisis paralyses Russia.

2000 Former city deputy governor, Vladimir Putin, becomes Russia's president. The city becomes the official capital of the Northwest Federal District.
2003 The city celebrates its 300th anniversary, marked by numerous infrastructure and restoration projects.
2004 Director of Russia's largest oil company, YUKOS, is imprisoned for tax evasion and the state seizes some of the company's assets.
2005 Russia and Germany agree a deal to connect the countries via a gas pipeline run under the Baltic Sea.
2006 After decades of tight monetary control, the ruble is allowed to become a convertible currency. Over $5-million worth of artefacts go missing from the Hermitage museum. ❏

LEFT: Peter I with his family in 1720.
RIGHT: a commander of the Red Army.

THE CITY TODAY

After years of neglect, St Petersburg is a rejuvenated city, thanks in no small part to President Putin favouring his home city at a time when Russia – thanks to the high price of oil – is reasserting its power in global affairs

During the hard-line communist coup of August 1991, the people of Leningrad massed onto Palace Square, in front of the Winter Palace, just as they did in 1917 when the fate of Russia was decided on these same smooth cobblestones. But this time there was no government in the palace, either to defend or to storm. This time it was Moscow that was the scene of the action.

One month later, the democratic forces, which had never really taken to being Leningraders, won the city's subsequent change of name back to St Petersburg.

Many of the democrats' hopes and dreams failed to materialise, however, and by the mid-1990s many were too consumed by persistent and overwhelming economic hardship to worry about high ideals. Survival in Russia's brutal capitalist world became the ultimate deadly game: businessmen had to dodge the bullets of organised crime, while workers were paid slave-like salaries – if paid at all.

The 1998 crash

After the August 1998 financial crash caused by an outdated tax code, low oil prices and huge government debt, St Petersburg's plight seemed hopeless. Receiving only 5 percent of all foreign investment (while Moscow gathered 80 percent), the city teetered on the brink of bankruptcy, the federal government shut down the city's only national broadcasting station, and the most talented people in town

were fleeing for Moscow, Europe or America. This great, former imperial capital had been reduced to a crumbling, provincial town. That all changed in the course of one night, in August 1999, when Vladimir Putin, an obscure government official who came from St Petersburg, was appointed Russia's prime minister. On 31 December of that year, he became Russia's acting president after Boris Yeltsin's resignation, and a few months later he won the presidential election.

Today St Petersburg is a boom town, and quickly becoming one of the most fashionable places in Europe thanks to its rich cultural, economic and technological potential.

LEFT: older citizens feel out of place in the New Russia.
RIGHT: tricentennial celebrations in 2003

The cost of living

There are plenty of stores with a wide assortment of goods and services. Though locals complain how little they earn, they clearly spend beyond their means, proving that most people are making their money off the books – tax evasion has become a national sport.

Many locals own their apartments, which were privatised for a pittance in what was a rare display of long-term thinking by the government, and their main expenses are food and clothing, both of which are affordable – unlike imported goods.

Foreign travel once a year is more feasible than before the mid-1990s, with a trip to St Petersburg. Putin has made the city the official capital of the Northwest Federal District, one of the seven federal districts created in 2000 as part of a plan to reform the country's government. The Northwest has one of the richest and fastest growing economies in the country, with numerous ports, increasing foreign manufacturing and the largest oil and natural gas deposits in Europe.

Vladimir Putin began his political career in 1991, serving as Sobchak's deputy mayor until the latter's defeat in the 1996 mayoral elections. Considered an enigma by many observers and analysts, Putin is indeed the ultimate St Petersburg sphinx, combining two

Turkey now costing as little as $350 a person for one week, a price which is equivalent to the average worker's monthly salary. The city's yuppie class is growing, with most employed in the new capitalist economy, in industries such as telecommunications, sales and trading, public relations and media, banking and real estate. A decade ago, these sectors barely existed and an unfeasibly high proportion of the population was employed in the defence industry.

The rise of Vladimir Putin

Most of the city's current prosperity is due to President Putin, who was born and raised in seemingly incompatible backgrounds: career KGB agent and top assistant to one of post-Soviet Russia's leading democrats.

With Putin's ascendancy to the Kremlin, St Petersburg's star is again on the rise. There is no reason to move the capital back to the banks of the Neva because, besides Putin, others from St Petersburg occupy many of the highest positions in his government, many of whom worked with the President in the early 1990s. Little wonder that the Russian government easily approved spending $1.7 billion over a three-year period to rebuild Russia's 'Window on the West' in time for the city's 300th anniversary in 2003.

Infrastructure projects

As part of the tricentenary projects, construction on the flood protection barrier *(see page 212)*, which began in the early 1980s, will continue with a boost of about $500 million and is scheduled to be completed in 2010. While flooding is an annual occurrence, primarily in the autumn, three times in the city's 300-year history – in 1777, 1824 and 1924 – St Petersburg has been hit by devastating floods. Another project is a ring road which, at a cost of just under $1 billion, will allow vehicles to avoid the city centre when travelling between city districts, as well as reroute heavy lorries between Finland and other major Russian cities.

million in 2003. Placed in perspective, such plans are a humble effort to rebuild a city centre that has more than 5,000 pre-1917 buildings, a large number of which are crumbling and dilapidated.

About 15 percent of city residents live in communal flats in the centre, among the worst slums in Europe. You can sometimes go into the entrance hall of an old apartment house; behind its brightly painted facade, you wander through an archway into the courtyard. Inside, by the huge front doors of each stairwell, are several door bells, perhaps four, maybe even eight. Some have handwritten messages telling callers to ring

Rebuilding the city

Among the main beneficiaries of federal largesse are the city's cultural mainstays: the Hermitage Museum, the Russian Museum and the Mariinsky (the former Kirov) Theatre. The World Bank will loan the city about $150 million for the reconstruction of the historical centre. Part of that plan envisages giving a boost to the hotel and tourism industry. The city has few western-grade hotels to accommodate the growing number of foreign visitors, which totalled about 2.6

a signal of two long buzzes and one short for a particular person.

These are the communal flats with a separate family to every room, where they share a common bathroom and kitchen. Often in former, extravagant tsarist-era quarters, the new Russian rich, as well as an influx of foreigners, now covet these flats for between $1,300 and $5,000 a square metre. The buyers must also pay to resettle the tenants, and renovations might cost just as much – if not more.

The crime rate

Like any big city, St Petersburg has its problems. The rise in the rate of crime has been

LEFT: many people find it difficult to make ends meet.
ABOVE: workers take a break from renovation.

accompanied by an increase in corruption among the police force that has made them ineffective in protecting the people, and sometimes even more of a threat than the criminals. The fear Russians have of their own police is shocking to Westerners. Russian police often extort, beat and harass people; locals recall lugubriously that nothing like it went on in Soviet times.

The police can work well, if you're willing to pay them for an investigation. They too are capable capitalists who have basically privatised justice.

In times of distress, poorer Russians are loathe to call the police, so they rely on

themselves and their friends for protection and to mete out justice when possible. All the same, St Petersburg is safer today than it was in the early 1990s. Most current crime concerns businessmen and rarely touches tourists, except for the pickpockets and gypsies who prey upon unsuspecting visitors in the summertime. As in any large city, it pays to be streetwise in St Petersburg.

Modern women

Flaunting wealth is a Russian pastime, and Russian men know it is what most readily catches a Russian woman's attention. Indeed, most Russian females aren't especially interested in Western ideas of feminism, but rather are on the look out for a successful husband to support them. And they do know how to snare their prey: indeed, the women of St Petersburg are considered to be the most beautiful in Russia. Little wonder that dozens of marriage agencies operate in the city, attracting Western men in search of the perfect Russian bride. This new phenomenon, the image of the Russian woman as sex-object, has largely been prompted by the Westernisation of Russian society through advertisements and film. The battle to achieve real equality of status for women is likely to be a long one.

The drinking revolution

More than 80 years on, a new revolution is brewing in St Petersburg. Of all the upheavals ripping through the fabric of Russian society in the past 15 years, one of the most significant is the rapid increase in beer consumption. It sounds like heresy to many older Russians, weaned on vodka and grain alcohol, but younger Russians are finding comfort in the better quality beers produced by almost a dozen domestic manufacturers that have appeared since economic liberalisation began in 1991.

Five years ago tens of thousands gathered to sample Russian beers at the first St Petersburg Beer Festival. The festival eventually became extremely popular, attracting well over 1 million people, mostly rowdy young men who were (unsurprisingly) keen to get drunk. It was held in the area around the Winter Palace and St Isaac's Square, and city officials feared rioting and the destruction of city monuments. In the end, the authorities banned it altogether.

Still, with St Petersburg being home to the country's leading brewers such as Baltika, Vena, Bochkarev and Stepan Razin, it's not surprising that the city has been christened Russia's beer capital.

Besides beer, in the 1990s St Petersburg became Russia's tobacco capital. The country's largest tobacco factories, such as Japan Tobacco are here, as well as that of Philip Morris, which recently surpassed Japan Tobacco to claim the title of the largest cigarette factory in the world outside the US.

Other industries

The city is also going back to what it does best – arms manufacture, especially naval vessels, and heavy engineering equipment for power plants and the oil and gas sector. China, India, and Iran are among the biggest clients. St Petersburg is also the Baltic Sea's largest and Russia's second largest port. Plans to modernise and expand the port will double capacity to 60 million tons a year and make it the largest port in the country.

But high-tech industries, especially those connected to computer programming and the internet, are rapidly growing and showing the city the way to future wealth. With its enor-

coveted status symbols that few possessed, while today nearly 60 percent of Petersburgers have mobiles and the city streets are choking from traffic jams with every third family owning a car. People are generally better dressed and groomed, and are starting to smile more, though this doesn't always come easy for some.

Of course, Russia's new prosperity is in large part tied to the high price of oil *(see below)*, of which Russia is the world's second largest producer. Whether or not the country can move away from such dependence and create a sustainable economy remains the chief question for the government. ❑

mous scientific potential and highly qualified workforce, St Petersburg has been named Russia's Silicon Valley.

In the mid-1990s, many computer programmers were lured to America and Europe with big salaries, as part of a so-called brain drain. Now, many others are finding well-paid jobs at home as the Russian economy posts its most spectacular growth in the past half century.

Indicative of this fact is that, in 2000, items such as mobile phones and cars were

LEFT: there are more opportunities for youth today.
ABOVE: nostalgic goods sell well to the tourist market.

ON THE ROAD WITH BLACK GOLD

Russia's economy and global influence hit rock bottom in August 1998 when the state was forced to default on its debt because of the collapse in world oil and natural gas prices. Government revenue and the price of oil and gas go hand-in-hand in Russia – the world's second largest oil producer. The oil and gas industry accounts for up to 25% of Russia's GDP. Russia's current economic boom is driven by high prices for oil and gas. The benefits are not just economic. As the conflict in Iraq stoked supply fears in the Middle East, Russia's global importance strengthened – its safe supply of oil made its economic voice impossible to ignore.

THE PEOPLE OF PETER

**Despite its ornate architecture and Venetian beauty,
St Petersburg is a tough city to live in, but now –
after decades of emigration – most of its inhabitants
wouldn't wish to live anywhere else**

The city successively known as St Petersburg, Petrograd and Leningrad has always been referred to as "Peter" by its inhabitants. They have suffered more than most in recent history but today they are busy creating a new St Petersburg, both to preserve and restore what's worth keeping, and to construct a modern city on this sturdy foundation.

Housing

Life in the so-called sleeping districts can seem frightful to foreigners, especially if they are home-owners. Most of the city's population live in poorly built pre-fab high-rises, occupying small apartments that are on average one-third the size of a West European apartment. Most Russians, however, see little point in complaining, and are thankful to have a secure living space.

Accustomed to seeking out the positive side, they sometimes boast about the clean air. It is indeed clean because most of the soulless housing estates are located towards the outskirts of town. Living there hardly feels like being part of St Petersburg, the former Imperial capital, but housing is cheaper on the outskirts and most of the available land in the city centre has been snapped up by real estate companies, as well as wealthy Russians who can afford to maintain the grandeur of a tsarist-era apartment.

Some old-style communal apartments still exist near the centre, though. Their residents are accustomed to sharing kitchens and bathrooms with their neighbours, and can only hope that those neighbours do not turn out to be alcoholic, loud or even violent. For others, especially students and migrants from provincial towns and villages, renting a room in a communal flat is a reasonable alternative to the high prices of the real estate market, and they are often happy to put up with irritating inconveniences – so long as they can stay in the city.

Old people

St Petersburg has one of the oldest populations in the nation, with 1.2 million inhabitants past retirement age. The majority have housing and health problems and are also burdened by increasing poverty as inflation eats away at their savings and Vladimir Putin's government cuts back on social security benefits. Such older people are resilient because they've always had to be: they still remember World War II, the 900 days of the blockade, the bombs and shells which destroyed 3,000 buildings and damaged another 7,000.

During the war, hunger claimed over 600,000 lives; air and artillery raids another 17,000. Some have seen frozen corpses in the streets and watched the lawns near St Isaac's being turned into vegetable plantations *(see picture page 36)*. Come Victory Day (9 May), the veterans march along Nevsky prospekt – the length of their column gets shorter with each passing year.

Petersburger, there are some dominant types who most likely define life in the city today.

Academics and students

St Petersburg was always known for its educated people, good manners and culture. Refined intellectuals from "Peter" have at times been attacked by outsiders (especially Muscovites) for their snobbery. It's true that the influence of Europe, which was preserved in the city's architecture, museums and history, helped give local intellectuals a degree of cosmopolitanism not found in Moscow during the Soviet period. Still, shut off behind the Iron Curtain, many of them

The new Russia

Russian society was relatively homogeneous in the Soviet period and even up to the early 1990s. Historically, there were several major social groupings – workers, peasants, intellectuals, and then the small, ruling Party elite.

Today, Russia has a vast variety of social groups, and that is even more pronounced in major cities such as St Petersburg. While it is impossible to specify who is a typical St

PRECEDING PAGES: catching a lift at the Winter Palace.
LEFT: winter temperatures fall well below zero.
ABOVE: taking advantage of a sunny summer in front of the Peter and Paul fortress.

A COSMOPOLITAN OUTLOOK

St Petersburg is the most northerly city in the world to have more than 1 million inhabitants. Nearly 5 million live here – not only Russians, who constitute the vast majority, but also Ukrainians, Belorussians and people from other nations of the former Soviet republics.

The atmosphere of old St Petersburg may be long gone, but in this city, designed as a cultural centre, many of the citizens consider themselves the most cultivated of Russians. In keeping with the city's traditional role as Russia's window on the world, they also pride themselves on maintaining a cosmopolitan outlook and on being receptive to cultural change.

lacked foreign language skills and worldly knowledge – in stark contrast to most of today's generation of 20-somethings.

The student population attending St Petersburg's 40 colleges, institutes and universities adds a distinct flavour to the city. Students here receive a state subsidy but it is too small to support them, so many take on a part-time job, while the richer ones are subsidised by their parents. Easy-going academic terms are interspaced with the usual excruciating exam periods and sleepless nights. Library facilities at least are adequate: the city has several large ones and some 1,700 regular libraries. So are the holidays: in the long summer break, many

students head for the Black Sea, either to the Crimea in Ukraine, or to Turkey, where a holiday can cost as little as $350.

You can recognise a member of the student tribe anywhere – despite the varying quality of the clothes they wear, the students of St Petersburg resemble their peers from Paris, Boston or Stockholm. Well, perhaps St Petersburg students are paler and more prone to colds.

The businessman

The businessman is the most maligned and conspicuous new character on the Russian demographic map. Often disparagingly referred to as New Russians by poorer people and those still holding Soviet political views, the country's businessmen have undeniably been accumulating great wealth, but their lives are far from rosy.

There are countless tales of rags to riches in today's Russia. Many young people, especially those who grew up in Soviet poverty, are eager to make something out of their life. Although international reporters have focused for much of the past decade on the so-called oligarchs – Russia's "robber barons" – the period since the 1998 financial crisis has seen the emergence of many honest businessmen striving to make the country work. Some are putting off marriage – which in Russia tends to happen before the age of 25 – in order to concentrate on their careers.

The businesswoman

The city's young female population has two roads to choose from. Some prefer to marry

THE RISE OF ORGANISED CRIME

Russia has been ranked fifth in the world, per capita, for murders, thanks mainly to the estimated 5,000 contract killings a year, most of them businessmen. Like many Western cities, St Petersburg society has become dramatically stratified, with the rich tending to live in certain districts and the poor in less desirable areas. Some districts, such as the city's southeast, are considered to be the most drug-infested in Europe, and are best avoided.

Tourists are fairly safe. Street crime in the city centre is limited to pickpockets and street vendors short-changing customers. Beggars have returned to Nevsky prospekt, with mothers in rags holding pallid, mute chil-

dren. Child labour – nothing new in Russia's history – is also back on the streets as kids, usually from poor homes, hustle to make some money for their families.

Organised crime has become more sophisticated and is more likely to use computer hackers than hardmen, and St Petersburg has some of the best hackers in the world.

For the most part, the mafia has gone legitimate and become part of the establishment. It's no secret that many politicians are on its payroll, and in some cases mafia bosses are in public office. Today they have legal control – originally gained through violence, of course – over some of the most profitable parts of the local economy.

and stay at home with the children. But a growing number of young women are proving themselves both capable and tough in the rough, male-dominated Russian world of business. Recent social surveys are showing that women are becoming increasingly prominent in mid- and upper-level management positions.

Post-Soviet working class

The post-Soviet working class bears little resemblance to what it was in Soviet times. Many factories, especially those tied to the collapsed defence sector, have long since closed or laid off more than half their work-

binge drinking torpedoes their chances of a placid old age. The average life expectancy for a man here is 59, while for women it is 73 – well below levels in the West.

Rest and relaxation

Yet optimism is hard to annihilate in St Petersburg. There's more to life, people argue, than the mundane matters of everyday economics. Something new happens daily on the culture scene. After Moscow, St Petersburg offers more to lovers of theatre, classical music, concerts and opera than any other Russian city.

Young people in particular tend to do their

ers. Many workers have become demotivated as a result of long years of idling, guaranteed wages and suppressed initiative. A lot of people over 45 are unable to come to terms with the demands of the new economy.

The situation has caused alcoholism to rise, with all the attendant social problems. Domestic violence is more prevalent, and some estimates claim that up to 15,000 women die at the hands of their men each year in Russia. Men do themselves plenty of damage, too, as

own thing, as evidenced by the publicity given to rave parties. Sports enthusiasts can watch their heroes – the Zenit football club and the Army hockey club. Local people love the countryside: St Petersburg has attractive environs, made famous by the former residences of the tsars which are very popular day-trip destinations, as are the forests and the lakes of Karelia, to the north of the city.

And if there's no time to get away to the beaches of the Gulf of Finland, you can enjoy the sun right in the city limits. You can join the locals, even during the winter, by sunbathing on the small beach near the Peter and Paul Fortress. ❏

LEFT: remaining war heroes commemorate the Great Patriotic War.
ABOVE: the city has always attracted artists.

THE INFLUENCE OF RELIGION

The number of churches in St Petersburg suggests
that Russia, like Italy, is a country united by faith.
However, the relationship between church and
state has often been an uneasy one, and remains so

The gradual rehabilitation of churches since the late 1980s, together with the congregations they attract and new members entering the priesthood, constitutes something of a religious revival in Russia. Some see it as a triumphant repudiation of the propaganda drummed into Russians over four generations by Soviet state organs such as the Society of the Militant Godless. Others draw comparisons with the recent rise of Islamic fundamentalism in the Asian republics of the former USSR – a manifestation of a society in upheaval looking to their more glamorous past for some kind of cultural anchor.

The contemporary role of religion in Russia is quite different from, for example, the current Roman Catholic renaissance in Poland. The latter is a more political and intellectual force, at loggerheads with everything atheistic Communism once represented. Russian Orthodoxy, on the other hand, was never as intellectualised as Western Catholicism by the likes of Thomas Aquinas in the 13th century. The Russian faith was and is rooted in worship, not scholastic theology, and it is not inconceivable that it could have contrived a modus vivendi with Communism as it did with tsarist absolutism if the opportunity had arisen.

Who goes to church?

Visitors to a Russian Orthodox service will be struck by the highly orchestrated ritual. There are no bibles or hymnals in evidence, and few

seem to know the procedure, nor understand the Old Church Slavonic, which dates back 1,000 years and is only a distant echo of contemporary Russian. Worshippers seem to cross themselves and bow at almost any moment. The air is thick with incense, the richly coloured icons hold pride of place, and there is close interaction between clergy and congregation, communicating with one another through a sonorous chant. Those familiar with the Greek Orthodox liturgy will recognise the common Byzantine source.

Anyone who visited Russia in Communist times will be struck not only by the large number of churches open today, but also by the age

---

LEFT: the *Mother of God* icon.
RIGHT: a baby is baptised.

range of the worshippers. Some churches even provide a carpet and toys for young children. Nearly all middle-aged and younger Christians, at least in the cities, are well-educated, while poorer, working-class people are to be found mostly in the few churches that undertake serious social involvement, such as the distribution of food and clothing. In addition, there are the sometimes bossy *babushkas* (grandmothers) and other elderly people who have maintained their faith through the decades of persecution.

A craze for getting baptised started in the late 1980s, and has produced many nominal Christians who no longer go to church; some of these, in particular, are inclined to look back

to times before Bolshevism with a view to reliving past glories of the Russian Empire. Russian culture under the tsars was closely interwoven with Christian values and symbols, that even Communism could not completely conceal. But such nostalgia can lead to alarming ideas. A small minority of Orthodox church-goers are monarchists and long for the restoration of an absolutist tsar.

The role of church and state

The Russian Church had a peculiar role in society, because it never went through the process which eventually separated Church and State to varying degrees in the West. Ivan the Terrible directed arbitrary horrors against the church in the 16th century (for which he undertook exaggerated penances), but the Church was not finally subjugated until the early 18th century, as part of the westernising reforms of Peter the Great.

Peter abolished the office of patriarch (the head of the church), and made the ruling synod an organ of State, which was presided over by a government official – not necessarily a Christian – who had power to appoint and remove bishops; parish priests were even required to report to the police some of the things heard in private confessions. In the 20th century, the Communists exerted even tighter control *(see panel below)*.

The power of solitude

The church built up an economic strength that made it an obvious target when the state needed funds. Russian monks could claim

THE THIRD ROME

When the Bolsheviks took power in 1917, they regarded themselves as the ultimate spiritual authority, in exactly the same way as they assumed control over the armed forces. The messianic manner in which they presumed to convert the whole world to Communism was uncannily reminiscent of the 15th-century phenomenon of viewing Moscow as "the Third Rome". (Constantinople became "the Second Rome" after Rome was overrun in the early 5th century.) Although the Russian Church had progressively distanced itself from its Greek origins by adopting Old Slavonic for liturgical purposes (the Cyrillic alphabet was invented specifically to facilitate the translation of Byzantine Greek

texts into Slavonic languages) and by replacing its Greek bishops with native Russians, the bonds remained close, if only as an alliance against the hostility of Western Christianity to the Eastern rites as a whole.

The fall of Constantinople to the Turks in 1453 was therefore a devastating blow to the Russian Church, and Ivan III decided it was Moscow's sacred duty to become "the Third Rome" – the beacon of the True (Eastern) Faith. This mission ultimately led to what were in large part religious wars with Roman Catholic Poland in which the latter was no less determined to win Russia for the Pope, Rome and the Western faith.

much of the credit for opening up vast tracts of the Russian interior. Taking after the desert fathers of Syria and Egypt, they went deep into virgin forests to find sites for secluded monasteries, such as the settlement at Kizhi *(see page 208)*. The forest was their desert. The tireless energy with which they made these remote areas habitable was their undoing because they were trailed by peasants pleased to exchange their labour for the right to settle on the monastic lands as tenants.

These arrangements were preferable to serfdom, and led to the monasteries becoming the biggest and richest landowners in Russia. Many monks were content to capitalise on their enterprise and become landlords, but others preferred to push the frontiers ever outwards and start all over again. The cycle repeated itself until monasteries ringed the White Sea and encroached on the fringes of Siberia.

St Sergius of Radonezh (Sergei Radonezhskiy, 14th century) is the best known and most popular of the monks who simultaneously Christianised and colonised Russia. His tomb is revered at Sergeyev Posad monastery, 50km (30 miles) outside Moscow, probably the holiest shrine in the country It resembles a walled fortress and contains no fewer than seven churches and one of the Orthodox Church's theological seminaries. There is also provision for visitors, with a museum and shops.

LEFT: two elderly parishioners.
RIGHT: a monk reads from an ancient text.

The Church under Communism

The Tsar's abdication in February 1917 was welcomed by the Church which saw its opportunity to break free from State control and to restore the office of patriarch after a gap of two centuries. Patriarch Tikhon, who had been metropolitan archbishop in North America, was elected. Some people welcomed the Bolshevik revolution in general and specifically Lenin's decree of 23 January 1918 which separated Church from State and schools from Church. This separation turned out to be rather one-sided, as the State took over all Church property and placed obstacles in the way of free association and travel for

OLD BELIEVERS NEVER DIE

In the mid-17th century Russia was plunged into a religious dispute which, unlike the Reformation, was about ritual rather than doctrine. Nikon, a peasant monk and a close friend of the Romanov Tsar Alexei Mikhailovich, became patriarch in 1652. He decided to bring Church ritual into conformity with contemporary Byzantine practice. In effect, this meant people crossing themselves with three fingers rather than two and a few changes in verbal formulas. But conservatives within the Russian Church, who became known as Old Believers, fought the proposals.

Nikon was authoritarian and uncompromising, and persecution was common and even cruel. It continued into the reign of Peter the Great when the Old Believers refused to surrender their beards in the interest of bringing Russian society into line with Western Europe, where men were in the habit of shaving. Old Believers fled to remote areas rather than shave.

Colonies of Old Believers still exist, and have at least two active churches in Moscow. When official persecution ceased, many Old Believers chose to remain in their remote colonies. They became famous for their hospitality, although if the visitors were not Old Believers any plates or glasses they used had to be smashed afterwards. Guests were expected to leave money for replacements.

its members and leaders. This was before serious persecution began.

The 1921–23 famine persuaded Patriarch Tikhon to hand over much of the Church's gold and silver plate, stipulating only that sacred vessels be melted down by Church authorities and handed over as bullion.

This was done, raising enormous sums, but accounts show that all the money went into Party funds, and none, apparently, to the famine victims. The Party, or often just local officials, wanted to take everything. Tikhon issued an appeal to resist the theft of Church property, and the result was 1,500 bloody conflicts, followed by exile to Siberia or execution for the culprits.

Tikhon was also arrested and ecclesiastical Communist sympathisers, who formed the Living Church, usurped his position. They declared the patriarchate void and called on "every faithful churchman… to fight with all his might together with the Soviet authority for the realisation of the Kingdom of God upon earth… and to use all means to realise in life that grand principle of the October Revolution." Most of the faithful proved to be unmoved by the call and stayed loyal to the patriarchate rather than the alternative Living Church offered to them.

Amidst this chasm, various groups amalgamated and the Communists saw this as an opportunity to split the weakened Church. They favoured the Living Church with privileges, including free travel, while maintaining restrictions on everyone else. Eventually the Living Church faded away, but has left to this day the suspicion that moves for change in the Church are tainted with Bolshevism.

Tikhon was urged to repent in order to resume his duties. "I was filled with hostility against the Soviet authorities," he said on his release in 1923. "I repent of all my actions directed against the government." Tikhon's confession reaffirmed the traditional, though compromising, solidarity of Church and State.

The Church moves underground

A similar statement made by Tikhon's successor, Patriarch Sergei, in 1927 had much more influence. Followers assumed that both these statements of alliance with the Soviet regime had been made under duress, so elements of the Church went underground. Modelling their

---

OTHER FAITHS AND DENOMINATIONS

All religions suffered repression and persecution under Communism. The Baptists, an active (though not so numerous) union of Protestants who trace their origins in Russia to 1870, were in turn tolerated and persecuted like the members of the Orthodox Church. Roman Catholics, who once numbered at least 50,000 in St Petersburg alone in 1914, were totally suppressed. Islam had a marginally easier time because most Russian Muslims live in communities which are ethnically not Russian, and less easy to control from Moscow. Jews were always an easy target of repression, and recent research suggests that Stalin was preparing his own genocide of the Jews, cut short only by

his sudden death. Today, Jews enjoy more freedom and acceptance, occupying important positions in the private sector and government. Even so, neo-Nazi forces are gaining ground among disenchanted young people, and they often have patrons among the state security forces.

There are Buddhists here too, and a well-established Buddhist temple can be visited in St Petersburg in Novaya Derevnya *(see page 162)*. Today, there are Pentecostal churches in many parts of Russia, missions from Mormons, and other sects, mostly from Korea and North America. The scale of this theological invasion has lately begun to alarm both Orthodox churchmen and some politicians.

organisation on former Communist cell systems, they used passwords to make themselves known to one another. Priests in plain clothes would pop up unannounced in villages, administer to the faithful, and as suddenly disappear.

In 1927, the year in which Lenin's first Five-Year Plan started, intellectuals and Christians were denounced as enemies of the revolution. Tax collectors swooped on churches and, if the sum demanded was not met, they were boarded up. Teaching religion to children under 18 was forbidden except in private houses and to groups of no more than three children at a time.

Stalin was forced to relax the ban on Church activities during World War II. Everyone could see that the Germans were allowing churches to open in the territories they occupied, and after they withdrew the churches remained open by popular demand. When the war was over, however, controls were reimposed in the form of intense anti-religion propaganda in schools, and general intimidation of anyone who aired religious convictions.

This persecution continued under Nikita Khrushchev and Leonid Brezhnev, when many believers served terms in prison for holding prayer meetings or conducting baptisms – not because they were crimes as such, but because they constituted anti-Soviet agitation. The few officially registered places of worship were infested with KGB informers. Bibles and other religious texts were unavailable except on the black market.

When Mikhail Gorbachev introduced *perestroika* in the 1980s, Christians of all denominations sensed freedom, and took every opportunity to come into the open. The millennium celebration of Russian Christianity, held in 1988, was a big, international event. The present Russian constitution makes a fairer separation between Church and State, but today's politicians seem to think that appearing in public in the company of the Patriarch or a bishop is a vote-winner.

The future for faith

Under pressure from right-wing nationalists, and with some support from the patriarchate, Boris Yeltsin passed laws which curb the religious activity not only of sinister sects such as Aum Shinrikyo (which allegedly gassed the Tokyo metro in 1995), but other non-Orthodox faiths.

Fears that the laws would damage established denominations such as the Roman Catholics and the Baptists have so far been unfounded. President Putin has made a point of keeping church leaders on side, but it is likely that his bureaucrats would find ways of making life difficult for any who voiced dissent. Meanwhile, many of the 70 percent of Russians who declare themselves Orthodox are probably inspired less by fervent beliefs than by an instinctive loyalty to religion as a symbol of national identity. ❑

POLICE HARASSMENT

Anti-religious persecution intensified in the early 1960s, and even more churches were closed under Nikita Khrushchev than had been under Stalin. The Communists went to great lengths to discourage religious observance. For example, at Easter, the high point of the Orthodox calendar, state television would schedule a rare night of rock music. Those who went to midnight mass would encounter police and volunteer militia whose job was to stop anyone under 40 from entering the church. They were not actually forbidden to enter, but it was made clear that names of those attending "cult events" would be noted by the authorities.

LEFT: an Orthodox ceremony performed outdoors.
RIGHT: portrait of a Roman Catholic nun, 1908.

ART AND ARCHITECTURE

Peter the Great created St Petersburg as Russia's cultural capital, and the results of his vision can be seen both in the iconic buildings and in the astonishing treasure trove held by more than four dozen museums

St Petersburg has played a unique role in the history of Russian culture. It was here that Alexander Pushkin wrote his greatest poems, that Mikhail Glinka composed his masterpieces, that Ilya Repin painted his best pictures and that Andrei Voronikhin designed his neoclassical structures. Until the demise of the former Soviet Union, however, the past was officially viewed through a prism of political correctness. Now the richness of St Petersburg's culture can be assessed on its own merits, and much of it is readily on show at more than 50 museums.

These treasure troves range from the renowned Hermitage, with over 1,000 rooms, and the Russian Museum, displaying its art in the magnificent Mikhailovsky Palace, to the Alexander Pushkin Museum, commemorating the great writer and poet, and the Dostoyevsky Memorial Museum, showing the rooms where he wrote *The Brothers Karamazov*.

The Russian Museum *(see pages 137–43)* is an encyclopedia of national art, from its origins in the 10th century to current experimental works. It is especially strong in 18th-century portraits, a reflection of the fact that the Imperial Court, which then resided in St Petersburg, attracted painters in search of lucrative commissions. Here also are some very large icons, including *Apostle Peter* and *Apostle Paul*, by the 14th-century master of the form, Andrei Rublev *(see page 138)*.

LEFT: *Anna Akhamatova* by Natan Altmann, 1914.
RIGHT: Cubism heavily influenced Russia's avant-garde in the early 20th century.

Icons are inescapable here, whether in museums or churches. The tradition of icon painting, imported from Byzantium, had been controversial in the 8th and 9th centuries, condemned by many as sacrilegious because it portrayed holy figures. The purpose of icon painting, however, was not to depict reality but to aid contemplation and prayer. This was achieved mainly through the harmony of the lines that composed the figure. So subtle are the differences between many of the early icons that only an expert can detect them, and most people can best appreciate their power by contemplating one or two classic examples, such as Rublev's.

Art in the 17th and 18th centuries followed the broad patterns of western Europe. At the end of the 19th century, increasing pressure for social reform stimulated a distinctively Russian form of modern art. This initially sought its inspiration from the traditional folk art depicting peasant life, but in the early 20th century urban influences made themselves felt as painters took their inspiration from factory life and produced increasingly abstract works.

After the revolution in 1917, political propaganda and a celebration of industrial might created a school known as Constructivism. Avant-garde painters found their style repudi-

ated by Stalinism, though their work has now been rehabilitated in the Russian Museum.

The evolving architecture

St Petersburg's buildings, however magnificent, are also the visible expression of absolute power. Peter the Great (1672–1725) used brute force to realise his dream of creating a city from the unhealthy Neva marshland.

He was the first European potentate to conceive and organise a city as an architectural whole, and he chose to break with Russia's architectural traditions, which were heavily influenced by religion, and turned his eyes westwards. Having first dreamt of modelling

it on Amsterdam, Peter changed his mind while visiting France. Paris became his ideal.

Creating one of the world's most beautiful cities from the deserted and rough woodland involved hundreds of thousands of soldiers who were turned into bricklayers. Swedish prisoners-of-war, Finns and members of ethnic minorities were brought in as forced labourers; they drove stakes into the marshy ground and transported blocks of granite and stone to the site with their bare hands. Soon St Petersburg ranked with Paris and Rome.

Its grandeur was augmented by Catherine II, the wife of Peter III. During her reign the transition from baroque to Classicism began with the creation of the Marble Palace, the Pavlovsk Palace and the Academy of Fine Arts. Using architects, sculptors and well diggers brought from France and Italy, the empress remodelled the Neva Islands; she had wide avenues and spacious parks laid out, large and small palaces built.

Alexander I's reign from 1799 to 1825 saw St Petersburg become Europe's diplomatic capital. During his reign the Italian architect Carlo Rossi built numerous yellow and white palaces as well as the marvellous Mikhailovsky Square, bordered by the Mikhail Palace and other Rossi creations.

Although subsequent tsars continued to commission new buildings in St Petersburg, these were no longer as unified and accomplished as in the earlier years. As the tsars worried about their increasingly tenuous grip on the reins of power, the era of the well-balanced architectural ensemble came to an end.

In recent years the city's architects have faced the same problems as their counterparts in many other countries. Conservative clients like the historicist approach, so that a new building can instantly look 100 years old. A mixture of lax town planning, corrupt business deals, poor-quality building materials and a general lack of money has not promoted excellence in architecture. But the tourist dollar makes its voice heard and, though the odd moulding may occasionally tumble to the ground, injuring a few passers-by, there is agreement that the city's magnificent visual heritage must at all costs be maintained. ❑

LEFT: the grand facade of Rastrelli's Winter Palace.

The Great Architects

I t is the architects of the 18th and 19th centuries, and not the statesmen, who brought worldwide fame to St Petersburg – which explains why so many streets and squares are named after them. They came from France, Italy, Switzerland, England and Germany, as well as from Russia, to design some of the finest baroque and neoclassical structures of their age.

Swiss-born Domenico Trezzini came when the city was founded and, between 1703 and his death in 1734, built the earliest churches, government offices, palaces and country villas. Their distinctive features are streamlined silhouettes with modest interiors, and a combination of austere and baroque elements. Trezzini designed Peter's Summer Palace (1710–14) and the Cathedral of St Peter and Paul (1712–33).

Italian-born Bartolomeo Rastrelli (1700–71), a master of Russian rococo, created the Great Palace at Peterhof (Petrodvorets), the Smolny Convent (1748–59), the Vorontsov Palace (1749–57) on Sadovaya ulitsa and the Stroganov Palace (1752–54) at the corner of Nevsky prospekt and the Naberezhnaya reki Moika. These architectural ensembles, magnificent in their design and solemnity, were built, Rastrelli said, for the glory of Russia.

Neoclassicism was championed by Vassili Bazhenov (1737–99), who designed the Mikhailovsky Castle (1799–1800) and Vincenzo Brenna (1745–1800) and Ivan Starov (1745–1808), who built the Tauride Palace (1783–89) and the Holy Trinity Cathedral of the Alexander Nevsky Monastery (1778–90).

The buildings designed by Giacomo Quarenghi (1744–1817), another Italian, are distinguished by their grand colonnades, which stand out against a background of smooth surfaced walls. The main building of the Academy of Sciences (1783–89), the Hermitage Theatre with the arch over the Winter Canal (1783–87) and the

Smolny Institute (1806–09) were built to his designs. Russian neoclassicism reached its peak in the early 19th century when Andrei Voronikhin (1759–1814), born a serf, built the Cathedral of the Kazan Icon of the Mother of God (1801–11) on Nevsky prospekt and the Mining Institute (1806–11) on the Neva Embankment.

When architect Andreyan Zakharov (1761–1811) rebuilt the Admiralty he created a jewel of Russian architecture. Thomas de Thomon (1760–1813) designed the majestic building of the Stock Exchange (1804–10), which now houses the Central Naval Museum, and the two

landmark rostral columns (1806) on the Spit (Birzhevaya Strelka, now Pushkin Square) on Vasilievsky island. Of great significance were the buildings designed between 1818 and 1834 by Carlo Rossi, especially the Ploschad Isskustv ensemble encompassing the Russian Museum, and the building of the General Staff Headquarters, with its monumental arch over Bolshaya Morskaya ulitsa.

Frenchman Auguste Montferrand created the inimitable St Isaac's Cathedral (1818–58) and the Alexander Column (1830–34), both massively proportioned yet austerely beautiful.   ❑

RIGHT: Bartolomeo Rastrelli, master of rococo.

THE PERFORMING ARTS

Ballet, opera and classical music remain as strong
as ever, and the city's beleaguered movie makers
are finally making an international comeback

St Petersburg is famous for its ballet. As
early as the beginning of the 19th century, ballets produced by the choreographer Charles-Louis Didelot (1767–1837)
were performed at the city's Bolshoi Theatre. Alexander Pushkin, who often attended
the theatre, saw in Didelot's ballets "a lively
imagination of extraordinary charm". In the
early 20th century, Anna Pavlova (1881–
1931), Waslaw Nijinsky (1889–1950) and
Michel Fokine (1880–1942) danced to great
acclaim on the stage of the Mariinsky
Theatre *(see page 132)*.

But the best years of those inimitable
dancers were spent abroad, where they performed in the ballet troupe called the Russian
Seasons, formed in 1907 by the choreographer
Sergei Diaghilev (1872–1929). The ballerinas
Galina Ulanova and Maya Plisetskaya started
their careers in Leningrad, and it was also here
that Rudolf Nureyev, Natalia Makarova and
Mikhail Baryshnikov won their fame.

The city's opera and ballet companies were
founded by imperial command in 1742, but it
was only in the creation of the Mariinsky
Theatre a century later that they found a wor-
thy home, with its majestic facade and a dazzling auditorium with gilt-moulded
decorations and white sculptures. The Mariinsky is headed by Valeri Gergiev, one of the
most formidable cultural figures in St Petersburg. He has single-handedly raised the Mariinsky's opera from near obscurity in the
mid-1990s to international acclaim, successfully staging about 15 premieres a season.
Among his most prominent recent works have
been stagings of Wagner's *Der Ring des
Nibelungen* and Tchaikovsky's *War and
Peace*, in collaboration with Russian-Ameri-
can film director Andrei Konchalovsky.

Drama

For the past decade, St Petersburg's theatres
have produced some of the country's finest
drama, taking home many awards at Russia's
most prominent theatre ceremony, the Golden
Mask, held each spring. Yet, paradoxically,
drama in the city is in crisis. The problem is
that, while fine work is being produced by a
small number of stage directors, the average
quality merits little applause.

The city's theatre life is based not so much around a number of venues, but around individual actors and directors. "There are no great movements being made in theatre in St Petersburg, especially in comparison to Moscow which has always had a more vibrant theatre scene," according to local theatre critic Aleksandr Ures. "In St Petersburg, there are no interesting theatres *per se*, but rather interesting stage directors, actors and individual plays."

For almost three decades, for example, the best work produced was by the Bolshoi Drama Theatre (BTD) on the Fontanka, headed by Georgy Tovstonogov. But, after the death of its director and some of its leading performers, the BTD fell into crisis, though there are signs that it is enjoying a renaissance as new, young talent flocks to this venerable theatre.

Most theatres are state-financed, but in the past 10 years a number of privately financed, independent theatres have sprung up. One of the most interesting is the Farces Theatre, run by stage director Viktor Kramer. He is unhappy with the old, Soviet-era theatre system, which he thinks is moribund and failing. While many theatres are now in financial crisis, determined individuals such as Kramer have been able to secure financing, mostly from friends and contacts in the business world. Though the theatre system seems to be breaking down there is no lack of creative ideas in Russian theatre, which is powered by strong and outstanding individuals who are dedicated to what they do.

Making music

Opposite the Mariinsky Theatre is the St Petersburg Conservatoire, where some of the world's best orchestral performers are trained. Meanwhile, Yury Temirkanov, who worked at the Mariinsky for many years, now heads the famous orchestra of the St Petersburg Philharmonic, which, though it spends a good deal of its time playing abroad, remembers its loyal audience and plays frequently in St Petersburg. The Hermitage Theatre *(see page 226)* is also an important concert venue for both Russian and foreign orchestras.

Coming to grips with the post-Communist world has left some Russian composers uncertain about the direction their music should take. But, given the city's strong links with the great composers of the past *(see page 65)*, it is not surprising that many perceive a spirit of renaissance that will inspire new talent.

The cinema scene

Independent film production companies such as the St Petersburg-based CTB Film Co. are reporting a healthier demand for Russian films, but it's an uphill struggle when 70 percent of the movies on the nation's screens hail from Hollywood. Even some local successes, such as Yegor Konchalovsky's 2003 hit *Antikiller 2 – Antiterror*, sound conceived in Beverly Hills.

The 1990s were the worst ever decade for Russian films. Producers and directors found that their new freedom of expression was not accompanied by ready sources of finance. Many people lost the habit of cinema-going, preferring to watch videos (often pirated) at home rather than go out to underfunded cinemas with poor projection and sound facilities. A film magazine that had sold 1 million copies in the 1980s found its print run reduced to 50,000. Some film makers fought back with derivative gangster movies or banal historical epics, and others embarked on international co-productions whose artistic compromises ensured that they appealed neither to Russians nor to anyone else.

LEFT: the St Petersburg ballet school.
ABOVE: portrait of Fyodor Shaliapin as Boris Gudunov.

But a new generation of film makers, with perhaps a greater regard for popular taste than their state-funded predecessors, was waiting in the wings, and, as economic crises eased, they became the beneficiaries of an increase in film funding from the Ministry of Culture. Films like the critically acclaimed anti-war movie *The Prisoner of the Caucasus* (retitled in the US *Prisoner of the Mountains*) didn't disguise its sympathy for the Chechens or its hostility to the Russian military. *Vozvrashcheniye (The Return)*, which portrayed an errant father being reunited with his two sons, gave local directors hope by winning an award at the Venice Film Festival and being nominated for a 2004 Golden Globe.

St Petersburg film makers have always favoured such low-key movies to the monumental epics beloved by Moscow. In St Petersburg, the camera looked at the rank-and-file participants in historic events rather than the Ivan the Terribles. Films made in the city had a soft and humane intonation, a certain modesty and a preference for realism and psychology over formal experiments.

The city's movie studio, Lenfilm, has a distinguished history, beginning as a small atelier in Aquarium Summer Garden and growing into the USSR's second largest movie company (after Mosfilm). Its golden era was between the two world wars.

The tradition lives on in the work of Lenfilm's younger generation. Alexei Balabanov directed *Brat* (Brother, 1996) and *Brat II* (2000), both dealing with the violent world of Russia's post-Soviet urban youth and both box-office hits. Alexander Rogushkin produced *The Peculiarities of the National Hunt* (1995), which tells the story of Russian men who go on a hunt but only spend their time drinking vodka. That film was followed by a sequel, *Peculiarities of National Fishing*.

A fresh look and profound analysis mark the films of Aleksei German: *Highway Inspection*, *Twenty Days Without War* (1977), *My Friend Ivan Lapshin* (1984), and his 1998 critically acclaimed film about Stalin's death, *Khrustelyev, Bring the Car*. German is a remarkable director whose work suffered in the era of stagnation: *Highway Inspection* was kept from the public for 15 years, and was salvaged only in 1988 by the conflict committee, which released more than 200 unshown films made in the period 1960 to 1980.

A new era

The fate of that film was shared by other St Petersburg productions – for example, *The Second Attempt of Viktor Krokhin* by Viktor Sheshukov (about a boxer disillusioned by the falsity of professional sport). Aleksei German and his younger supporters ushered in a new era of films such as *The Burglar*, *Gunpowder*, *Forgive Me* and *Freeze-Die-Arise*. Often, though, innovation was welcomed more warmly at international festivals than at the home box office.

Veteran filmmaker Alexander Sokurov has recently emerged as the most internationally acclaimed St Petersburg director. His *Russian Ark* (2002), a fantastical odyssey through the country's history shot in one take at the Hermitage Museum, was the most successful Russian film ever in Europe and America. His next work was the third part of a tetrology about the great dictators of the 20th century: having dealt with Hitler and Eva Braun in *Moloch* (1999) and with the last days of Vladimir Lenin in *Taurus* (2001), he turned his attention to the tense relationship between Emperor Hirohito and General Douglas MacArthur after Japan's surrender in 1945. ❑

LEFT: the Aurora cinema on Nevsky prospekt.

The Great Composers

Russian classical music is bound up with St Petersburg because it was here that the composers whose works constitute Russia's musical treasure trove created their masterpieces. Mikhail Glinka (1804–57), the founder of Russian classical music and the author of the operas *Ivan Susanin* and *Ruslan and Lyudmila*, wrote almost all of his works in the city. After the premiere of *Ivan Susanin* in 1836, Vladimir Odoyevsky, the musical critic and poet, wrote: "What has long been sought after and not found in Europe has come with Glinka's opera – a new wave in art and a new period in history has started, a period of Russian music."

In 1840 Glinka composed a series of romances, *Farewell to St Petersburg*, as a setting for Nestor Kukolnik's lyrics and dedicated them to the city.

An extremely creative group of composers lived in St Petersburg in the 1860s. Three attained world fame: Modest Mussorgsky (1839–81) was author of many vocal pieces and the deeply emotional operas *Boris Godunov* and *The Khovansky Affairs*; Alexander Borodin (1833–87), author of such epic works as the opera *Prince Igor* and the *Second Symphony in B Minor,* was also a master of chamber music; and Nikolai Rimsky-Korsakov (1844–1908), who wrote many operas based on history, like *The Tsar's Bride*, on fairytales, like *The Snow Maiden*, on epics, like *Sadko*, and on satires, like *The Golden Cockerel*.

The Russian Musical Society, which introduced regular concerts, was established in 1859 in St Petersburg on the initiative of the composer and pianist Anton Rubinstein (1829–94). In the same year the Society started its first musical classes, on the basis of which Rubinstein organised Russia's first conservatoire in 1862. Among the first graduates of the conservatoire was Peter Tchaikovsky (1840–93), the greatest of Russia's sym-

phony and opera composers, author of such masterpieces as the operas *Eugene Onegin* and *The Queen of Spades*, the ballets *Swan Lake* and *The Sleeping Beauty*, suites such as *The Nutcracker*, and symphonies such as the *Sixth (Pathétique)*. "Like Pushkin, he has become integrated into the very foundations of the Russian national conscience", wrote Dmitri Shostakovich (1906–75), the pre-eminent Russian composer of the 20th century and another graduate of the St Petersburg (Leningrad) Conservatoire.

Shostakovich lived in the city until 1942. Many of his best works were written and

performed here for the first time, in particular the opera *Lady Macbeth of Mtsensk* and the ballet *The Age of Gold*. He lived in Leningrad for the first months of the 900-day siege *(see page 36)*, during which he wrote his famous *Seventh (Leningrad) Symphony* which was performed in the besieged city by the Leningrad Radio Orchestra in 1942.

Igor Stravinsky (1882–1971), the Russian composer and conductor who lived in the US after 1910, also began his musical career in St Petersburg, as did another classic composer of the 20th century, Sergei Prokofiev (1891–1953). ❑

RIGHT: Shostakovich working on his Seventh Symphony in besieged Leningrad, 1941.

LITERARY LIONS

The elusive character of St Petersburg, "the most abstract and imaginary city" as Dostoevsky called it, inspired some of Russia's greatest writers

Acity that claims to have 1,700 public libraries serving a population of 4.7 million clearly takes its reading seriously. Writers have returned the compliment, for there is scarcely a major Russian author who has not been inspired to write about St Petersburg. In this sense, it is one of the most literary cities in the world.

Alexander Pushkin (1799–1837), sometimes described as "the Russian Shakespeare", spent most of his writing career in St Petersburg. He loved "Peter's creation" and he himself created an impressive poetic image of the city. Whole chapters of *Eugene Onegin* (1823–31), in which Pushkin described St Petersburg's high society and theatrical life, with its spectators and actors, captured it with the verisimilitude of a photograph. His unfinished novel, *Peter the Great's Negro* (1827), a title referring to the Ethiopian roots of Pushkin's mother, depicts the city at the time of Peter the Great.

In Pushkin's mind, St Petersburg symbolised a new, unshakeable and powerful Russia. After the failure of the Decembrists' uprising in 1825 *(see pages 30–1)*, however, he began to think of the city as a place of "ennui, cold and granite" and his later works contain the theme of peasant rebellion. Indeed, if he had not at the time been temporarily banished to his mother's estate at Pskov for a flippant declaration of atheism, Pushkin might have been one of the demonstrators who were gunned down in Senate Square that December day.

Count Uvarov, the Minister of Education, remarked that he would only get a good night's sleep when literature ceased to be writ-

ten. But Pushkin, who didn't conceal his sympathy for the rebels, escaped such threats by being put under the unexpected custody of Tsar Nicholas's patronage. Despite this restraint, he turned his hand from poetry to drama with *Boris Godunov*, to prose with *The Captain's Daughter*, whose plot concerned a peasant uprising, and then back to poetry with *The Bronze Horseman*, dealing with the contentious topic of Peter the Great.

The tsar's tolerance may have stemmed partly from his being transfixed by the beauty of Pushkin's wife, Natalia Goncharova. Her looks, however, led to Pushkin's eventual downfall. Baron Georges d'Anthes, a French officer serving in the Russian forces, also became besotted with her; Pushkin challenged him to a duel and was mortally wounded. He died at No. 12, Naberezhnaya reki Moika, at the age of 37 *(see page 160)*.

Gogol's satire

The work of Nikolai Gogol (1809–52) is also associated with St Petersburg, where he lived from 1829 to 1836 before departing to Italy for 10 years. It was in the city that he wrote his best works, including *The Government Inspector* (a masterly farcical drama sending up government procedures), and *Dead Souls* (a satire on serfdom and the evils of bureaucracy).

Gogol created an image of St Petersburg as a smart European and a dandy. But it was against the background of all this that unusually strange happenings, such as a member of the gentry awakening to find he has turned into a nose, took place. In Gogol's stories, everything breathed deception and the fantastic became commonplace. He was on the brink of madness when a fanatical priest told him to destroy the manuscript of a second volume of *Dead Souls*. He complied and died shortly afterwards, perhaps intentionally, aged 42.

LEFT: Pushkin, the "Russian Shakespeare".
ABOVE: Gogol, scourge of the bureaucrat.

Dostoevsky's view

Fyodor Dostoevsky (1821–81), who was born in Moscow, wrote almost all of his novels in St Petersburg. With his brother he edited the magazines *Vremya* (Time) and *Epokha* (Epoch) here. In St Petersburg he saw "a mixture of something purely fantastic and perfectly ideal, and at the same time insipidly prosaic and common."

St Petersburg's dream and ideal did not seem lofty for Dostoevsky; he did not feel "a common unifying thought in the crowd, all were by themselves". For Dostoevsky, St Petersburg was "the most abstract and imaginary city." His greatest works – *Crime and Punishment* (1866), *The Idiot* (1869) and *The Brothers Karamazov* (1880) – found acclaim around the world.

Literary inspiration

At various times Leo Tolstoy (1828–1910), who contributed his first works to the journal *Sovremennik* (Contemporary), the playwright Alexander Ostrovsky (1823–86), who also contributed to St Petersburg's literary journals, and Anton Chekhov (1860–1904), who had his plays staged at the Alexandrinsky Theatre, came to St Petersburg on short visits.

St Petersburg also figured prominently in the works of the great Russian poet Alexander Blok (1880–1921), who spent almost his whole life there. In the poem *Retribution* (1910–21), Blok wrote about the St Petersburg of the late 19th century as a city in which irresistible anti-autocratic forces were in the making.

No matter what Blok wrote about St Petersburg, he did so with a deep love. Anna Akhmatova (1889–1966), Osip Mandelshtam (1891–1938) and many other poets and writers wrote affectionately about the city which had become the heart and soul of Russian literature.

But where are the present-day Pushkins? Despite all those libraries, a finalist in one recent Russian literary competition sounded a pessimistic note: "The new reader has not appeared yet, and it will take a long time for the present generation to tire of Stock Exchange news and James Bond novels, and start to want literature". There are signs, though, not least in the flowering of literary magazines, that St Petersburg has once again begun to cast its spell over Russia's writers. ❑

FOOD

Traditional cuisine – and that means more than potatoes
and cabbage – is regaining popularity as Russian restaurants
compete for custom alongside multinational chains

The cliché that Russians survive on a diet of potatoes and beetroot alone, with a healthy portion of *ogurtsi* (small cucumbers) and vodka to aid the digestion is, like many clichés, sometimes not that far from the truth. These are indeed national favourites. The imperatives of tourism, however, have encouraged restaurateurs to be more adventurous, both in their presentation of local dishes and those from the rest of Russia.

Foreign influences

In the 19th century, St Petersburg was in thrall to all things French, and the Gallic influence is still felt in a penchant for thick sauces for meat, complicated salads, and in the huge variety of cream-filled tortes to be eaten at the end of the meal with *chai* (tea). One such cake is the *ptiche moloko* (bird's milk), so called because it is supposed to be so fine that it cannot possibly be created by humans.

The years since *perestroika* have seen a renewal of European influences in the kitchen and a more relaxed approach to eating out. In summer the streets buzz with café life, and trendy bars do a brisk trade below street level. In addition to such foreign fads, there is a strong revival of traditional Russian restaurants catering for every pocket, from the modest student stipend to the extravagant, no-holds-barred, *novy-Russky* (new-Russian) men who carry their cash in handbags.

Certainly, there's no lack of variety in the cuisine. From the Ukrainian *borshch*, that infamous but delicious beetroot soup normally served in a *gorshok* (deep clay pot) with *petrushka* and *smetana* (fresh parsley and sour cream), to the frozen *sibirskie pelmeny*, a small boiled pastry parcel of meat, mushrooms or potatoes, the national cookbook is as comprehensive as the country is vast.

Central Asian specialities

Russians can also call on the spicy southern, almost Mediterranean traditions in food. The cuisines of Armenia, Georgia and Azerbaijan, as well as Uzbekistan, Kazakhstan and Kyrgizstan – which make liberal use of typical Central Asian ingredients such as coriander leaf, fruit and meat cooked together, walnuts, vine leaves, chillis, beans and flavoured breads – can be found in the Russian home as well as on the menu in restaurants.

Meat in these Central Asian eateries will more often than not be boiled – with the tasty exception of *shashlik* (kebabs), which is normally made from sheep or pork, and grilled over hot charcoal. This favoured dish is known throughout Russia, and the chef, normally the man of the house, is likely to be passionate about the preparation and cooking of what some may simply call a barbecue.

The *pelmeny* pastry parcel puts in an appearance everywhere in Russia – even in Siberia, where it's smaller than usual but made in vast quantities for the winter. There is also the large,

ture of tomatoes and cucumbers, but green salads comprise *travky* (literally "grasses") which in reality can be a refreshing plate of fresh basil, dill and other green herbs.

Traditional dishes

The Russian cookbook may now have become as cosmopolitan as any other, but the traditional dishes are presented today much as they would have been in the reign of the tsars. *Kisel* (blancmange), made from oatmeal, was the basis of most meals and was eaten with both savoury and sweet foods. *Shchi*, a soup made from *kislaya kapusta* (sauerkraut) and meat or fish, would probably feature in every main

flat, fried style known as *cheburek* throughout Central Asia and the Transcaucasus, or *manti* in Kazakhstan; the more wholesome version in Georgia is known as the *khinkali*.

All of these are found on the *zakuski* section of the menu, and some restaurants specialising in regional food will have them waiting on the table when customers arrive. Other *zakuski* include *zhulien* (julienne), thin slices of smoked and non-smoked red and white sturgeon, and *kolbasa* (salami-like spicy sausages). *Salat* (salad) is often simply a mix-

LEFT: *solianka* (stew) and *borshch*.
ABOVE: Caucasian cuisine adds spice to Russia's diet.

WHAT TO DRINK

The big restaurants serve tea, mineral water, fruit juices, beer, vodka, *Ukrainian dessert wines, Moldavian, Azerbaijani, Armenian and Georgian cognac, and Crimean sparkling wine. In summer *kvas*, a light, fermented drink made out of dried black bread with yeast and raisins, is sold on the street.

Russian vodka, of course, is ubiquitous. Various kinds can be recommended: Russky Standart, Stolichnaya, Zolotoye Koltso, Starorusskaya and Sibirskaya.

In mid-June, the St Petersburg Beer Festival offers the chance to try up to 40 varieties of Russian beer, such as Baltika and Nevskoe.

meal of the day. The fruits of Russia's abundant forests have long been harvested. Berries such as *brusnika*, *chernika*, *klyukva*, *zemlinika*, *golubika*, *malina* and *yeshevika* (foxberry, bilberry, cranberry, wild strawberry, blueberry, raspberry and blackberry respectively) were gathered and used to make preserves, jams, desserts and drinks – as indeed they are still today. Vegetables such as *brukva* (swede), *redka* (radish), *markov* (carrot) and *chesnok* (garlic) were staple foods, too.

What remains traditional is the *blin* (pancake), which is eaten both as a savoury and sweet dish. Bliny with lots of honey, smetana and red caviar are natural choices of filling for hungry Russians. Bliny are eaten at Maslinitsa, the week leading up to the *veliki post* (great fast of seven weeks) before Easter. The festival itself is celebrated with a *kulich*, a light, Easter cake similar to the Italian Christmas panettone. A delicious sweet dish, *paskha*, synonymous with the celebration of Easter, is prepared from *tvorog* (soft cheese) with dried fruits and sugar added for sweetness.

The upper echelons of society would have known a different menu, one that surprised many visiting dignitaries with its richness and quality. Carp in smetana, baked *osyotr* (sturgeon) and *okorok* of ham (baked leg of ham in pastry with fruit and spices) were some of the

A TOAST TO HOME COOKING

If you are invited to dine at home with a St Petersburg family, it's an offer worth accepting. The only drawbacks are Russian generosity and a liking for hearty meals. It is traditional to load the dinner table in advance with an enormous variety of delicious *zakuski* (hors d'oeuvres). The *zakuska* plays an important role in lining the stomach in preparation for the likely onslaught of alcohol.

The ritual of endless toasting is still common. Toasts can last for minutes and the formula to remember is to toast your host, the women present and the spread of food.

In fact, the *zakuski* are the main event of the meal, and it is as daunting as it is appetising to contemplate a table laden with red and black caviar, a selection of cold meats, garlic sausage, smoked sturgeon, salmon, an array of potato salads, mushrooms in sour cream, bowls of pickled cabbage, beetroot vinaigrette, goat's cheese, plus the usual liquid ensemble of deep-chilled vodka, *shampanskoye* (champagne), and syrupy Georgian wines.

Popular favourites include *seledka pod shuboi*, literally "salted herring in a fur coat", a delicious combination of fish, beetroot, boiled (and grated) egg and mayonnaise, and *domashni piroshki* (homemade pies), which can be stuffed with a variety of cabbage, meat, mushrooms or apricots. And then the second course arrives…

dishes served to important visitors and the ruling class. Large pies of fish and meat, *zapikanky* (bakes) of rice, smetana, eggs and sugar and *kulebyaki* (more pies) with fillings of cabbage, mushrooms and meat, or fish, were enjoyed by those who could afford them. *Khren* (horseradish sauce) was often the only addition to the natural juices that the dish was cooked in. *Kholodets* (aspic) is another favourite method of preparing meat and fish.

Welcome treats

Possibly the greatest sign of respect that can be shown to a guest is the giving of *karavai*, an intricately decorated bread shaped like a

when the two newly related mothers prepare the *karavai* for the newlyweds' return.

A real treat when visiting St Petersburg is tasting the *ikra* (caviar) which comes in *chornaya* and *krasnaya* (black and red) and is sold by the kilo to the rich and in small tins to tourists. It's prudent to check the date stamped on the packaging before making a purchase. Red caviar is best eaten on white bread spread with a generous layer of butter, and black from little egg-baskets (made from the white of hard-boiled eggs, carefully cut into a basket form). Despite being significantly cheaper than in the West, black caviar in a restaurant can still push up a bill dramatically.   ❑

cake, which is traditionally presented at the border of a village or as a guest enters the house, and is accompanied by a small pot of salt. This ritual symbolises the wealth of the village or host. One is expected to break off a corner, dip it in the salt and taste it before advancing.

As bread was eaten with every meal and was the staple food during hard times, it was seen as an appropriate way of indicating readiness to welcome newcomers. It is a tradition often observed at weddings, even in the city,

LEFT: celebratory pie; barbecue time.
ABOVE: making a birthday wish.

THE MAGIC OF MUSHROOMS

The *gribok* (mushroom) is at the heart of a traditional pastime still popular in many parts of the country: whole families will spend a weekend together in the countryside, gathering mushrooms to preserve for the rest of the year in various concoctions of vinegar, spices and herbs. The culture of mushroom-gathering is one still familiar to many children and people will sometimes be able to recite a lengthy list of edible and deadly varieties. The marinading of *griby* and *ogurtsi* (mushrooms and cucumbers) is another Russian passion, and one of the few occasions when the men are likely to roll up their sleeves and help out in the kitchen.

SHOPPING

The vast department stores offer good value and
spectacle, and the markets are fun – but beware
of counterfeit vodka, which can be lethal

The days of breadlines and empty shelves
are long gone. Now St Petersburg's historic department stores are filled with
fashionable boutiques and plenty of Western
brands. They cater mostly to the tourist trade
and the wealthy new Russians. Most locals
still favour markets where cheap clothes,
pirated compact discs and traditional foods are
more reasonably priced.

Department stores

Three well-stocked department stores are
located in historic buildings worth a visit for the
spectacle alone. The most famous is Gostiny
Dvor, an imposing yellow building at Nevsky
prospekt 35 that has been the city's largest trading centre since the 18th century *(see page
114–115)*. Trekking through the whole of it,
however, can take an entire day. The ground
floor sells workaday items; the first floor has
more exclusive shops and designer boutiques.

Passage, at Nevsky prospekt 48, is smaller
than Gostiny Dvor, but occupies a more stylish building with a beautiful facade and a 180-
metre-long glass roof. It sells more upmarket
and more expensive clothes, jewellery, souvenirs and household items.

Dom Leningradskoi Torgovly (Leningrad
House of Trade), better known as DLT, on Bolshaya Konyushennaya 21–23 just off Nevsky
prospekt, is modelled on the late 19th-century
department stores of Paris, and contains an
open ground floor surrounded by balconies that
line each level. The ground-floor souvenir section, has a vast choice of wooden toys, lacquered boxes, matryoshka dolls, painted eggs,

traditional painted wooden bowls, amber jewellery and much more. This is the best place in
town to do your gift shopping in one go and at
an unbeatable price.

Savvy souvenirs

Souvenirs can be found over the city, at wildly
differing prices and of varying quality. An outdoor market behind the Church of the Saviour
on the Spilled Blood has good-quality mer-
chandise. Vendors are often cash-strapped artists

ABOVE: modern goods and designer shops
on Nevsky prospekt.
RIGHT: searching for souvenirs at a streetside stall.

who paint souvenirs themselves. There you will find matryoshka dolls of all sizes and colours, beautiful hand-made chess boards and lacquered boxes as well as fur hats, Soviet memorabilia and jewellery. Vendors – all of whom speak English – tend to initially state outrageous prices, but bargaining is expected.

Markets

Because the main stores are pricey for the average Russian, you'll find more Russians in the markets. A stroll through the food market on Kuznechny pereulok 3 *(see page 119)*, the best of its kind in St Petersburg, is a colourful introduction to Russian cuisine and a fun way

to spend a few hours between viewing the nearby Dostoevsky or Arctic museums *(see page 119)*. Expect the vendors' more subtle techniques to include yelling in your direction and offering you a free taste of their products. It's worth trying the honeys, the traditional milk products such as smoked cottage cheese and the market's mouth-watering pickled produce – particularly the cucumbers and apples.

For the more adventurous, the rundown Apraksin Dvor market on Sadovaya 28–30 offers just about everything, from cheap clothes made in China or Turkey to kebabs and DIY. The atmosphere is usually animated, to put it mildly, so hold on to your valuables as you are sure to get jostled about in the crowd.

Cheap CDs and DVDs tend to be an integral part of what tourists returning from Russia bring back in their suitcases. Pirate discs – and more rarely licensed ones – can be found everywhere in town, but for music lovers who want to buy them by the ton, the outdoor market near the metro station Avtovo (from there, catch one of the many minibuses going to "Yunona market") is the place to go.

Russian specialities

For caviar and other Russian delicacies, visit more specialised venues such as Firmennaya Torgovlya, on Nevsky prospekt 21, which sells a wide range of caviar, smoked fish and alcohol. Caviar, chocolate and liquors are also sold at Yeliseyevsky Gastronom at Nevsky prospekt 56, a legendary gourmet shop decorated in art nouveau style with marble counters and chandeliers. ❑

PLACES

A detailed guide to St Petersburg
with the principal sites clearly
cross-referenced by number to the maps

St Petersburg is a magnificent misfit. Conceived by Peter the Great
as a showpiece city, a capital to rival the great cities of western
Europe, it is an echo of the West that reverberates in a harsh Russian landscape. As you gaze along the city's embankment, the perfectly
rectangular buildings gradually fade from sight into the vast flat Russian
expanse. This is where the finest European architecture meets Russian
swampland and, by any standards, it is an extraordinary achievement.

The Winter Palace, once home to Catherine the Great, sits on the cold
banks of the Neva. Inside its walls, one of Europe's finest collections of art
documents much of mankind's creativity, from Grecian ruins and Leonardo
da Vinci to the Impressionists and the abstract Futurists. Its treasures are
rivalled only by the nearby Russian Museum, which displays the world's
largest collection of Russian icons.

Opposite the Winter Embankment lies the Peter and Paul Fortress, the
city's first defensive structure and final resting place for the former tsars
of the Russian empire. Its walls once held prisoners who dared to question
the regime's ways. Now residents casually lean against these walls while
catching the fleeting rays of the sun. Its beaches, no longer patrolled by
security forces, have made way for games and an annual sand castle building competition. It's as if Alcatraz had rebranded itself as a mini-Majorca.

Vasilievsky Island, which splits the Neva in half, serves as the city's academic hub. On the Vyborg side of the river, outside Finland Station, stands
a solitary statue of Lenin – a reminder of a world-changing revolution.

But the most vivid life of the city, now as when the satirist Nikolai
Gogol portrayed it in the 19th century, is on Nevsky prospekt. This busy
boulevard stretches from the spire of the Admiralty on the Embankment to
the consecrated grounds of Alexander Nevsky Lavra, one of Russia's most
important monasteries. Along its length you can find St Petersburg in a
nutshell: breathtakingly ornate churches, historic facades and the bustle
of a city reinventing itself after decades of neglect and celebrating a turbulent history that it has laboriously transcended.   ❏

PRECEDING PAGES: Beloselsky-Belozersky Palace; crossing the Neva in style.
LEFT: workers polish the symbol of St Petersburg before the tricentennial celebrations.

ALONG THE EMBANKMENT

To walk along the Neva is to experience one of Europe's most palatial sections of river. From the grand homes of the tsars to historic squares, the Embankment is St Petersburg at its finest

L ike Amsterdam and Venice, St Petersburg is a city built on water, with a complex network of canals and waterways, spanned by countless bridges. The River Neva, which cuts a swathe through the historic centre, is its main artery. The south bank – made up of **Dvortsovaya naberezhnaya** (the Palace Quay), **Admiralteyskaya naberezhnaya** (the Admiralty Quay) and **Anglyskaya naberezhnaya** (the English Quay) – is lined with sumptuous palaces, reminders of St Petersburg's imperial past. A good way to begin a tour of the city is to take a walk along one of the grandest waterfronts in Europe.

The English Quay

Tours of St Petersburg traditionally begin at the Bronze Horseman, an equestrian statue of Peter the Great on Decembrists' Square. We recommend that you break with tradition and start your tour further west, at the beginning of **Anglyskaya naberezhnaya** ❶ (English Quay), a row of splendid mansions overlooking the river. All these buildings are closed to the public, so tour guides and even guidebooks tend to bypass them, but this once fashionable stretch of the Embankment is well worth a look. The palaces along here, as yet untouched by modern

restoration, offer a real insight into how St Petersburg must have looked in the 19th century, at the height of its imperial glory.

The quay is named after the English merchants and craftsmen who settled here in the early 18th century, along with their cousins from the American colonies. Initially, the waterfront was lined with stores and taverns, but by the 19th century they had been replaced by aristocratic mansions. The English Quay remained one of the city's most

Map
on pages
82–3

LEFT: crossed by graceful bridges and lined by historical facades, the Neva provides the city's most romantic views.
BELOW: Romany children relax in the Summer Gardens.

Peter the Great is usually represented as a young man (as here), but in the grounds of Peter and Paul Fortress there is a sculpture by Michael Chemyakin portraying him in later life.

desirable addresses until the Bolshevik Revolution, when its name was changed to the naberezhnaya Krasnovo Flota (Red Fleet Quay). The original name was restored in 1996, to commemorate Queen Elizabeth II's visit to the city and in recognition of better relations between Britain and Russia.

Heading east along the Embankment, towards the Winter Palace, the first building of interest is **Dvorets Barona Stiglitsa** (Baron Stieglitz Palace), at No. 68. It was built in the late 19th century for a powerful Russian-German industrialist, who was also one of the foremost patrons of the arts. Stieglitz established the first independent arts academy in Russia, which remains a reputed institution, rivalling the Academy of Arts just across the Neva *(see page 173)*.

Further on, the impressive building at No. 56 was the former English church. It was designed in 1814 by Giacomo Quarenghi, architect of many imposing neoclassical buildings in the city. He also designed No. 32, an elegant building with a partially colonnaded facade, which once housed the Military Academy of the Russian General Staff. A little further along No. 28, with its rusticated facade, was built for a rich family of financiers. It then became the Collegium of Foreign Affairs until that moved to Palace Square in the first half of the 19th century.

Shortly after the Bolsheviks took power, the building was converted into the **Dvorets Brakosochetaniye ②** (Palace of Weddings) where, for the first time in Russian history, people could marry in civil ceremonies. It still serves this function and, when you pass by, chances are you'll see crowds standing outside with champagne, ready to toast the newlyweds, married at a conveyor belt speed of about one couple every 15 minutes.

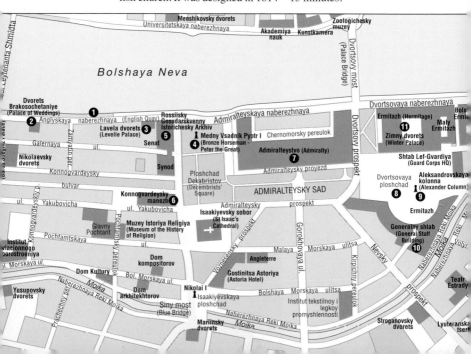

Map below

Just before reaching Decembrists' Square, the second to last building on this quay, No. 4, was originally called the **Lavela dvorets** ❸ (Lavelle Palace). In the early 19th century the Lavelles ran a popular literary salon frequented by the most illustrious writers of the day – Ivan Krylov, Nikolai Karamzin, Alexander Griboyedov, Mikhail Lermontov and Alexander Pushkin. They would have walked in the footsteps of the Roman elite, as the floors are laid with tiles from the royal residence of Emperor Tiberius, on the island of Capri.

Today the building belongs to the Russian State Historical Archives, which also occupy the Senate and Holy Synod buildings on Decembrists' Square.

Decembrists' Square

The English Quay becomes Admiralty Quay at **Ploschad Dekabristov** (Decembrists' Square), the site of Russia's first revolution. On 14 December 1825, the inauguration day of Nicholas I, troops fired on some 3,000 mutinous soldiers (and spectators) during their abortive attempt to force the new tsar to accept a constitutional monarchy *(see pages 27)*.

The square is dominated by **Medny Vsadnik** ❹, the magnificent equestrian statue of Peter the Great, known more commonly as **the Bronze Horseman**. The historical and literary importance of this statue should not be underestimated. The horseman astride his rearing steed has come to symbolise the conflicting opinions about the city's founder, who was a visionary, but ruthless in the pursuit of his ambitions. The many lives lost in the building of this city and the speed with which Peter pushed for its completion has never been forgotten and, for some, the menacing nature of the statue serves as a reminder. The Bronze Horseman gets its name from Pushkin's epic poem of the same name (1833) in

Celebrations for St Petersburg's 300-year anniversary included military presentations, formal events with invited heads of state and, of course, many parties.

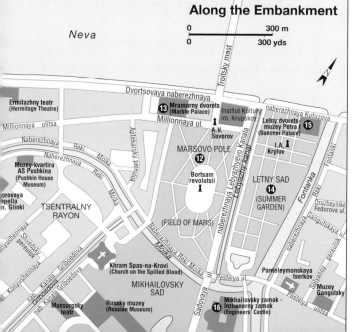

Along the Embankment

Neva

0 _____ 300 m
0 _____ 300 yds

Ermitazhny teatr (Hermitage Theatre)

Millionnaya ulitsa

Naberezhnaya

Muzey-kvartira AS Pushkina (Pushkin House Museum)

orovaya apella n. Glinki

TSENTRALNY RAYON

Dvortsovaya naberezhnaya

Troitsky most

Millionnaya ul.

Reki Moika

Reki Moika

Aptekarsky pereulok

❸ **Mramorny dvorets (Marble Palace)**

A.V. Suvorov

MARSOVO POLE ❷

Bortsam revolutsii

(FIELD OF MARS)

Naberezhnaya Reki Moika

Moika

Institut Kultury im. Krupskoy

naberezhnaya Kutuzova

Lebyazhyevo Kanala

naberezhnaya Lebyazhny Kanal

Letny dvorets-muzey Petra (Summer Palace) ❺

I.A. Krylov

LETNY SAD

❹ (SUMMER GARDEN)

Fontanka

Oruzheynike Fedorova ul.

naberezhnaya Reki Fontanka

Gangutskaya ul.

Gangutskaya ul.

pereulok

Shvedsky pereulok

yushennaya pereulok

nab. Konyushennaya

Kanala Griboedova

nab. Kanala Griboedova

Khram Spas-na-Krovi (Church on the Spilled Blood)

MIKHAILOVSKY SAD

Mussorgsky teatr

Russky muzey (Russian Museum)

Pestelya ul.

Sadovaya

Pantelemonskaya tserkov

Pestelya

Solyanoy pereulok

Muzey Gangutsky

Pestelya ulitsa

❻ Mikhailovsky zamok - Inzhenerny zamok (Engineers' Castle)

The gleaming spire of the Admiralty building serves as an important landmark to help guide you through St Petersburg's winding streets.

BELOW: the Bronze Horseman – a memorial to Peter the Great and a reminder of the regime's darker side.

which the statue comes to life, and relentlessly pursues the hero, a poor clerk called Evgeny. The poem was inspired by the great flood of 1824, when the whole city was submerged.

Catherine the Great commissioned the statue in 1768. An inscription appears on either side in Latin and Russian "To Peter I from Catherine II". The mammoth task took French sculptor Etienne Falconet 12 years to complete. In accordance with the empress's wishes, Falconet's aim was to personify enlightened absolutism, depicting the monarch leading the country along the road of progress.

Falconet became totally absorbed in his task. Accomplished horsemen reared their mounts – prize stallions from the royal stables – in full gallop, so he could study their movements. Grooms held the horses motionless on a specially made platform so he could sketch them. An illustrious cavalry general, who resembled Peter in body and build, endlessly posed for him. Work was painstaking, with the mould alone taking Falconet three years to make. The casting finally took place in

1775, and almost ended in disaster when bronze spilled out of a crack in the mould. Had Falconet's craftsmen not managed to seal the crack and save the statue, they would have probably lost their lives.

For the next three years, they worked on the statue. Then came the difficulty of moving the immense pedestal. The 1,600-ton block of granite took nine months to transport from the Gulf of Finland. The statue was finally unveiled in 1782.

South of the square is the gilded dome of St Isaac's Cathedral, the third largest in Europe *(see page 127)*. On its western side, linked by a monumental arch, stand the imposing yellow buildings originally constructed for the **Imperial Senate and the Holy Synod** by the Italian architect Carlo Rossi in 1829–32. Most of Rossi's buildings are painted yellow, as are many of the government institutions in the city. In 1955 the buildings were requisitioned by the **Rossiisky Gosudarstvenny Istorichesky Arkhiv ❺** (Central State Historical Archive of Russia), which holds millions of documents

relating to the activities of central state authorities, going back as far as the early 18th century. However, the archives' days at this grand address are numbered. Despite widespread protest, President Putin plans to relocate the archives and take the buildings over for government use.

South of the archive buildings, two marble columns, each crowned with a bronze angel, mark the beginning of Konnogvardeysky bulvar (a filled-in canal), which runs alongside the **Konnogvardeysky manezh ❻** (Horseguards' Manège; opening hours vary according to exhibition; entrance charge). It was built at the turn of the 19th century by the architect, Quarenghi, who based his design on the Quirinale Palace in Rome. It features an impressive eight-columned portico.

The statues of Castor and Pollux, Zeus's twin sons, taming wild horses are a reference to the building's original function as an indoor riding school for the Cavalry Guard. Today the building is used to host art and photography exhibitions, as well as trade fairs.

The Admiralty

Carrying on along the waterfront, east of the square, you come to **Admiralteystvo ❼** (The Admiralty). The Admiralty's origins date to the beginnings of the city itself. In 1707 Peter ordered the construction of a fortified shipyard where a mighty Russian fleet was to be built. The original fortress was replaced in the 1820s by Andreyan Zacharov's neoclassical Admiralty building.

Soon after, shipbuilding activities were transferred elsewhere, and the building became the navy's administrative headquarters. The tremendous 400-metre (1,300-ft) facade that looks on to the Neva is awash with sculptures and reliefs glorifying the Russian Navy. The central arch is crowned by a statue of Victory with flags. A little higher, in the centre of the bas-relief entitled *Virgin of the Russian Fleet*, Peter the Great accepts Neptune's trident as a symbol of supremacy on the high seas. The corners of the rectangular tower are topped with sculptures of the great military leaders of antiquity – Achilles, Ajax, Pyrrhus and Alexan-

Map on pages 82–3

Dvortsovaya ploshchad (Palace Square) is a popular venue for rock concerts during June's White Nights Festival.

BELOW: decorative reliefs on the Admiralty facade.

der the Great. Atop the tower, the Admiralty's gleaming needle spire is crowned by a frigate-shaped weathervane that has become the city's emblem. The Admiralty has been home to a naval college since 1925. The cadets can often be seen exercising outside, or on cleaning duty in the adjacent park.

Admiralty Quay ends at **Dvortsovy most** (Palace Bridge), which crosses the river to Vasilievsky island, one of the oldest parts of the city *(see page 165–77)*. Beyond the bridge is St Petersburg's number-one attraction: the **Winter Palace**. Home of the Romanov dynasty for almost two centuries, it is one of four buildings that make up the magnificent Hermitage Museum, one of the world's most important art collections *(see page 88 for the Winter Palace and pages 97–105 for a run-down of the Hermitage collection)*.

Palace Square

Behind the Winter Palace is the impressive **Dvortsovaya ploshchad** ❽ (Palace Square), a key landmark in the city's turbulent history. In 1905 it was the scene of the so-called "Bloody Sunday" massacre when tsarist troops opened fire on thousands of unarmed strikers, sparking the 1905 Revolution. The square also took centre stage in the build-up to the second revolution: on 25 October 1917, following the signal shot fired from the cruiser *Aurora*, a small army of Bolsheviks stormed the Winter Palace from here, seizing power in a coup d'état. *(The Aurora is open to the public as part of the Naval Museum – see page 154)*.

Palace Square has remained a place for political rallies and ceremonies. When human-rights activist Andrei Sakharov died in 1989, hundreds of people came here to mourn him in a candle-lit vigil *(see box on opposite page)*. And in August 1991, when hard-line communists tried to stage a putsch against Mikhail Gorbachev, over 100,000 people flooded into the square to oppose this attempt to crush Russia's nascent democracy. In the same year, the changing of the city name from Leningrad to St Petersburg was hotly debated here during the referendum.

One account of the invasion of the Winter Palace says that when the Bolsheviks' main forces of the operation stormed the palace they found a unit of revolutionary seamen already there. Apparently the sailors had infiltrated the building through the sewer system.

BELOW: General Staff Building – once home to the secret police.

Today, Palace Square is more of a social than a political forum. It is a popular meeting place, bustling with tourists, students and teenagers on skateboards. It is occasionally used to stage a festival or concert.

The Alexander Column

In the centre of the square stands the **Aleksandrovskaya kolonna** ❾ (Alexander Column). In September 1812, it was decided that a triumphal monument should be erected here to commemorate the victory of the Russian Army over the French during the Napoleonic War. Ironically, the design that won the contest was by a French architect, Auguste Montferrand (who also designed St Isaac's; *see page 127*). The towering column is made from a granite monolith transported from the northern shore of the Gulf of Finland.

In 1832, supervised by the craftsmen who had installed the columns of St Isaac's, over 2,000 volunteers (mostly veterans of the Napoleonic Wars) and 400 builders raised the column on the pedestal, using a complex system of scaffolding, ropes and pulleys, similar to that which would have been used by the Pharoahs in Egypt *(see picture below)*.

The column is one of the highest monuments of its kind in the world. At 47.5 metres (156 ft) it is taller than many of its rivals, including the 44.5-metre (146-ft) Trajan's Column in Rome and the 46-metre (151-ft) Vendôme Column in Paris. The bronze angel that crowns it symbolises the peace that came to Europe following the final defeat of Napoleon's armies. The base is decorated with bas-reliefs of figures representing the great rivers Russian troops had to cross in pursuit of Napoleon on his march to Moscow, along with allegories of Wisdom, Plenty, Victory, Peace and Justice. The column is not actually attached to the pedestal, but stands freely, balanced under its own 650-ton weight.

The General Staff Building

The south side of Palace Square is taken up by the sprawling **Generalny shtab** ❿ (General Staff Building). Alexander I commissioned his favourite architect, Carlo Rossi

Map on pages 82–3

Sceptics said that Rossi's arch on Palace Square would collapse under the weight of the bronze statues on top. On the day the scaffolding was removed, the architect climbed to the top of the arch to demonstrate its sturdiness, proclaiming that if the arch went he would go with it.

BELOW: the erection of the Alexander Column in 1832.

Andrei Sakharov

Known more for his human-rights campaigning than his work on the hydrogen bomb, Andrei Sakharov's essays laid the foundation for reform in the 1990s. After publishing *My Country and the World* in 1975, Sakharov won the Nobel Peace Prize for his fight "not only against the abuse of power and violations of human dignity... but also for the ideal of a state founded on the principle of justice for all". He was swiftly exiled. When he returned in 1986, the then president, Gorbachev, engaged him in reforming the struggling Soviet system. Days before his death in December 1989, he drafted a new constitution for the Union of Soviet Republics of Europe and Asia.

Private boat hire makes an excellent way to tour the city's tiny canals.

BELOW: the baroque facade of the Winter Palace.

(rumoured to be the illegitimate son of Tsar Paul I and a ballerina) to undertake the aggrandisement of Palace Square. Rossi's sweeping neoclassical building was intended to symbolise the vast extent of the empire and the power of its ruler. All the houses that faced the square were demolished to make way for the grand building that would be visible from the Winter Palace opposite. The curvaceous wings of the yellow facade are joined in the middle by a triumphal arch, another monument commemorating Napoleon's defeat. On top of the arch, Rossi installed an impressive 10-metre (33-ft) sculpture of a winged Victory in her chariot drawn by six horses and flanked by warriors.

Originally the headquarters of the Russian Army, the General Staff Building then housed the Foreign Ministry and the Ministry of Finance. In Soviet times it became a training academy for agents of the NKVD, the dreaded Stalinist secret police.

Today the west wing of the General Staff Building is still occupied by government offices, but the **East Wing** belongs to the Hermitage Museum (opening hours vary, separate entrance charge or with combined ticket for the main museum). The main focus of this wing of the Hermitage is as space for touring exhibitions and for works by the Nabis (notably Bonnard, Denis, Vuillard and Vallotton), a symbolist group of post-Impressionist painters; many of these paintings were commissioned by the industrialist Morozov, for his Moscow mansion. Restoration of the General Staff Building is continuing, and the long-term plan is to transfer the Impressionist collection from the Hermitage to here.

The Winter Palace

Next we come to the magnificent green, white and gold **Zimny dvorets ⑪** (Winter Palace; *for opening times see page 97*). Superbly situated on the banks of the Neva River, it is the grandest and most lavishly decorated building in the city and at the heart of a stately complex of four buildings which make up the **Ermitazh muzey** (Hermitage Museum; *see pages 97–105*).

The Winter Palace was, in fact, the fourth palace to be built on this stretch of the Neva. The first two – one in timber replaced with one in stone – were built for Peter the Great where the Hermitage Theatre now stands. Peter's niece, Empress Anna, commissioned a young Italian architect, Bartolomeo Rastrelli, to build a third palace in the 1730s.

When Peter's daughter, Elizabeth, came to power, she commissioned a now more experienced Rastrelli to replace her predecessor's palace with something grander that would reflect Russia's might. Construction of the Winter Palace began in 1754 and was not completed until 1762. Elizabeth died just months before Rastrelli completed his masterpiece of Russian baroque.

Catherine the Great was the first in a long line of tsars and tsarinas to take up residence in the palace. Unlike her predecessor, she did not care for the baroque interiors and had them remodelled in the more sober classical style. The lavish ornamentation and abundant statuary of the exterior, however, remained untouched.

Special rooms in the palace were assigned to art works bought by Peter. Catherine, an art lover and avid collector, added a neoclassical annexe to the palace. Known as the Small Hermitage *(Maly Ermitazh)*, it served both as her private retreat, a place for entertaining guests and home for the ever-expanding imperial collection of art. She then added a further wing, known as the Large Hermitage *(Bolshoy Ermitazh)*, on the waterfront, followed by a theatre. Built by Quarenghi from 1783–7, the **Ermitazhny teatr** (entrance at Dvortsovaya nab. 34; tel: 710 9030) is separated from the main building by a canal and can be reached via a raised gallery, reminiscent of Venice's Bridge of Sighs.

The theatre was built over the remains of Peter the Great's Winter Palace (which can also be visited on a guided tour) and is today used for concerts and exhibitions.

In 1837, a great fire raged through the Winter Palace. Thankfully, it did not reach the art-filled annexes. However, the State Rooms were devastated, but restored to their former grandeur just 15 months later.

Map on pages 82–3

TIP

From August–October tours along the Neva and trips to Peterhof *(see page 191–5)* leave from the Winter Palace Embankment.

BELOW: a "walrus" taking a dip in the Neva.

Aptly named, only aristocrats could afford to make their home on Millionaire's Street – a prime location for courting favour from the tsar.

BELOW: the eternal flame on the Field of Mars.

Nicholas I added the New Hermitage, purpose-built for exhibiting the imperial collection. In 1852, he opened the New and Large Hermitages as a public museum. Ten giant granite figures of Atlantes sculpted by Alexander Terebenyev support the southern facade, the original entrance to the museum. Today's Hermitage Museum, entered from Palace Square, is made up of these buildings, together with the Winter Palace and the Small Hermitage.

For more about the history of the Hermitage and how to find your way around its monumental collection, see the following chapter.

Millionaire's Street

Behind the Hermitage, **Millionnaya ulitsa** (Millionaire's Street) leads from the north-eastern corner of Palace Square to the Field of Mars. The street, which runs parallel to the river, gets its name from the wealthy aristocrats, court dignitaries and members of the imperial family who lived in the residences that stand between the River Neva and the River Moika. On the Embankment side **dom Uchyenikh** (The House of Scholars) at No. 26 Dvortsovaya naberezhnaya was designed for Alexander II's son, Vladimir, president of the Academy of Arts and commander of the Guards' Troops who gave the order to shoot on Bloody Sunday in January 1905. No. 16 is the old English Club, so frequently mentioned in Tolstoy's *Anna Karenina*. And it was at No. 12 that Nicholas II's brother signed the abdication papers in 1917, thus bringing the Romanov dynasty to an end.

The Field of Mars

When the city was founded, the marshy piece of land sandwiched between the Moika and the Neva rivers was ignored by the builders. It wasn't until 1710, when the Summer Garden was laid out, that the marshes were drained to create a flat field. But nothing ever grew here and the area was dubbed the Sahara of St Petersburg. In the 19th century it was used as a military parade and exercise ground. Hence its name **Marsovo pole** ⑫, or Field of Mars, after the Roman god of war.

In March 1917, a crowd set out for the Field of Mars to mourn those who had fallen in skirmishes with troops loyal to the deposed tsar. To the accompaniment of a burial march and 180 rifle salvos, the remains of 180 revolutionaries were buried here and a foundation stone for a memorial was laid. In 1957 the eternal flame, which still burns today, was lit in the centre of the monument in honour of the 1917 Revolution's 40th anniversary.

Since the fall of communism, few Russians apart from the occasional newlyweds come here to pay their respects. It has become the nighttime domain of boisterous youths who gather round the flame to drink, keep warm and play music. Though periodically dispersed by the police, they soon regroup.

The Marble Palace

On the corner of the Field of Mars and Millionaire's Street rises the majestic **Mramorny dvorets** ⓭ (Marble Palace; open Wed–Sun 10am–6pm, Mon 10am–5pm, entrance charge). The palace was commissioned by Catherine the Great as a gift for her lover, Grigory Orlov, who was instrumental in bringing her to power in 1762, but he died before its completion. The neoclassical building, erected between 1768 and 1785, is faced with marble, unusual in this city of plaster facades. It was designed by Antonio Rinaldi, and is considered to be his masterpiece. Rinaldi's interiors were remodelled in the 1840s, but his original grand staircase and Marble Hall remain.

Through the 19th century, the Marble Palace was the home of various grand dukes. It remained empty and neglected after the Bolshevik Revolution until 1937, when it was turned into the city's Lenin Museum. Now the palace belongs to the Russian Museum *(see pages 137–143)*, which lies south of the Field of Mars, and exhibits modern Russian and international art from the **Ludwig Collection**, donated to the museum by leading German art collectors, Peter and Irene Ludwig. Their bequest consisted of 118 pieces of art, among them works by Pablo Picasso, Roy Lichtenstein, Jeff Koons, Jasper Johns, Andy Warhol and Moscow conceptualist Ilya Kabakov. These are shown on a rotational basis. The ground floor is used for temporary exhibitions.

The Suvorov statue

Back on the waterfront, on the south side of **Troitsky most** (formerly Kirovsky Bridge) stands the 8-metre (26-ft) statue of Russian general Alexander Suvorov. On the granite pedestal, beneath the figures of Glory and Peace, the inscription "Prince of Italy, Count Suvorov-Rymniksky, 1801" is a reference to the Italian campaigns he fought against Napoleon. The slim, youthful warrior portrayed by sculptor Mikhail Kozlovsky (creator of the Samson fountain at Peterhof, *see page 194*), bears little resemblance to the famously portly general.

Map on pages 82–3

The Marble Palace was intended for aristocrat and statesman Grigory Orlov, one of Catherine the Great's favourites, but he died before he could take up residence.

BELOW: the soaring spire of Peter and Paul Fortress is visible from the Embankment.

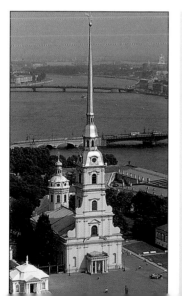

City of Islands

St Petersburg is Russia's largest seaport and second-largest city with an official population of just under 5 million. It lies 60°N, on the same latitude as Alaska, Hudson Bay, the southern tip of Greenland and Oslo. While the city originally straddled 101 islands at the mouth of the River Neva, which sweeps majestically through its centre, many have since disappeared as the rivers, streams and canals have been filled in. Today, the "Venice of the North" is situated on 42 islands linked by 432 pedestrian, vehicle and railway bridges. Twenty of these are drawbridges, some of which rise each night between 2am and 5am, from the months of April to the end of November, to allow the passage of sea-going ships.

The Neva flows westerly from Lake Ladoga, 74 km (46 miles) to the east, into the Gulf of Finland. Here, where it branches into three arms, separating the Petrograd side and Vasilievsky island from the mainland, the main channel is 400 metres (437 yards) wide. Today, granite embankments contain the 68 rivers, canals, channels and streams which separate the islands.

Street performers in Palace Square and all along the Embankment make a decent living entertaining tourists.

BELOW: detail from Mikhailovsky (Engineer's) Castle.

The Summer Garden

To the east of the Field of Mars flows the Lebyazhy Kanal (Swan Canal), channelled in 1715 to link the Moika to the Neva. Originally swans nested here, hence the name. The canal divides the Field of Mars from **Letny Sad** ⓮ (the Summer Garden; open daily 10am–9pm; closed Apr; entrance charge).

This green oasis is nearly as old as the city itself. It was laid out by a team of French landscape gardeners between 1704–12 on the initiative of Peter I who wanted to create his own Versailles. Peter the Great's westernisation of Russia was not just about military advances and trade reforms, but also about encouraging the arts. Unlike Christianity in western Europe, which fostered and even financed the arts, the Orthodox Church had a stranglehold on artistic development in Russia. The strict code of laws banned, among other things, statues, portraits and musical instruments. Breaking this stranglehold and promoting the arts was perhaps the most important of Peter's reforms.

The garden was planned for the summer residence of the royal family, and the tsar spared no expense in making it as beautiful as possible. The avenues were lined with trees and the grounds were decorated with an abundance of marble sculptures by Italian masters, summer houses, fountains and pavilions. The conservatories, ponds, cages of rare birds, labyrinths and rare flowers, were the tsar's pride and joy.

In the middle of the 19th century, Nicholas I issued a decree restricting access to the nobility, army officers and those adhering to a strict dress code. It wasn't until the end of the century that access to the general public was granted. The garden was much favoured by writers and artists. Its shady paths attracted and inspired the likes of Pushkin, Gogol, Tchaikovsky and Mussorgsky. On the eastern side of the central avenue is a monument to the fable-writer Krylov (1768–1844), whose works have been translated into over 50 languages. Krylov, the Aesop of Russian literature, loved to go walking in this garden and often met with Pushkin here. Decorating the pedestal of his monument are some charming reliefs depicting various animals from his fables.

Today, the original arrangement of the park is only visible in old engravings, but the park is no less beautiful and remains a very popular strolling ground. Entrance is on the northern Neva side, through the lovely wrought-iron gate on the Embankment, or from the south side, near the Engineer's Palace.

The Summer Palace

On the Fontanka Embankment, bordering the eastern side of the garden, is **Letny dvorets** ⓯ (the Summer Palace; open May–Nov, Wed–Mon 10am–6pm, closed 1st Mon of month; entrance charge; tel: 314 0456), one of St Petersburg's first

stone buildings. Built for Peter the Great by Domenico Trezzini in 1710–12, it is a modest palace, with only 14 rooms and a simple, relatively unadorned facade. Peter moved in before the decorators had finished working on the place and spent all his summers there until the day he died in 1725.

Today the Summer Palace is a museum, housing a permanent collection of Peter's personal belongings. The layout is simple; the rooms, which were all restored after World War II, are positioned almost identically on both floors. The first floor of the palace was intended for Peter's wife, Catherine I, who reigned for two years after his death.

South of the palace are two pavilions: the **Tea House**, a neoclassical pavilion now used for exhibitions and the nearby **Coffee House**, which is a shop and café.

Mikhailovsky Castle

Across the Moika River, which borders the southern end of the Summer Garden, looms **Mikhailovsky zamok** ⑯ (Mikhailovsky Castle,

also known as Inzhenerny [Engineers'] Castle; open Wed–Sun 10am–6pm, Mon 10am–5pm; tel: 570 5112), a brooding building which Pushkin referred to as "a tyrant's menacing memorial." The fortified palace was built for the notoriously paranoid emperor, Paul I, son of Catherine the Great. Paul's hatred of his mother was so intense that when he succeeded her to the throne, he pursued policies more out of spite than reason, trying to undo everything she had done, and ruining all those she had embraced. He liberated those Catherine had imprisoned and filled his court with people who had been out of royal favour during her reign. In so doing he made many enemies.

The tsar sensed that conspiracy was afoot, and feared for his life. He disliked the Winter Palace; it reminded him of his mother and its endless rooms fuelled his paranoia. In 1797, Paul ordered the castle to be built on the southeastern edge of the Field of Mars. The castle was planned as an impenetrable fortress whose water-filled moats, dirt walls, draw-

Map on pages 82–3

TIP

St Petersburg is the world's most northerly large city. It stands at such a high latitude that for a whole month in summer the sun never sets below the horizon, a phenomenon known as the White Nights. During this period crowds gather at 2am on both sides of the River Neva, near the Hermitage, to watch the bridges being raised to allow sea-going vessels to pass.

BELOW: relaxing in the leafy Summer Garden.

Map
on pages
82-3

*A view of the
Fontanka River in the
19th century when
wooden boats were
the city's main
mode of transport.*

BELOW: restoring
the glory of the
Summer Garden.

bridges and secret passageway out of the castle, could protect him from conspirators. Since the castle was only protected by natural waterways on the north side (the Moika) and the east side (the Fontanka), canals were dug along its southern and western facades. (These have since been filled in, but part of the old moat has been recreated at the main entrance.)

The castle was completed in 1801. But, as fate would have it, just 40 days after moving in, Paul was strangled in his bedchamber by soldiers of his own household guard, and his son, Alexander I (a conspirator in his demise) became tsar.

Unsurprisingly, in the ensuing years none of the Russian emperors wished to set up residence in Mikhailovsky Castle. For a brief period it was used as an alms house for widows until it was taken over by the Military Engineers' College, hence the name by which it is commonly known today, Inzenerny zamok (Engineers' Castle). In 1838, the 16-year-old Dostoevsky was sent here as a cadet. It was while studying in the gloomy castle that he first began to write. After the Bolshevik Revolution the castle was used to house archives and administrative offices.

When the adjoining land was redeveloped in 1958, this opened up a magnificent view of the south facade of the palace, where a bronze equestrian statue of Peter I was erected in 1800. The model for the statue was prepared in 1715, during Peter I's own lifetime, by Bartolomeo Rastrelli, son of the Winter Palace architect.

The castle is now part of the **Russian Museum** *(see pages 137–43)* and is undergoing restoration. It houses a **Portrait Gallery**, filled with paintings of Russian royals, aristocrats and dignitaries from the late 17th century to the early 20th century. Other rooms are used to exhibit art from the Russian Museum collection, and there are a number of areas dedicated to the era of Paul I's reign. The castle also houses temporary exhibitions.

South of the castle, **Klenovaya alleya** (Maple Alley) runs to the former military parade ground. ❏

Gregorian Calendar

The Russian Orthodox Church observes the Gregorian Calendar known as "old style". This means that church festivals are 13 days later than in the West – so, for example, Christmas Day is on 7 January rather than 25 December. The Church Council of 1918–9 decided to follow the state and adopt the Julian calendar ("new style"). Obviously every diocese had to lose the 13 days simultaneously, but state persecution and the arrest of bishops prevented it from being announced. Recent suggestions for change have met strong resistance from the majority of churchgoers, but there can be no doubt that it will happen eventually.

RESTAURANTS & BARS

Restaurants

Borsalino (Angleterre Hotel), $$$
Bolshaya Morskaya ulitsa, 39
Tel: 494 5115
Open: B, L & D
Borsalino serves up good international cuisine in a chic setting more reminiscent of New York or London than Russia. It often stages live music; the regular jazz sessions are particularly popular. Great breakfast and Sunday brunch.

Da Vinci, $$$
Malaya Morskaya ulitsa, 15
Tel: 315 9334
Open: L & D
Da Vinci offers a mixture of Mediterranean and Russian cuisine and cabaret-style entertainment while you eat. In summer there are pavement tables, which are not always a wise idea since Russian cars still run on leaded fuel.

Hermitage, $$$$
Dvortsovaya ploshchad, 8/6
Tel: 314 4772
Open: L & D
When it comes to decor, the sumptuous interior of the Hermitage Museum's official restaurant lives up to expectations. Unfortunately, the same cannot be said for the food, which is mediocre for the price. Definitely a case of style over substance.

Nikolai, $$$
Bolshaya Morskaya ulitsa, 52
Tel. 571 5900
Open: L & D
Not far from St Isaac's Cathedral, this smart restaurant in the wood-panelled basement of the House of Architects serves up fine Russian and European cuisine. It specialises in seafood dishes, with salmon imported fresh from Finland, and has a good selection of salads and vegetarian dishes.

Pizzacato, $$
Bolshaya Morskaya ulitsa, 45
Tel: 315 0319
Open: L & D
Good Italian restaurants are few and far between in St Petersburg. Pizzacato is one of a handful that do an acceptable job, offering good pizza made in a brick oven. It is located in the basement of the ornate 19th-century House of Composers.

Tandoor, $$$
Voznesensky prospekt, 2
Tel: 312 3886
Open: L & D
This long-established Indian restaurant serves a wide range of meat and vegetable dishes, which are tasty if not as spicy as some might prefer. Prices are reasonable and it makes a welcome change from Russian cuisine.

Victoria, at the Taleon Club, $$$$
Moiki naberezhnaya reki, 59
Tel: 324 9944
Open: L & D
Victoria is the elegant rooftop restaurant in the mansion built for wealthy 19th-century merchant, Yeliseev. The cuisine is refined, the wine list comprehensive, the decor sumptuous and the views stunning. A serious splurge. Lunch and Sunday brunch are more affordable.

Bars and Cafes

Olivia, $$
Bolshaya Morskaya ulitsa
Tel: 314 6563
Open L, D
A large Greek restaurant with a sunny interior that will make you feel as though you have left Russia for the warmth of Greece.

Pushka Inn, $$
Moiki naberezhnaya reki, 14
Tel: 314 0663
Open: B, L & D
A western-style pub that's more popular as a watering hole, but its Russian and European dishes are worth trying. Not far from Dvortsovaya ploshchad, it's an ideal place to stop by after a visit to the Hermitage.

PRICE CATEGORIES

Prices for a three-course dinner per person with a half-bottle of house wine:
$ = under $15
$$ = $15–$35
$$$ = $35–$80
$$$$ = over $80

RIGHT: the city's cafés offer quick bites at cheap prices.

THE HERMITAGE

The Hermitage Museum is one of the world's most magnificent repositories of art treasures. So vast is its collection that only one-twentieth can be put on display at any one time

Top of every visitor's list of things to see in St Petersburg has to be the **Hermitage Museum** (open Tues–Sat 10.30am–6pm, Sun until 5pm; entrance charge; tel: 710-9625; www.hermitagemuseum.org). This vast repository of art and artefacts draws 3 million visitors from all over the world every year. The opulence of its halls and the astonishing array of masterpieces it contains seldom fail to inspire awe in first-time visitors. Its hundreds of rooms cover 20 km (12 miles) and yet can only accommodate 5 percent of the 3-million strong State Collection.

Although renowned for its collections of Western European art, including early 13th-century Italian works, French Impressionists and modern art, the Hermitage has other important departments, notably the prehistoric cultures, Oriental and classical antiquities, as well as an exhibition of gold treasures that are among the finest in the world. Of equal interest is the architecture of the interior and the opulent State Rooms: the Jordan Staircase, the Malachite Hall and the Hall of Twenty Columns, to name but a few of the highlights.

The Hermitage complex is, in fact, made up of four buildings. At its heart is the Winter Palace *(see pages 88)*, former winter residence of all the tsars and tsarinas of Russia since Catherine the Great. The Small Hermitage, the Large Hermitage and the New Hermitage were all added subsequently, to accommodate the ever-expanding imperial collection *(see page 100)*. As you wander between the galleries spread across its three floors it's often hard to tell which building you are in.

Navigating the treasures

Enter the inner courtyard of the Winter Palace from **Palace Square** and buy your ticket at the main entrance

Map on Back Cover

LEFT: many visitors speed through the Hermitage's impressive collection of ancient artefacts to leave more time for exploring the Impressionists.
BELOW: Rastrelli's Jordan Staircase.

Many of the ancient Greek artefacts in the Hermitage come from the Crimea region. The Black Sea coast was once controlled by Greek city-states. Pantikapae (now Kerch in Ukraine) was the fourth-largest ancient Greek city.

BELOW: the Winter Palace's Raphael Loggia.

to the museum. (Be prepared for long queues, especially in the summer – *see tip on page 99*). To help you find your way through the maze of corridors and halls, pick up a free map of the museum from the information desk or refer to the floor plan on the inside back cover of this guide. Room numbers are indicated above the door frames, but remember that Russians label their floor levels in the same way as the US – so the ground floor is the first floor, the first floor is the second and so on.

It is said that if you looked at each work of art in the museum for just a few seconds it would take eleven years to see it all. With this in mind, it's a good idea to decide what you want to see beforehand *(see the quick reference list on page 105)*. Renting an audio-guide will help you to focus your journey. These are available in English, French, German, Italian, Spanish and Russian, and offer a selection of themed tours including 17th-century Dutch and Flemish painting; the period from Impressionism to Picasso; the State Rooms and a tour of the museum highlights.

The Jordan Staircase

The starting point of most tours is the Jordan Staircase. Built by Rastrelli in 1762, this beautifully curved twin staircase, made of Carrara marble, with decorative balustrades and gilded and mirrored walls, survived destruction both by Catherine the Great (who was not a fan of Rastrelli's baroque flourishes) and the fire of 1837 (it was the one area faithfully restored by Nicholas I's architect Vasily Stasov – *see next page*). The staircase, once used by ambassadors and dignitaries on their way to an imperial audience, sweeps up to the State Rooms on the first floor.

Ancient artefacts

The ground floor rooms are devoted to the art of ancient civilisations from ancient Egypt, Greece and Rome to Siberia and ancient Asian cultures. A marvellous collection of finds from prehistoric Russian settlements is spread across several rooms on the first floor of the Winter Palace's dusty west wing. Prize exhibits among the well-preserved **Altai and Scythian relics and arte-**

facts include an intricate woollen carpet and a wooden burial cart, preserved by the thick layer of frozen ground covering the burial mound they were excavated from.

Among its most valuable treasures is the Hermitage's collection of ancient jewellery, from exquisite Scythian and Greek pieces to Byzantine and Mughal treasures. These are kept (under tight security) in the **Golden Treasure Galleries**. Room 42 contains finely crafted Scythian gold from around the 7th century BC. Of particular note are a beautiful deer and panther, thought to have been used as centrepieces on shields. The treasure galleries can only be visited on a guided tour, and will cost you an extra 300 rubles. You should book ahead of time as places are limited (tel: 571 8446).

The corridor to the right of the Jordan Staircase leads past the shops to the **Egyptian Hall** (Room 100), which has some remarkable Egyptian mummies, funerary objects and papyruses. Beyond the hall another corridor leads through the Small Hermitage to the ground-floor rooms

of the Large Hermitage where you'll find the **Classical Antiquities** collection: an array of Greek sarcophagi, figurines and vases, and Roman statuary, portrait busts and antique cameos. Don't miss the monumental 19-ton Kolyvan Vase and the Hall of Twenty Columns – dating from the 1850s its mosaic floor and wall decorations are inspired by ancient Roman designs.

The State Rooms

Before tackling the art collections, climb the Jordan Staircase to visit the magnificent State Rooms, the glittering stage of many a state ceremony, grand ball and historic event. In 1837 the imperial palace was devastated by fire. Nicholas I immediately put architect Vasily Stasov to the task of restoring its opulent rooms to their former glory. Stasov rose admirably to the challenge and with the help of a team of eminent architects and a 10,000-strong army of workers took 15 months to complete the restoration. In most cases, however, the replicas were not exact and Stasov's preference for a more restrained neoclassical style is evident. The aforementioned Jordan Staircase is most representative of the Winter Palace as it was before the fire.

Climb the stairs to the first floor and the north river-facing front of the palace, known as the Neva Enfilade. Directly in front of you at the top of the staircase, an antechamber leads into the **Nikolaev Hall**, also known as the Great Hall. This magnificent gold-and-white room, hung with monumental crystal chandeliers, is the largest in the palace. In Russia's imperial heyday it was the scene of many a lavish ball. The **Concert Hall** next door displays Russian silverware from the late 17th to the early 20th centuries. The centrepiece is Alexander Nevsky's silver sarcophagus. Empress Elizabeth had this richly ornamented tomb made in

Map on Back Cover

 TIP

Save time queuing by booking your ticket online (www.hermitagemuseum.org). Note that the museum tends to be less busy in the afternoons, as the majority of tour groups visit before lunch. The cost of a ticket for the State Hermitage is 350 rubles. Entrance to each of the other buildings in the complex costs 200 rubles. These are: the General Staff Building on Palace Square (see pages 87), the Museum of Imperial Porcelain, the Winter Palace of Peter the Great, and the Menshikov Palace (see page 172). You can save money by buying a combined ticket though you might find it a bit of a challenge to visit more than the Hermitage in a day. Entry is free on the first Thursday of every month.

LEFT: *Madonna with Flower*, by Leonardo da Vinci.

The Birth of a Collection

Work on Rastrelli's new Winter Palace began in 1854 on the request of Elizabeth Petrovna, Peter the Great's daughter, who reigned for 20 years (1741–61), but died just a few months short of its completion. The empress and the Italian architect shared the same preference for the Russian baroque. Rastrelli's vast palace was unashamedly ornate. Its 1,050 rooms, 1,787 windows and 117 staircases were festooned with stucco, statues and colonnades, and awash with marble, malachite, jasper, bronze, fine wood, rock crystal and gemstones.

Catherine the Great came to the throne in 1792, just one year after the palace was finished. She immediately set about enhancing the reputation of the Russian court abroad and, in the tradition of her forebears, began to collect great works of art. She put her Russian ambassadors at the European courts to the task, sparing no expense for the purpose, acquiring not just individual paintings, but entire collections.

Catherine did not share her predecessor's passion for the baroque and had many of Rastrelli's original interiors in the Winter Palace remodelled in the more sombre classical style. She also wanted a more intimate space and added a small pavilion to be a "Hermitage" with room for her art and tables for private dinners. She then added a second pavilion and galleries, forming the Small Hermitage (1764–7) and a Large Hermitage along the waterfront (1771–87). Here she hung her fast-growing collection, played billiards, and, after the addition of the theatre (1783–7), allowed guests to wander around after performances.

In 1837, the palace was devastated by a raging fire, but the art collection was miraculously saved from destruction. Within 15 months the palace had been restored to its former grandeur and Tsar Nicholas I commissioned a new hermitage to be built. Catherine the Great's collection had been further enhanced by artworks acquired largely from Napoleonic victory spoils. By the time Nicholas opened the New and Large Hermitages as a public museum in 1852, the Russian imperial collection was one of the finest, and richest in Europe.

The imperial collection continued to expand through the 19th century, right up until the October Revolution. In 1917 the Winter Palace and the Hermitage were declared museums of the state. At first, the Bolshevik confiscations of aristocratic estates brought more art into Hermitage vaults. But by the mid 1920s, in order to finance their revolutionary dreams, the communists began to sell off valuable works at bargain prices to Western collectors.

During World War II, the imperial collection was saved from destruction for a second time. As the Germans advanced on Leningrad, an emergency evacuation of the museum's treasures to Siberia saved the collection from dispersal. In 1948, the Hermitage acquired over 300 very important paintings from the former collections of industrialists, Shchukin and Morozov. These paintings (together with a substantial Nazi horde confiscated by the Red Army) form the basis of the Hermitage's most popular gallery of French Impressionist and post-Impressionist art. ❏

LEFT: the stately Malachite Room was refurbished after the great fire of 1837.

Map on Back Cover

1752 out of the imperial coins minted from the first 1,474 kg (3,250 lb) of silver mined in Kolyvan, Siberia.

A door in the corner connects this room to the **Malachite Hall**, arguably the most impressive of all the State Rooms. Designed by Bryullov in 1839 as a drawing room for Nicolas I's wife, Alexandra, it is decorated with more than 2 tons of vibrant green malachite brought from the Urals. Return to the Jordan Staircase via the **Portrait Gallery of the Romanovs**, hung with paintings of the Russian royal family.

Backtrack to the top of the Jordan Staircase and turn right into the east wing, or Great Enfilade. The first room you enter is the **Field Marshall's Hall**, named after the portraits of Russian military heroes that hung here until they were destroyed by the 1837 fire. The state carriage on display in the corner was made in Paris and used for the coronation of Catherine I and Catherine the Great. This white hall leads to a suite of rooms beginning with the **Small Throne Room** dedicated to Peter the Great. The walls are lined with crimson velvet from Lyon and strewn with Romanov eagles. The silver-gilt throne was crafted in England in 1731 for Empress Anna. Next is the galleried **Armorial Hall**, the second-largest room in the palace. Here, official ceremonies were conducted beneath bronze chandeliers bearing the coats of arms and heraldic emblems of all the Russian provinces.

The long thin room parallel to the Armorial Hall is the **1812 War Gallery**. Its walls are lined with portraits of military leaders instrumental in the defeat of Napoleon. The other side of the gallery opens into the imposing **Hall of St George**. As the main throne room, it was lavishly decorated with marble and laid with an intricate parquet floor, made with 16 different types of wood, that mirrors the motifs on the ceiling.

Italian art

The Hermitage's extensive collection of 13–18th-century Italian art is spread over 30 rooms (207–38). These works made their way to imperial Russia when members of the aristocracy, who often visited and even

As it is best known for its collection of European art, the Hermitage's collection of Russian artefacts and icons is often overlooked. It is spread across the west wing of the first floor of the Winter Palace (rooms 151–73). Also worth a look are the Russian Palace interiors (rooms 175–87) decorated in the style of various periods from the early 19th century to the Bolshevik Revolution.

BELOW: vase in the Gold Drawing Room; Raphael's *Holy Family*.

maintained residences in Italy, spared little expense in acquiring fine art. To access this popular section, cross over from the Winter Palace to the river-facing wing of the Large Hermitage, via the **Pavilion Room** (Room 204). The centrepiece of this magnificent room adorned with gold and white marble is the 18th-century peacock clock, made in England, which spreads its feathers and crows every Wednesday at 5pm.

The stars of the Italian section (which begins beyond the Council Staircase in Room 207) include **Leonardo da Vinci**'s *Madonna Litta* (*c*. 1491), a striking canvas depicting the Virgin suckling the baby Jesus; two among many great works by **Raphael**, in the Raphael Loggia – the *Holy Family* and *Madonna Conestabile*; and a marble sculpture, *Young Boy Crouching* (*c*. 1530) by **Michelangelo**. Other Renaissance masterpieces include **Titian's** *St Sebastian* and *Penitent Mary Magdalene*; **Giorgione**'s *Judith*; and several works by **Botticelli**. The two Venetians, **Tintoretto** and **Veronese**, are well represented

and there are some fine works by **Caravaggio**, of which the best known is *the Lute Player* (1595).

Flemish and Dutch

The range and quality of Flemish and Dutch masters on display in the Hermitage is astonishing (rooms 244–254, 258, 261–262). There are over 40 paintings by Rubens and two dozen by Rembrandt, making this one of the most important collections of its kind in the world. Paintings by **Rembrandt** are grouped in Room 254. Worth singling out are the dramatic *Abraham's Sacrifice* (1635), the luminous *Danae* (1636) (painstakingly restored after its near-fatal attack in 1985 by a madman) and the deeply emotional *Return of the Prodigal Son* (1668–9) painted shortly before his death. Works to look out for in the **Rubens** gallery include the *Descent from the Cross* (1611–4) the sensual *Union of Earth and Water* (1618) and a corpulent *Bacchus* (1636–40). A room dedicated to **Van Dyck** includes a fine self-portrait (1622–3) and his *Portrait of Court Ladies* (*c*. 1638), painted in England.

TIP

The internet café on the first floor, across from the Jordan Staircase, is one of the best places in St Petersburg to go online. It also serves coffee, sandwiches, bagels and pastries. Along the corridor is a cluster of shops selling books, postcards, prints and souvenirs. The toilets are nearby.

A Legacy of Restoration

Following the collapse of the Soviet Union in 1991, a run-down and cash-strapped Hermitage was in dire need of restoration. With UNESCO backing, Hermitage director Mikhail Piotrovsky set out to give the museum a facelift ahead of St Petersburg's 300th anniversary in 2003. Restoration work quickly gathered pace: the Danish Government donated a new and more economical heating system; Finnish sponsors installed a state-of-the-art plumbing system, while Canadian sponsors helped create an electronic database of the museum's collection and installed ultraviolet film over 2,000 windows to protect paintings from the sun. A new storage facility was opened and the General Staff building, across Palace Square, was incorporated into the Hermitage complex. The Rembrandt Hall was refurbished thanks to Dutch sponsors and fitted with a brand-new roof and a new lighting system. In addition, the Dutch Friends of

the Hermitage led a $5-million project to recreate the Hermitage's lavish 18th-century Hanging Gardens.

On the night of the city's 300th anniversary, the Hermitage opened its newly renovated gates on Palace Square and let in visitors for free.

But the renovation process is far from complete. Funding is a perennial problem, though a number of Russian and international corporate giants have made substantial contributions and the international network of Friends of the Hermitage are active fundraisers. The task is a Herculean one, but with luck, work will be completed in time for the museum's 250th anniversary in 2014. In 2006 it emerged that $5-million worth of artefacts were missing from the museum's collections. Some of the items, reportedly stolen by museum staff, have since been recovered and an investigation is underway.

Spanish Collection

Although much smaller, the Spanish Collection (rooms 239–40) counts several gems such as **Murillo**'s *Boy with a Dog* (1650s), **Goya**'s *Portrait of the Actress Antonia Zarate* (1811) and **El Greco's** *Apostles Peter and Paul* (1587–92).

French and German art

Catherine's private apartments in the south-east corner of the Winter Palace were inhabited by the empress (who installed her lovers on the level below) during the winter and it was here that she died after suffering a stroke in 1796. Although a few rooms are given over to German artists (including **Dürer**, **Cranach** and **Holbein**), the majority are dedicated to her great collection of French art, with works by 17th-century artists **Poussin** and **Lorraine** and great painters of French rococo, **Watteau** (look for his *Savoyard with a Marmot*, 1716); **Boucher**, whose *Pastoral Scene* is very characteristic of the period; and **Fragonard**, painter of the delightful *Stolen Kiss* (*c*. 1780).

Impressionists and post-Impressionists

Much of the second floor is given over to European art of the 19th and 20th centuries. The pride and joy of the Hermitage, and its biggest attraction after the State Rooms, is the comprehensive collection of Impressionist and post-Impressionist paintings displayed here. Most of these were assembled in the early 20th century by two wealthy Muscovite industrialists, Morozov and Shchukin.

All the big names are here, each represented by several paintings. **Monet**'s *Lady in the Garden* (1867) is a fine example of the Impressionists' attempt to record reality in terms of light and colour, while **Renoir's** *Portrait of Jeanne Samary* (1878) and **Degas'** balleri-nas and women washing illustrate the artists' common passion for painting women. **Van Gogh** is present with his vivid *Ladies of Arles* (1888) and *Cottages* (1890), and there are 15 paintings by **Gauguin** from his Tahitian period. **Cézanne** occupies a prominent place in the collection. His *Mont Ste-Victoire* (1896–8) and *Smoker* (1890–2) demonstrate what was then a ground-breaking representation of shapes and volumes that influenced many painters after him.

The Hermitage also owns the world's largest collection of paintings by **Matisse**, central to which are *Dance* and *Music* (1910), two works commissioned by Shchukin for his Moscow mansion. The museum is equally proud of its **Picassos**. Look out for *Absinthe Drinker* (1901), his earliest work here, and *Woman with a Fan* (1908), a sober geometrical portrait from his cubist period. Another room is dedicated to **Kandinsky**.

This floor also displays **Chinese, Iranian** and **Byzantine** art, and a part of the museum's 90,000-strong **Numismatic Collection**. ❏

Map on Back Cover

Portrait of the actress Jeanne Samary (1878), one of six paintings by Renoir in the Hermitage collection.

BELOW: the floodlit Winter Palace from the Neva Embankment.

THE HERMITAGE: ART AS POWER

The Hermitage's rich collection of Old Masters, sculptures, antiquities and archaeology is a powerful symbol for Russia

Art has always been political in Russia. Catherine II bought her first collection of 225 paintings in 1764 to get one up on Frederick of Prussia, who could not afford them. She went on to purchase vast national collections one after another – the Campana collection in Italy, the Crozat collection in France and the Walpole collection in England – until she had more than 4,000 paintings and 10,000 drawings. The sale of these works of art to Russia aroused storms of disapproval and political censure but, in each case, it also proved Catherine's wealth, power and cunning in the international arena. The 19th century added rich archaeological collections – archaeology being a patriotic and political science important in proving the glory of the Russian land – and more paintings and applied art. All this came to the Hermitage, heir to the imperial collections, along with thousands of confiscated works including, after 1917, those of the Impressionists. During the Soviet era the Hermitage collection was a symbol of Soviet learning and magnificence, and today, with its 3 million pieces, it remains a great source of pride to Russians everywhere.

LEFT: Scythian Stag. Book a guided tour to see the magnificent collection of golden treasures, from 7th-century BC Scythian and ancient Greek items to Oriental daggers and jewellery.

ABOVE: 19th-century Russian silverware, part of the Russian collection of art and artefacts on the first floor of the Winter Palace. Because the Hermitage is better known for its collection of Western European art, the Russian section of the museum is often, undeservedly, overlooked.

ABOVE: *Ladies of Arles.* The stunning display of Impressionist and Post-Impressionist canvases includes this painting by Van Gogh, as well as work by Monet, Renoir and many more.

THE COLLECTIONS

A quick reference guide for what to see where:

Ground Floor
The Winter Palace Ancient Cultures: Prehistoric Russia; the Scythian and Altaic cultures; Eastern Europe in the Iron Age; the Caucasus; the Golden Treasures Gallery; Ancient Egypt.
Highlights: 4th-century BC carpet and funeral cart (Room 26); Scythian jewellery (Room 42, guided tours only); Egyptian mummies
The New and Large Hermitage Classical Antiquities.
Highlights: the Tauride Venus (Room 109); the Gonzaga Cameo (Room 121); the Kolyvan Vase (Room 128); the Hall of Twenty Columns (Room 130).

First Floor
The Winter Palace The State Rooms; French painting of the 18th century; German art; Russian culture of the 18th century; Russian palace interiors.
Highlights: the Jordan Staircase; the Malachite Hall (Room 189), the Great Hall (Room 191), the Small Throne Room (Room 194), the Hall of St George (Room 198); the Poussin Room (Room 279), Fragonard's *Stolen Kiss* (Room 288);
The New and Large Hermitage Italian painting of the 13th to the 18th century; Dutch and Flemish masters; Spanish art.
Highlights: Leonardo da Vinci's *Madonna Litta* (Room 214), the Raphael Loggia (rooms 226 and 227), *The Lute Player* by Caravaggio, the Rembrandt Room (Room 254), the Rubens Gallery (Room 247); self-portrait of Van Dyck (Room 246).

Second Floor
The Winter Palace French, Western European and American art of the 19th and 20th centuries; Chinese and Central Asian art; Byzantine, Iranian and near Eastern art; the Numismatic Collection.
Highlights: the Impressionist and post-Impressionist Collection (rooms 316–320, 343–350); Sassanid Silverware (Room 383).

ABOVE: the Winter Palace. Rastrelli's baroque palace (1754–62) dominates the central body of the Neva and the immense Palace Square. It is at the heart of the complex of four buildings that makes up the Hermitage.

LEFT: *Saskia as Flora* (1634) One of 23 masterpieces by Rembrandt in a room dedicated to his works. Other famous paintings include *Return of the Prodigal Son* (1665–69), *The Holy Family* (1645), *Danae* (1636) and *Descent from the Cross* (c. 1634).

LEFT: the Jordan Staircase. Once, foreign ambassadors ascended this magnificent staircase to be received at court. Today, visitors can admire the stunning white marble and gold interior before embarking on their visit of the museum.

NEVSKY PROSPEKT

"There is nothing better than Nevsky Prospekt. It is the city's essence, it shines in all ways and is the most beautiful thing in our capital."
– Nikolai Gogol, *Nevsky Prospekt*

Nevsky prospekt begins in the heart of St Petersburg, just beyond the southern corner of **Dvortsovaya ploshchad** ❶ (Palace Square), and more than any other street it defines the soul and rhythm of the city. Its energy is exhilarating, though sometimes frustrating, as one can easily feel overwhelmed by the constant stream of people. Since it is the city's business and entertainment hub, most major transport arteries lead to Nevsky prospekt. Not to have walked Nevsky, as the locals refer to it, is not to have visited St Petersburg.

If you are not in the mood to cover the entire 4.5 km (2½ miles) from the Admiralty to the Alexander Nevsky Monastery, try at least to walk the 2 km (1½ miles) to Anichkov Bridge over the Fontanka. There are many handsome buildings to see along this stretch of the road. You can then board a bus to Ploshchad Vosstaniya (Uprising Square) – named in honour of the liberal February 1917 Revolution and not the Bolshevik seizure of power in the following October – before moving on to the Alexander Nevsky Monastery, one of Russia's most important religious centres.

The Great Perspective Road

In the Middle Ages, the marshy territories of the Neva estuary – the cradle of the future city – were a part of the lands settled by Finnish tribes but controlled by the Russian city-state of Novgorod *(see page 19)*. To the east of the estuary lay the Novgorod Road, which ran along today's Ligovsky prospekt and led to Novgorod.

In the early 18th century, following Peter the Great's conquest, construction of the Admiralty Yard on the Neva demanded easy access to wood, metal and other materials. It was therefore necessary to link the

Map on pages 108–9

LEFT: the Cathedral on the Spilled Blood.
BELOW: a street musician makes a decent living.

The sign near No. 14 Nevsky prospekt reads "This side of the street is most dangerous during shelling". It is a relic of World War II, when such signs were put up on the northwest sides of all streets to reduce casualties during German bombardments.

Yard to the major transport artery connecting Peter's young capital with the more developed cities of Russia's interior. Thus, between 1709–10, the Great Perspective Road was cut through the forests covering the area between the Novgorod Road and the Admiralty.

At this time, St Petersburg was still centred on the Petrograd side by the Peter and Paul Fortress and along the Spit of Vasilievsky island. It would be almost three decades before the Great Perspective Road became the city's chief thoroughfare. In 1738 the Empress Anna renamed it Nevskaya perspektiva, or Nevsky Perspective, after the River Neva. From this time on, Nevsky began its reign as the city's central spine.

Banking boulevard

Before the 1917 Revolution, Nevsky prospekt and the neighbouring streets were called the City of St Petersburg, and like the City of London in England it controlled the heart of the country's financial sector. Twenty-eight of Russia's largest banks and insurance companies had their headquarters between the Admiralty and Anichkov Bridge, and the area had the city's – if not the country's – most expensive real-estate values, something which is again true today.

Remnants of this period are still visible near the Admiralty. The magnificent Art Nouveau building at Nevsky No. 1, dating from 1911, once housed the St Petersburg Private Commercial Bank and is today owned by **Bank Menatepa**. To make way for the bank, the Hotel London, a popular place for 19th-century foreign visitors, was torn down.

Nevsky No. 9 was the former headquarters of the Wawelberg Bank, built in 1911–12 by the architect Marian Peretiatkovich, who

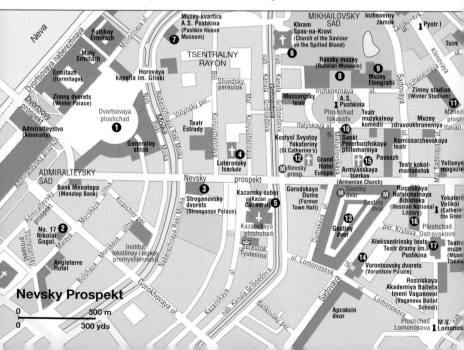

Nevsky Prospekt

0   300 m
0   300 yds

fashioned its distinctive arcades after the Doge's Palace in Venice. Beyond Malaya Morskaya stands **Bolshaya Morskaya No. 15**, once the headquarters of the Russian Trade and Industry Bank. Built in 1915–16 by the city's leading architect of the early 20th century, Fedor Lidval, it was not only the largest and most magnificent bank building of this period but also one of the last buildings erected in St Petersburg under the command of a tsar.

Gogol's flat

The first street that crosses Nevsky prospekt is Malaya Morskaya. Nikolai Gogol lived in a modest three-room apartment at **No. 17 ❷** between 1833 and 1836. In this house, which is marked by a plaque, he wrote *The Government Inspector*, *Taras Bulba*, a satirical story about the Cossacks, and the early chapters of the prose-poem *Dead Souls*. In 1835 Gogol penned the

story *Nevsky prospekt*, which is still quoted by locals as witness to Nevsky's unchanging eternal soul.

No. 15 Nevsky prospekt is referred to simply as the "house with columns". It was built in 1760 for the St Petersburg Chief of Police, Nikolai Chicherin. In 1858 it was bought by the wealthy Yeliseev family, who redecorated it and slightly altered the facade.

The Stroganov Palace

Just east of the Moika, **Stroganovsky dvorets ❸** (Stroganov Palace; open Wed–Sun 10am–6pm, Mon 10am–5pm; waxwork display open daily 11am–6.30pm; entrance charge; tel: 571 8328) was built by Bartolomeo Rastrelli in the mid-1750s for Count Stroganov, whose coat of arms is still visible over the gates. A fine example of Russian baroque, the palace is now a branch of the Russian Museum and is under restoration. Temporary exhi-

The short section of Bolshaya Morskaya that looks towards Dvortsovaya ploshchad (Palace Square) was planned by Carlo Rossi (above) to run exactly along the Pulkovo Meridian. On a sunny day, you know when it is noon: the houses have no shadows.

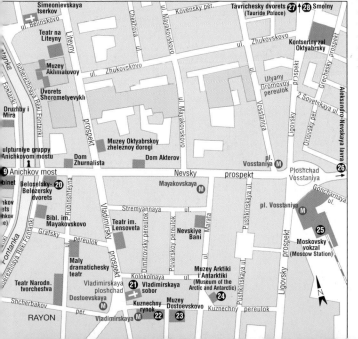

The sign of an antique book dealer – Russians spend a vast amount of their time reading.

BELOW: relaxing on the steps of Kazan Cathedral.

bitions are held in the completed rooms and there is also a modest waxwork display.

Be wary of a sign in front of the palace advertising the "Museum of Chocolate". It is not a museum at all, but a shop in the palace's basement. Still, it's worth a look since the chocolate comes in unusual forms and can make a nice gift to take home.

Unorthodox churches

Until Peter the Great began inviting Europeans to settle in St Petersburg in large numbers, the population of central Russia was entirely adherent to Orthodoxy. Suddenly, Protestants and Catholics appeared in large numbers and, though the Orthodox Church was bitterly opposed to their presence in the country, the will of the sovereign was paramount.

Peter gave permission for members of these other religions to build houses of worship; in fact he was godfather to the first-ever Catholic baptised in Russia, the son of the city's chief architect, Domenico Trezzini.

None of the original Protestant and Catholic churches has survived, but later structures still stand along Nevsky prospekt. No. 20 used to house a Dutch church; today it is home to the district's public library, named after Alexander Blok. Nearby (Nos 22 and 24) is the **Luteransky tserkov** ❹ (Lutheran church; Sunday services).

After 1917, the church was converted into a storage house for vegetables and later became a swimming pool. Today the Lutheran congregation has restored it to a place of worship.

Kazan Cathedral

Opposite the Lutheran church, across Nevsky prospekt, is one of St Petersburg's architectural masterpieces – the **Kazansky sobor** ❺ (Kazan Cathedral; open daily 10am–8pm, but large groups are prohibited during mass – services daily at 10am and 7pm), built between 1801 and 1811 by Andrei Voronikhin, who was clearly inspired by Bernini's colonnade for St Peter's in the Vatican.

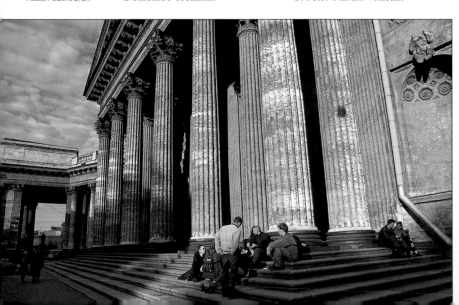

The cathedral's colonnade comprises 96 columns which stand 13 metres (42 ft) high. Huge, 15-metre (49-ft) long bas-reliefs at both ends of the building depict biblical themes. The statues of generals on each side of the portico were installed in 1837 to commemorate the 25th anniversary of the victory over Napoleon. One depicts Field Marshal Kutuzov, his sword pointing towards the imaginary enemy, and the other pensive figure is Barclay-de-Tolley – one of Russia's finest generals. Kutuzov, the commander of the Russian forces that opposed Napoleon, is buried here in a vault in the northern chapel.

Opposite Kazan Cathedral, the house with a globe on its corner tower was once the Russian headquarters of the New York-based Singer sewing machine company. It has since been the home of the city's most important book store, **Dom Knigi** (House of Books), which occupied the building from 1919. Enormous and always busy, the shop has recently reopened after extensive renovation.

Church of the Spilled Blood

On the right-hand side of Griboedov kanal opposite Kazan Cathedral is the **Khram Spasa-na-Krovi ❻** (Church of the Saviour on the Spilled Blood; open Thus–Tues 11am–7pm; entrance charge), which is also known as the Church of the Resurrection of Christ. Designed by the Russian architect of English descent, Alfred Parland, the church was built on the order of Alexander III, between 1883 and 1907 in memory of his father.

The reference to blood is a reminder that members of the revolutionary Narodnaya Volya (People's Will) group murdered Alexander II on this spot in a terrorist bomb attack on 1 March 1881; the explosion tore the tsar's legs off and left him bleeding to death.

The church was paid for by the imperial family and private donors. Construction dragged on for almost 24 years due to a member of the tsar's family embezzling the funds.

Some of Russia's leading artists of the day, including Mikhail Nesterov and Victor Vasnetsov (*see box*

Map on pages 108–9

Kazan Cathedral is the seat of the Metropolitan of St Petersburg and Ladoga, the highest-ranking church official in the city and one of the most powerful in Russia.

BELOW: the Singer symbol above the Dom Knigi building; Gogol reading to a group of friends.

Detail of the intricate mosaics that decorate the Church on the Spilled Blood.

BELOW: the fantastic domes of the Church on the Spilled Blood.

and margin text, page 113), decorated the church. The architecture contains elements of the Russian Revival style and is reminiscent of St Basil's Cathedral in Moscow.

The exterior is embellished by nearly 7,000 sq. metres (75,300 sq. ft) of mosaic portraits of the saints, while the central mosaic depicts scenes from the Old Testament. Adding to the colourful exterior are 20 granite plaques recording the historic events of the reign of Alexander II, and five domes covered with jewellers' enamel. The interior of the church, reopened in 1998 after more than 20 years of restoration to repair the vandalism of the Soviet era, is entirely covered by mosaics based on paintings by famous Russian and religious artists.

Pushkin Museum

Not far from the Church on the Spilled Blood, walking west along the course of Naberezhnaya Reki Moiki, you come to house No. 12, the **Muzey-kvartira A.S. Pushkina ❼** (Pushkin House Museum; open Wed–Mon 10.30am–5pm; entrance

charge). It was here that Pushkin wrote his novel *The Captain's Daughter* and his great poem *The Bronze Horseman*. The poet spent his last days in this house after being mortally wounded in a duel *(see page 160)*. He died on 29 January 1837, and every year on the anniversary of his death devotees of Russia's greatest poet come to the house to pay tribute; the queues of people can stretch down the street.

Square of the Arts

Walking south along Griboedov kanal from the Church on the Spilled Blood, take the first left on to Inzhenernaya ulitsa (Engineering Street) which leads to **Ploshchad Iskusstv** (Square of the Arts), so named during Soviet times. The centre of this architectural ensemble is the yellow Mikhail Palace, now home to the **Russky muzey ❽** (Russian Museum; open Wed–Mon 10am–6pm; entrance charge), built for Nicholas I's younger brother, Mikhail, in 1819–25. At the end of the 19th century, the palace was rebuilt and redecorated; fortunately

the entrance stairway and the white column hall managed to escape this extensive remodelling.

In 1898, under Nicholas II, the palace was opened to the public as the Imperial Russian Museum; today the museum houses one of the world's greatest collections of Russian art *(see pages 137–43)*.

Between 1910 and 1912, two huge edifices were built alongside the palace. The left wing is now part of the Russian Museum, while the right originally acted as the ethnography section. In 1934 this section became a museum in its own right – the Museum of Ethnography of the Peoples of the USSR, now known simply as the **Muzey Etnografii** ❾ (Museum of Ethnography; open Tues–Sun 10am–5pm, closed last Fri of every month; entrance charge).

The museum has more than 450,000 pieces in its collection, documenting the customs, rituals, languages and religion of practically every nation in the former Soviet Union. Among the exhibits are Ukrainian and Belarussian embroi-

deries, Turkmenian carpets, amber from the Baltic republics, Vologda lace and so on.

Directly in front of the museum is Mikhail Anikushin's monument to Alexander Pushkin (1957). The house on the south side of the square, where the Assembly of the Gentry used to meet, is now home to the **Sankt Peterburzhskaya philomarniya** ❿ (St Petersburg Philharmonic), one of the world's great orchestras. Standing tickets sell for as little as 50 cents – though foreigners should expect to pay more to gain entrance – and the spectacular 19th-century interior is unrivalled in the city.

Manezhnaya ploshchad to the east of Ploshchad Iskusstv along Italianskaya ulitsa is a charming little square with many nice cafés and restaurants. On the north side is the **Zimny stadion** ⓫ (Winter Stadium; entrance charge for events and exhibitions), built in the 1820s as an imperial riding school and converted into a sports stadium in 1948. On the corner where the square meets the pedestrianised

Victor Vasnetsov, who worked on the Church on the Spilled Blood, made his reputation by producing grand scenes based upon Russian fairy tales. His masterpieces include The Three Bogatyrs, The Tale of Sleeping Beauty *and* The Unsmiling Tsarevna, *and are on display at the Russian Museum and the Tretyakov Gallery in Moscow.*

BELOW: unusual photo opportunities are available for a price along Nevsky prospekt.

Mikhail Nesterov

Mikhail Nesterov, one of the chief artists to work on the Cathedral on the Spilled Blood, was born in 1862 in Ufa in the Urals and became a master of monumental and landscape painting. He entered St Petersburg Academy of Fine Arts in 1881 and participated in the Wanderers society.

He married a fondness for nouveau style with a dedication to religious subjects. One of his masterpieces, *Taking the Veil*, is on display in the Russian Museum *(see page 143)*. Mostly he is known for his mosaics and frescoes. His commissions took him all over Russia, from the Church of Alexander Nevsky in Georgia to St Petersburg.

*Getting a bite to
eat outside
Gostiny Dvor,
St Petersburg's main
shopping centre.*

BELOW: lighting a
candle for prayer;
the Armenian church.

Malaya Sadovaya (Lesser Garden) and Italianskaya (Italian) ulitsas is a neo-Renaissance building housing the offices of St Petersburg State TV and Radio.

St Catherine's Church

Return to Nevsky prospekt and the point where it crosses the Griboedov kanal. **Kostyol Svyatoy Yekateriny**  (St Catherine's Catholic church; open for services) was built by Jean Baptiste Vallin de la Mothe in 1763–83. The last king of Poland, Stanislaw August Poniatowski, who lived out his days in St Petersburg, was buried here, but after Poland became an independent state in 1918, his remains were repatriated to his family's crypt. The church also housed the tomb of Marshal Moreau, who emigrated from France after Napoleon seized power, and who later fought in the Russian Army against Napoleon. He lost a leg in the Battle of Dresden in August 1813 and died the next day. His body was then buried, with honours, in the crypt of St Catherine's Church. The church was reopened as a place of worship in 1991, but is currently under reconstruction, with services held daily in the morning and evening.

Next to the Catholic church is the **Grand Hotel Europe**, the city's grandest and most expensive hotel *(see Travel Tips, page 222)*. Across the street is the former **Gorodskaya Duma** (Town Hall and municipal council), crowned with a pentagonal turret. In its day the turret was used as a fire-tower, from where firemen sounded the alarm in the event of fire, flood or a particularly vicious frost. Ironically, the tower itself caught fire in 2000 and has recently been repaired.

Gostiny dvor

In past times, travelling merchants stayed at special establishments where they were given room, board and an opportunity to ply their individual trades. Such a place was called a *gostiny dvor* (merchants' yard), deriving from the Old Russian word for merchant, *gost* (not to be confused with the modern

Russian word meaning guest). On the site of just such a complex Vallin de la Mothe built the splendid **Gostiny dvor** ⓭ between 1761–85.

The length of its facade totals nearly 1,000 metres (3,300 ft). The rectangular, neoclassical building had such a felicitous design that it was copied when similar establishments were built in other cities. The place retains its trading function to this day – it is now one of the city's largest department stores, along with the more upmarket Passazh, opposite, at 48 Nevsky prospekt (*see Shopping, pages 72–73*).

Vorontsovsky Palace

Vorontsovsky dvorets ⓮ (Vorontsov Palace; closed to the public) on the southeast side of Gostiny dvor was designed by Bartolomeo Rastrelli; it contains the famous Malteeskaya kapella (Maltese Chapel), which occasionally opens to the public for classical concerts (see local newspapers). The palace is now occupied by the Suvorov military academy for young boys.

Armenian Church

On the opposite side of Nevsky prospekt to Gostiny dvor, between houses 40 and 42 (set back from the road), is the light-blue neoclassical building of the **Armyanskaya tserkov** ⓯ (Armenian Church; open daily), built by Yuriy Velten in 1780. It closed in the 1930s when it was used as a workshop but it reopened as a church in 1993.

Legend has it that construction was financed by an Armenian businessman, Yokhim Lazarev, who raised the money from the sale of a single Persian diamond to Catherine the Great, for her lover, Grigori Orlov.

Russian National Library

Gostiny dvor's neighbour along Nevsky prospekt is the **Rossiskaya Natsionalnaya Biblioteka** ⓰ (Russian National Library; open Sept–June daily 9am–9pm; July and Aug Mon and Wed 1–9pm, Tues, Thur–Sun 9am–7pm; tel: 310 7137), whose main facade looks over the nearby Ploshchad Ostrovskovo. This library, which is the second

Map on pages 108–9

The winter climate in St Petersburg is harsh, with strong winds and snow between November and late March. In summer, from the end of May to early July, there is an air of festivity due to the extraordinary White Nights, when the sun sets for no more than two hours.

BELOW: the city's canals turn into grand, white avenues every winter.

Fur hats make a popular souvenir and are on sale throughout the city.

BELOW: the National Library – home of Voltaire's library.

largest in the country after Moscow's Russian State Library, was opened in 1814. It served as a place to work for St Petersburg writers, scientists, composers, architects and revolutionaries – Vladimir Ilyich Lenin among them.

Among its treasured possessions is the second-oldest surviving hand-written book in Russian, the 11th-century Ostromirov Gospel; Voltaire's library, comprising 6,814 volumes; and the world's smallest printed volume, the size of a postage stamp, containing Krylov's fables. The print in the latter is so clear that it can be read with the naked eye. The oldest manuscripts in the library date from the 3rd century BC and include ancient Chinese, Tibetan and Hebrew scrolls. In 1994 the library was the victim of one of the most daring thefts in history *(see box opposite)*.

Ostrovskovo Square

In the centre of Ploshchad Ostrov-skovo stands the **Pamyatnik Yeka-terine Velikoi** (Monument to Catherine the Great, 1873). The great empress is surrounded by her faithful supporters and favourites – Prince Potemkin-Tavrichesky, with a Turkish turban underfoot; Gener-alissimo Alexander Suvorov; Field Marshal Pyotr Rumiantsev; Princess Ekaterina Dashkova; the President of the Russian Academy of Sci-ences, book in hand; the poet and statesman Gavriil Derzhavin; Admi-ral Chichagov and other policy-makers of 18th-century Russia.

Most of the men were Cather-ine's lovers, and some recent his-torical research claims that even Dashkova, the only female of rank in Russia other than the empress, was a target of Catherine's vora-cious sexual appetite in the early years of her reign.

Aleksandrinsky Theatre

The **Aleksandrinsky teatr** ⑰ (also known as the Teatr dramy im. Pushk-ina or the Pushkin Drama Theatre; tel: 312 1545), on the south side of Ploshchad Ostrovskovo, was built in 1823 and named after Alexandra, the wife of Nicholas I. The building behind it is the **Vaganova Ballet**

School, founded in 1738. Its neighbour is the **Teatralny muzey** (Museum of Theatre, currently closed for renovation), which before 1917 was the building of the Imperial Theatres' Management. The collection has over 400,000 items, including photographs, sketches of scenery, sheet music and original items belonging to the stars of the Russian stage, such as director Vsevolod Meyerhold, stage artists Alexander Benois and Leon Bakst, as well as Kasemir Malevich, and ballet stars such as Anna Pavlova, Vladislav Nijinsky and Mikhail Baryshnikov.

On the other side of the theatre is Ulitsa Zodchevo Rossi, which is one of the most stunning, though shortest, streets in the city. Its proportions are precise: two identical buildings face each other, each measuring 220 metres (720 ft) in length and 22 metres (72 ft) in height, while the distance between them is also 22 metres (72 ft).

Lomonosov Square

Ulitsa Zodchevo Rossi leads into **Ploshchad Lomonosova** (Lomonosov Square) with a monument to Lomonosov, one of Russia's greatest scientists (see page 169).

(see page 169)

Map on pages 108–9

Anichkov Palace

Back on Nevsky, opposite Ploshchad Ostrovskovo you will see **Yeliseyevsky magazin** (Yeliseev's Store; open daily), a splendid example of Art Nouveau and a wonderful emporium of fine foods since tsarist times.

Further along the right-hand side of Nevsky, deep in overflowing greenery, stands **Anichkov dvorets** ⑱ (Anichkov Palace; open for special events). Its construction was started in 1741 for Count Razumovsky, the lover of the Empress Elizabeth, and was made the imperial residence during the reign of Alexander III, who disliked the Winter Palace. Alexander's son, the future Nicholas II, spent his youth in this palace. After the Bolshevik Revolution, it was turned into the Palace of Pioneers and Youth. Now the Palace of Youth Creativity, it hosts many classes and activities for children, as well as concerts and special events.

Old newspapers and propaganda posters are sold in stalls along Nevsky prospekt.

BELOW: Aleksandrinsky Theatre – home of the Pushkin Drama Theatre.

Book Burglars

Since the collapse of the Soviet Union the Russian National Library, along with other cash-strapped museums in the city, has struggled to cope with security. As a result, they have often been targeted by thieves. The most spectacular heist took place in 1994 with the theft of 47 medieval European and 45 ancient Chinese, Mongolian, Tibetan and Hebrew manuscripts, valued at around $300 million.

The theft was carried out to order by the former head of the library's rare manuscript department, who had emigrated to Israel. A joint operation by Russian and Israeli police rounded up the culprits, and the items were quickly recovered.

Traders at Kuznechny Market sell all sorts of goods. Much of the produce is grown at their dachas*, providing a steady income for the elderly whose pensions have been destroyed by inflation.*

BELOW: one of Klodt's horses on the Anichkov Bridge.

Over Anichkov Bridge

Nevsky crosses the Fontanka over **Anichkov most** ⓳ (bridge), named after Anichkov, the engineer who supervised the construction of the first wooden bridge over the Fontanka in 1715.

The bridge is best known for its four horse sculptures. When Pyotr Klodt first cast the statues for the city, Emperor Nicholas I impulsively gave them to the Prussian king. In Prussia, the statues were installed near the Great Palace in Berlin and Klodt was made an honourary member of the Berlin Academy of Arts, and then of the respective institutions in Rome and Paris. Meanwhile, plaster-cast statues were installed on Anichkov Bridge. Klodt replaced them with bronze ones, but not for long: Nicholas once more decided to give them as a present – this time to the King of Naples.

Klodt was told to make bronze copies from the old moulds, but he thought that the central bridge of the capital deserved better. In 1850, a new set of statues was installed on the bridge and remained there until World War II. During the Blockade, Klodt's horses were removed and buried in the garden near Anichkov Palace, to protect them from shelling. In 2000, the statues were given a fresh cleaning and can now be seen in their original grandeur.

On the east side of the Fontanka is the beautiful pink facade of the **Beloselsky-Belozersky dvorets** ⓴, part of which now houses offices of the Russian President's Administration in St Petersburg, as well as the newly opened **muzey Pervovo Mayora Severnoy Stolititsy Anatolya Sobchaka** (Museum of the First Mayor of the Northern Capital, Anatoly Sobchak; guided tours available, tel: 117 1706).

Sobchak became mayor of St Petersburg in 1991, and led the city through its most difficult period since World War II. One of his deputy mayors was an unassuming former KGB officer who, on resigning from the agency, had contemplated taking a job as a taxi driver, using his own car for the purpose. That man was Vladimir Putin.

The building also contains an exhibition of wax figures, entitled "Russia and Power" (open daily noon–6pm), featuring models of the country's rulers.

Vladimir Church

Further along Nevsky prospekt, the road crosses Liteyny prospekt (leading north to the Neva) and Vladimirsky prospekt (to the south). The latter comes to an end in front of **Vladimirskaya sobor** ㉑ (St Vladimir Church; open 9am–8pm), a functioning Russian Orthodox church on Vladimirskaya ploshchad (St Vladimir's Square).

A magnificent monument to 18th-century Russian baroque architecture, the church has an impressive bell tower, five domes, and two separate churches inside.

Kuznechny Market

Nearby, in Kuznechny pereulok, is the bustling **Kuznechny rynok** ㉒ (Kuznechny Market; open Tues–Sat 8am–8pm, Sun 8am–7pm), a farmers' fruit and vegetable market. The prices in this always-busy and colourful market are quite steep by Russian standards, but it sells produce from all over the former Soviet Union and beyond. It also provides some good photo opportunities.

Dostoevsky Museum

Just beyond the market at No. 5 Kuznechny pereulok is the basement entrance of the **Muzey Dostoevskovo** ㉓ (Dostoevsky Museum; open Tues–Sun 11am–6pm, closed last Wed of the month; entrance charge; tel: 571 4031). Dostoevsky lived in this small apartment from 1878 until his death on 28 January 1881; he wrote *The Brothers Karamazov* here. After his death, his wife Anna Grigorievna had photographs taken of his study and these were used to recreate his work space when the house was restored. There are many of the novelist's personal belongings on display, including his hat. On Sunday afternoons, film adaptations of his novels are shown downstairs. Tour information and headsets are available in English.

Museum of the Arctic

The **Muzey Arktiki i Antarktiki** ㉔ (Museum of the Arctic and Antarctic; open Wed–Sun 10am–6pm; entrance charge; tel: 571 2549) at the junction of Kuznechny pereulok and Marata ulitsa, is housed in the former Old Believers church of St Nicholas on Marata ulitsa. The museum is one of only a few such museums in the world, with 75,000 exhibits relating to the Arctic and Antarctic, some dating from the 16th century. Most of the collection is devoted to the history of Russian expeditions and imperialist settlements in the polar regions. The museum is popular with children, who like the self-explanatory dioramas, stuffed polar bears and other wildlife, but it is interesting for adults too.

Map on pages 108–9

Vladimir Church is divided between two floors. In the past the top was used for winter services and the lower for summer – today only the top one is open.

BELOW: the baroque Beloselsky-Belozersky Palace before renovation.

The unique cross of the Russian Orthodox Church.

BELOW: inside Alexander Nevsky Monastery.

Moscow Station

A short walk north along ulitsa Marata then east along Nevsky prospekt takes us to Ploshchad Vosstaniya, where the eye is inevitably drawn towards the imposing **Moskovsky vokzal** ❷ (Moscow Station). Every day some 100 long-distance trains connect St Petersburg with the rest of the country. The station was built in 1851 when the first trains ran from St Petersburg to Moscow, but was rebuilt 100 years later, preserving the external appearance, though the interior is modernised.

There is a small garden in the centre of the square, where an Egyptian-style obelisk to the "Hero City of Leningrad" stands. This was erected in 1985 on the 40th anniversary of the victory over Nazi Germany. From this point, there is a splendid view along the lower part of Nevsky all the way to the Admiralty's spire.

Alexander Nevsky Monastery

Nevsky prospekt terminates at the **Aleksandr-Nevskaya lavra** ❷ (Alexander Nevsky Monastery). The word *lavra* is a title reserved for the highest-ranking monasteries. Although Russia had many monasteries before the Bolshevik Revolution, there were only four *lavras*: Kievo-Pecherskaya, Sergeyev Posad (to the north of Moscow), Pochayevskaya and the Alexander Nevsky.

The monastery complex includes **Troitsky sobor** Ⓐ (Trinity Cathedral), built between 1778 and 1790 by Ivan Starov in neoclassical style. The interior is worth exploring for its iconostasis. The two-storey house to the left of the entrance (by Starov and Trezzini) contains two chapels – the Alexander Nevsky Chapel above and the Khram Uspeniyo Bogoroditsy (Church of the Dormition of Our Lady) below.

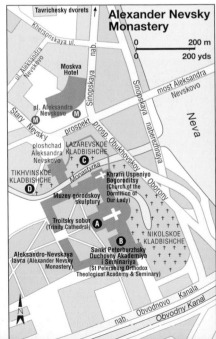

Alexander Nevsky Monastery

Walking though the park near the monastery, you will notice a large yellow building behind a fence. This is the **Sankt Peterburzhsky Duchovny Akademiya i Seminariya ⑧** (St Petersburg Orthodox Theological Academy and Seminary), where both clergymen and regents of the church choir (specialists in religious music) are trained.

Graves of the famous

The Alexander Nevsky Monastery is particularly known for its necropolis containing the tombs of many famous Russians. It includes the graves that lie inside the churches as well as several large cemeteries – Tikhvinskoe, Lazarevskoe, Nikolskoe (outside the monastery's limits) and the small cemetery near Troitsky Cathedral. These are interesting not only for their famous inhabitants but also for their monumental mausoleums and elaborate funerary art.

The **Lazarevskoe kladbishche ⑨** (Lazarus Cemetery) is the oldest in town. It was founded in 1716,

when Peter the Great buried his sister, Natalia Alekseevna, here. It is also the final resting place of Mikhail Lomonosov, the architects Andrei Voronikhin, Andreyan Zakharov, Carlo Rossi and Giacomo Quarenghi and the builder of the monastery, Ivan Starov.

In front of the Lazarus Cemetery is the **Tikhvinskoe kladbishche ⑩** (Tikhvin Cemetery), containing the remains of a number of artistic geniuses, including the composers Tchaikovsky, Mussorgsky and Rimsky-Korsakov, the actress Vera Komissarzhevskaya, the writers Dostoevsky and Krylov and the sculptor of the Anchikov Bridge horses *(see page 118)*, Pyotr Klodt.

Today, the cemeteries are part of the **muzey Gorodskoy Skulptury** (Museum of City Sculpture; open Fri–Wed 9.30am–5pm; entrance charge).

Southwest of the monastery, at No. 30 Rastannaya ulitsa, lies another important necropolis – the **Literatorskiye Mostki** (open Fri–Wed 11am–5pm). This is the last resting place of the writers and

Maps on
pages
108 & 120

The fine baroque architecture of the Alexander Nevsky Monastery.

BELOW: taking a break at Tauride Gardens.

literary critics Ivan Turgenev, Mikhail Saltykov-Schedrin and Vissarion Belinsky, the chemist Dmitry Mendeleev (the father of the Periodic Table, *see page 171*), the physiologist Ivan Pavlov *(see page 158)*, the "Father of Russian Marxism" Plekhanov, and some members of Lenin's family, including his mother.

Tauride Palace and Gardens

The **Tavrichesky dvorets ㉗** (Tauride Palace; not open to the public) was built by Catherine II for her long-term favourite, Count Grigory Potemkin (1739–91), whom she made Governor-General of the Crimea *(see Potemkin's Villages, below)*. After Catherine died, Paul I, seeking revenge against the late favourite of his mother, destroyed the lavish interiors and built stables in the grand halls.

When Paul died, the stables were removed, the palace was redecorated, and it once again became a residence of the royal family. Alexander I lived here for a time in the first few decades of the 19th century, and he was followed by the heir to the Persian throne. The palace then stood empty until 1906, when the state Duma (Russian Parliament) took it over.

Today, the palace belongs to the Inter-parliamentary Assembly of the Commonwealth of Independent States.

In the south end of **Tavrichesky sad** (Tauride Garden), now a park, where Kirochnaya ulitsa crosses Tavricheskaya ulitsa, is the newly refurbished **Memorialny muzey A.V. Suvorova** (Alexander Suvorov Memorial Museum; open 10am–5.15pm, closed Wed, Thur and last Mon of each month; entrance charge).

The museum contains many military items, mementos and documents connected to the life of the great general. Suvorov (1729–1800) was one of Russia's greatest military leaders, best known for beating the Turks and suppressing rebellion throughout the empire. But when he was fighting the French armies in 1798–99, he was ignominiously forced to retreat across the Alps, an act which – as unbelievable as it may sound – Russians consider a great victory. The highly nationalistic museum offers a somewhat idealised view of his life and achievements.

Smolny

One of St Petersburg's most interesting historical ensembles is found not too far away on **Ploshchad Rastrelli**. It is simply called **Smolny ㉘**, on account of it once being the Smolyanoi (Tar) Yard, where tar was prepared for the shipyards. The yard was later moved to another location, and Peter's daughter Elizabeth decided to found a convent on the spot.

The first buildings were built by Rastrelli in 1764 and are among the finest baroque structures in the city. The crowning glory is the light-

Potemkin's Villages

Grigory Potemkin was a man of formidable talent. He commanded military expeditions into the Crimea, and succeeded where many had failed by finally annexing the peninsula to Russia. His greatest talent, however, was his ability to pull the wool over the eyes of his beloved mistress Catherine the Great – and get away with it. When Catherine set out to inspect the Crimea – the newly added pearl in Russia's crown – the clever count decided that the unpleasantness of everyday existence of peasant life which Catherine was certain to encounter on the road would disappoint the empress.

So Potemkin arranged for the old huts to be substituted with freshly whitewashed cottage facades along the entire route of the imperial journey (most of which lay through his vast estates). Peasants were dressed up in pretty clothes for the day and ordered to smile, sing songs and generally act in a respectably pastoral manner as soon as they saw Catherine's carriage. Meanwhile, 10 steps away from the road, their dirty shacks remained as before. Catherine was pleased, and Potemkin rejoiced.

blue coloured Smolny Cathedral, also known as the **Khram Voskresenya Gospoda** (Resurrection Cathedral; open Fri–Wed; entrance charge), which rises to almost 100 metres (328 ft), and has five onion domes and a central cupola. Rastrelli's design was never fully realised, however; among the unfulfilled plans was a 150-metre (492-ft) bell tower that should have stood in front of the cathedral.

The cathedral holds services over the weekend and occasional concerts during the summer.

It was in the 1780s, under Catherine the Great, that the monastery became Russia's first educational establishment for women – the Institute of Noble Maids. But the Noble Maids found the monastic cells too small, and in 1806–8 a separate building was erected in the monastery grounds. It took the form of a classical palace.

The Smolny Institute existed until August 1917, when the Noble Maids were forced to give way to the Bolsheviks, who installed the Military Revolutionary Committee here prior to their coup. Today, the governor of St Petersburg and City Hall occupy the building. Several rooms have been made into a public museum, but tours must be reserved ahead of time (open Mon–Fri 11am–4pm; tel: 576 7461).

Two symmetrical pavilions serve as the entrance to the park in front of the Institute. One of them bears an inscription from the Communist Manifesto: "Workers of the world, unite!" In the park are bronze busts of Karl Marx and Friedrich Engels, and a 6-metre (20-ft) high statue of Lenin stands in front of the City Hall building, which itself is adorned with the tsarist two-headed eagle. Soon these symbols could be overshadowed by Gazprom's new headquarters, an ultra-modern skyscraper.

While this collage of Soviet, tsarist and modern may perplex some visitors, it is in fact a fitting representation of the identity crisis plaguing contemporary Russia – its unique heritage consistently playing second fiddle to the new economy. ❑

Map on pages 108–9

Smolny became the headquarters of the Military-Revolutionary Committee. It was here that the Bolshevik putsch was prepared and carried out in October 1917.

BELOW: the Smolny Cathedral.

RESTAURANTS

Restaurants

Bistro Garcon, $$$
Nevsky prospekt, 95
Tel: 277 2467
Open: B, L & D
Without a doubt, Bistro Garcon serves the best French cuisine in town, its décor is reminiscent of the Parisian Left Bank, and hence it tends to be much more popular with wistful European and American ex-pats than Russians or tourists.

Blow Up, $$
Griboyedova kanal, 22
Tel: 314 5800
Open: L & D
Don't be alarmed by this restaurant's name. It is a cinematic, rather than a militaristic reference. Blow up is a bistro,

sushi bar and photo gallery all rolled into one. It is also one of the chicest places in town serving great food and maintaining a friendly atmosphere.

Chaika, $$$
Griboedova kanal, 14
Tel: 312 4631
Open: L & D
Founded in the heady days of the 1990s, the Chaika (The Seagull) was St Petersburg's very first foreign-owned restaurant. The dining room is trimmed with brass and leather, and the menu offers a combination of typical German and Russian dishes including sausage, pickled herring, goulash and caviar.

Il Patio, $$
Nevsky prospekt, 30
Tel: 380 9183
Open: L & D
Il Patio serves the best pizzas in town, plus other Italian dishes. Centrally located, not far from the Russian Museum. It is very popular, so it's best to reserve a table.

James Cook, $$
Shvedsky pereulok, 2
Tel: 312 3200
Open: B, L & D
The six-dollar breakfast, with good coffee and tea, makes an excellent alternative to some overpriced hotel breakfasts. Other meals

are quite good too, but James Cook is more popular as a café than a restaurant.

Kavkaz Bar, $$$
Karavannaya ulitsa, 18
Tel: 312 1665
Open: L & D
Exotic Caucasian interior of Russia's south. Try the succulent shish kebabs on the grill, as well as the delicious aubergine and walnut salad.

Laima, $
Nevsky prospekt, 30/16
Tel: 315 5545
Open: B, L & D
Laima is a modern bistro open 24 hours a day providing quality

BELOW: Laima cafe, a 24-hour harbour for the hungry.
RIGHT: a mural depicting food and drink typical of 19th-century peasant life.

Russian food at democratic prices. It's popular with the late-night crowd after clubbing in the city centre. The bliny are perfect for a light breakfast.

Mama Roma's, $$
Karavannaya ulitsa, 3
Tel: 314 0347
Open: B, L & D
A change from Russian fare; although the pizza leaves much to be desired. The business lunch is a great buy and features a salad bar. One of the few places in town to serve breakfasts.

Marius Pub, $$
Marata ulitsa, 11
Tel: 315 4880
Open: B, L & D
A traditional Swiss pub serving fine German food. One of the few places in the city that is open 24 hours a day.

The breakfast buffet will fill you up.

SevenSkyBar, $$$
ulitsa Italianskaya, 15
Tel: 449 9462
Open: L & D
A trendy bar and restaurant located on the top floor of the Grand Palace shopping centre. It offers a roof-top view and a European/Asian fusion menu. In comparison with the surroundings, the food is fairly average.

Rossi's (Grand Hotel Europe), $$$$
Mikhailovskaya ulitsa, 1/7
Tel: 329 6622
Open: L & D
Superb Italian restaurant reaching the high standards set by the Grand Hotel Europe. The service is excellent and the location is perfect for people-watching. The tiramisu here is fabled.

Silk, $$$
Malaya Konyushennaya, 4
Tel: 311 5078
Open: L & D
Silk offers great Russian and Japanese cuisine, with probably the best and most expensive sushi in town. Sophisticated and relaxing interior makes it a great place to go with a close circle of friends.

Tinkoff, $$
Kazanskaya ulitsa, 7
Tel: 718 5566
Open: L & D
Tinkoff is a hip club and restaurant for Russian yuppies out for a roaring time. The eclectic menu features great borscht, salads, pizza and sushi. Has own microbrewery that makes eight types of the Tinkoff brand of beers. Live music and huge TV screen for sport.

Valhalla, $$$
Nevsky prospekt, 22
Tel: 571 0024
Open: L & D
Valhalla offers a hearty Russian dinner right on Nevsky prospekt for those looking for a rowdy night out. Live music and hard drinking make it popular with Russians.

Mekong, $$
Malaya Sadovaya ulitsa, 1
Tel: 314 3965
Open: L & D
Inexpensive Vietnamese cuisine in cheerful Buddhist surroundings. Just a few metres off Nevsky prospekt.

PRICE CATEGORIES

Prices for a three-course dinner per person with a half-bottle of house wine:
$ = under $15
$$ = $15–$35
$$$ = $35–$80
$$$$ = over $80

FROM ST ISAAC'S TO ST NICHOLAS

In this square kilometre sits St Isaac's Cathedral, with one of Europe's largest domes; Theatre Square, home to Russia's rising stars; and Yusupov Palace, scene of Rasputin's notorious demise

The golden domes of St Isaac's and St Nicholas cathedrals anchor either end of the area covered in this chapter. Alongside the grandiose St Isaac's, Yusupov Palace is a major attraction, with its sumptuous interiors and crowd-pleasing exhibition on the notorious mystic, Rasputin, who was murdered here.

Teatralnaya ploshchad (Theatre Square) should be the first stop for those seeking fresh interpretations of Russian culture. Few productions are in English, but a ballet at the Mariinsky or a concert at the Rimsky-Korsokov Conservatory require no language skills to appreciate. The nearby Astoriya and Angleterre hotels play host to the most pampered visitors. For a taste of a more authentic and down-to-earth old St Petersburg, head west beyond the wealthy residences of Bolshaya Morskaya ulitsa to the old naval quarter of Kolomna.

St Isaac's Cathedral

The gleaming golden dome of **Isaakiyevsky sobor** ❶ (St Isaac's Cathedral; open Thur–Tues 11am–7pm; entrance charge plus photography fee; tel: 315 9732) soars majestically over **Isaakiyevskaya ploshchad** ❷ (St Isaac's Square) and is visible for miles around. The cathedral is the fourth version of the Church of St Isaac of Dalmatia, built

on this spot to honour the Byzantine monk whose feast day (30 May) was the birthday of Peter the Great. St Isaac lived in the 4th century and was tortured and imprisoned for his faith by the Roman emperor Valens but was later set free by the Christian emperor Theodosius.

In 1818, a little-known French architect, Auguste Montferrand, was commissioned by Alexander I to build a much grander cathedral than the one which stood on the site. Initial attempts to lay the foundations

Map on page 128

LEFT: traditional Russian dancing in the theatre district.
BELOW: the gleaming dome of St Isaac's Cathedral is visible throughout the city.

went horribly wrong due to the city's soft and wet soil. Inspired by techniques used for building on the Venetian lagoon, Montferrand drove thousands of wooden piles into the ground to form a solid foundation. Forty years later, in 1858, the colossal cathedral was completed. Montferrand died just a few months afterwards. His last wish was to be buried in St Isaac's, but Nicolas I refused to allow the burial of a Roman Catholic in an Orthodox church, so Montferrand's wife took his body back to Paris.

St Isaac's Cathedral can accommodate up to 14,000 visitors.

The cathedral was decorated by some of the leading artists of the day, including Peter Klodt (who also sculpted the monument to Nicholas I outside and the horses on Anchikov bridge – *see page 118*) and Karl Bryullov. Forty-three types of stone and marble were used in the lavish interior, including lapis lazuli and tons of malachite for the columns of the iconostasis. The dome, which

rises 101 metres (331 ft) above the city, is plated with about 100 kg (220 lb) of pure gold. No wonder its construction cost ten times that of the Winter Palace.

The bas-reliefs in the cathedral are exceptional. On the southern pediment is *The Adoration of the Magi* by Ivan Vitali, a study of Mary and Jesus surrounded by the kings of Mesopotamia and Ethiopia. The relief above the western portico, *The Meeting of St Isaac of Dalmatia with the Emperor Theodosius*, is also by Vitali, who was undoubtedly courting royal favour by endowing Theodosius and his wife with the features of Alexander I and his spouse. The semi-recumbent figure in the corner holding a model of the cathedral is Montferrand.

The exterior **kolonnada** (colonnade observation point; open Thur–Tues 10am–7pm summer, 11am–3pm winter; entrance and photography charge) around the dome (the

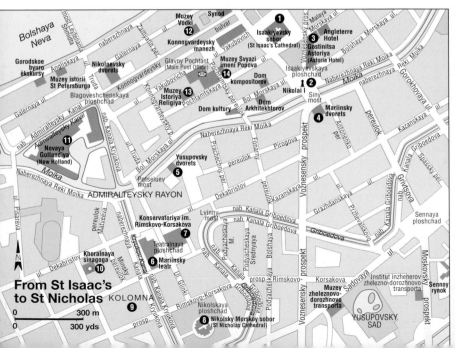

third-largest cathedral dome in Europe) offers spectacular views of the city centre.

In the centre of St Isaac's Square, in front of the cathedral, is an equestrian monument to Nicholas I (1859, by Klodt and Montferrand). According to a Russian saying commenting on the obvious parallel with The Bronze Horseman statue of Peter I on Decembrists' Square *(see page 83)*: "The fool [Nicholas I] chases the wise man [Peter I] but St Isaac's stands in between."

Grand hotels

To the east of St Isaac's, on Voznesensky prospekt, stands the **Gostinitsa Astoriya ❸** (Astoria Hotel, *see page 221*). Built 1910–2, the seven-storey Astoria was the most modern and luxurious hotel in town before 1917. It was first patronised by the tsarist army's top brass. After the 1917 Revolution, it was the turn of the Communist Party leaders to enjoy its luxuries. Lenin and the delegates of the Second Communist International stayed here, as did the writer H.G. Wells

in 1934. After the war, Soviet soldiers rummaging through a Berlin archive found printed invitations to a dinner party in the Astoria's banqueting hall to celebrate what the Nazis believed would be the imminent fall of the city.

Another fashionable hotel, the **Angleterre** *(see page 221),* is annexed to the Astoria. Despite efforts by round-the-clock protestors to save it from destruction, the original building was razed to the ground in 1988 following a ruling by the Leningrad Executive Council. The rebuilding of the historic hotel in the 1990s was funded by foreign investors. In December 1925 one of Russia's most popular poets (husband of the dancer Isadora Duncan) Sergei Yesenin, was found dead in one of the old Angleterre's rooms, next to a farewell poem written in his blood. As a young man, Yesenin was an active supporter of the October Revolution, but he soon became disillusioned with the Bolshevik Government and criticised them openly. The Soviet authorities claim he committed suicide, but

Fabergé had their shop at No. 24 Bolshaya Morskaya ulitsa. The famous Russian jewellers are best known for the exquisitely crafted imperial Easter eggs they made each year for the tsar and tsarina from 1884 until the Bolshevik Revolution.

BELOW: the Blue Bridge over the Moika.

Grigory Rasputin

Grigory Efimovich Rasputin (1869–1916) was the son of peasant farmers from a small Siberian village. As a young man, with a growing reputation for drunkenness and debauchery, Rasputin came across a mystical sect of the Orthodox church which believed that the best way to drive out sin, was to sin and repent. For one so dissolute, this doctrine held enormous appeal and he entered the monastery, re-emerging as a *staretz* (holy man). Dressed in his monk's robes he took to the road, satisfying his sexual appetites by convincing women that through sinning with him, a carrier of particles of divinity, they could achieve salvation.

In 1907, the Rector of the St Petersburg Spiritual Academy introduced Rasputin to the tsarist court. Within a few months the "saintly sinner" had gained recognition and a small following. He was introduced to the devout Empress Alexandra by her trusted companion, Anna Vyrubova. According to contemporary reports the self-styled mystic and faith healer possessed an almost hypnotic power which he used to put the royal family under his spell. He established a particularly strong hold over the empress, who believed that only the prayers of the "holy man" could save the life of her haemophiliac son, Prince Alexei, and help her beleaguered husband, Nicholas II, with affairs of state. Nicholas and Alexandra took Rasputin into the bosom of their family and within a few years he had become one of the most influential men in the Russian government. For a fee, Rasputin could dispense with ministers, organise deals and distribute state orders. The tsar and tsarina seemed oblivious of Rasputin's notoriety outside the court. Stories of his sexual antics spread far and wide, and the gossips fuelled the fire with rumours that he'd seduced the empress and her daughters.

As his influence strengthened, so his enemies increased. For those who disapproved of Tsar Nicholas II's policies and appointments but dared not confront the tsar himself, Rasputin was the ideal scapegoat. In an attempt to save the crumbling monarchy and lead the country away from disaster, a group of patriotic aristocrats led by prince Felix Yusupov decided to rid the nation of Rasputin and his sinister influence.

In the small hours of 17 December 1916, he was lured to Yusupov Palace to be assassinated. The "mad monk", however, was a hard man to kill. First he was fed with poisoned cakes, but when the cyanide didn't seem to have any effect, he was shot at repeatedly. He managed to escape his captors clutches briefly, only to be caught again and brutally beaten, tied up and thrown into the icy river. When his body was discovered some days later, it was evident that he had managed to extricate himself from the ropes. The water in his lungs indicated that he had died by drowning.

Yusupov Palace *(see opposite)* now houses an exhibition dedicated to the life and times of Rasputin and includes a reconstruction of the circumstances of his grim death. But the grisliest exhibit of all can be seen at St Petersburg's Museum of Erotica where Rasputin's pickled penis is on display. The 30-cm (12-inch) organ was apparently cut off by his brutal killers. ❑

LEFT: the notorious mystic Rasputin exercised a great influence over Russia's last tsar and tsarina.

now scholars believe he was murdered, or at least forced into suicide.

Montferrand's buildings

While building St Isaac's, Montferrand found time to complete several other grand designs – all of them in the immediate vicinity. From 1817–20, he built the **Lobanov-Rostovsky Palace**, the huge triangular building on the eastern edge of St Isaac's Square, where it meets Malaya Morskaya ulitsa. It is currently under reconstruction and is destined to house government offices. Montferrand also built a couple of smaller mansions on the fashionable Bolshaya Morskaya ulitsa, west of St Isaac's Square, for the wealthy industrialist Demidov and princely Gagarin family (at Nos 43 and 45 respectively). The Gagarin palace is now called the **Dom Kompositorov** (House of Composers) and is occupied by the composers' trade-union headquarters.

Next door, No. 47, is the birthplace of the great Russian novelist Vladimir Nabokov, author of *Lolita*. Across the road at No. 52, **Dom Arkhitektorov** (the House of Architects), built by Aleksandr Pel in the 1830s, is another handsome mansion with a splendid interior (and restaurant). Montferrand's own house at Naberezhnaya Reki Moika No. 86 (one street further south), may not be as grand as those he built for his wealthier clients, but is impressive nonetheless.

The Blue Bridge

South of St Isaac's Square, on the opposite bank of the Moika stands **Mariinsky dvorets** ❹ (Mariinsky Palace), home to the city's Legislative Assembly. It was built between 1839 and 1844 by Andrei Stakenschneider for Nicholas I's daughter, Maria. The **Siny most**, or Blue Bridge (so called because its underside is painted blue) links the palace to the square and is the widest in the city. The corner building next to the Mariinsky Palace on Antonenko pereulok, is the house where the sixth president of the United States – John Quincy Adams – lived while serving as the first American Ambassador to Russia from 1809 to 1814.

Yusupov Palace

Further west along the Embankment, the long yellow colonnaded building overlooking the River Moika is **Yusupovsky dvorets** ❺ (Yusupov Palace; Naberezhnaya Reki Moika, 94; guided tours daily 11am–6pm, entrance charge; tel: 314 8893). The palace was built in the 1760s by Vallin de la Mothe, and from the early 19th century until the Bolshevik Revolution, it was the principal residence of the Yusupovs, one of the wealthiest families in Russia, and close friends and allies to the imperial court. After the Winter Palace, Yusupov Palace has the most spectacular interiors in the city. The most popular of the lavish interiors is the exotic Moorish room, complete with a fountain and

Map on page 128

The elegant interior of the Yusupov Palace theatre.

BELOW: window shopping for Russian brides.

Theatre Square has plenty of bars and cafés to have a drink and relax before or after a performance.

BELOW: statue of nationalist composer, Rimsky-Korsakov, outside the conservatoire which honours his name.

mosaics. The exhibition in the cellars (visited on a separate guided tour) recounts the story of the infamous Rasputin murdered here by a group of aristocrats led by Prince Yusupov *(see box, page 130)*. Concerts are held regularly in the palace's jewel-box of a theatre.

Theatre Square

Just west of Yusupov Palace, Ulitsa Glinki leads south from the river to **Teatralnaya ploshchad** (Theatre Square). Dominated by the Mariinksy Theatre on one side and the Rimsky-Korsakov Conservatoire on the other, this square is a cultural hub and one of the most beautiful architectural ensembles in the city.

In 1825, an enormous new theatre called the Bolshoy was inaugurated in Moscow. This glittering stage drew the greatest names in ballet and opera of its day. But St Petersburg was not to be outdone by Moscow. In 1859 Albert Cavos, the Bolshoy's architect was commissioned to restore a burnt-down theatre, which he transformed into the imposing **Mariinsky teatr** ❻

(Mariinsky Theatre; open for performances only; www.mariinsky.ru; tel: 326 4141). It was named in honour of Alexander II's wife Maria, who saw its first performance the following year.

The dazzling auditorium became a formidable rival to Moscow's Bolshoy and a healthy rivalry between the two has existed ever since. During its golden age, around the turn of the 20th century, Russia's top ballet stars graced the Mariinsky's stage, including Anna Pavlova, Matilda Kseshinskaya, Vatslav Nijinsky and Tamara Karsavina.

After the Bolshevik Revolution many members of the troupe emigrated and the Mariinsky fell on hard times. Things picked up again during the Soviet era when the theatre, renamed the Kirov (after the Secretary of the Leningrad Communist Party from 1926 to 1934), regained popularity thanks to composers Prokofiev and Khachaturian, ballet stars Galina Ulanova and Vakhtang Chabukiani, and conductors Yevgeny Mravinsky and Vladimir Dranishnikov. Today, although the theatre has resumed its original name officially, it is still referred to internationally as the Kirov.

The Mariinsky continues to thrive under the stewardship of Valeri Gergiev, who has added many new productions to the operatic repertoire. Every June, Gergiev presides over the month-long White Nights Festival, which brings top international names in opera and ballet to St Petersburg. The theatre is currently in the throes of a US$150 million expansion and modernisation programme, which includes the building of a brand-new performing arts centre across the canal, due for completion in 2008.

Opposite the theatre stands the **Konservatoriya imeni Rimskovo-Korsakova** ❼ (Rimsky-Korsakov Conservatoire; open for performances only; tel: 312 2129). It was

founded in 1862 by the composer Anton Rubenstein as Russia's first institution for higher musical education. Tchaikovsky, Prokofiev and Shostakovich were among its most precocious students. In 1944, the conservatoire was renamed after the nationalist composer Rimsky-Korsakov, one of the school's most influential teachers.

St Nicholas Naval Cathedral

South of Theatre Square, alongside the Kryukov kanal is **Nikolskaya ploshchad** (St Nicholas Square), dominated by the blue, white and gold **Nikolsky Morskoy sobor ❽** (Cathedral of St Nicholas; open daily for services). Built between 1753 and 1762 for the use of navy employees, this cathedral is also known as the Sailors' Church. St Nicholas is often compared with Rastrelli's Smolny Cathedral – its architect, Chevakinsky, was one of his pupils – and is considered to be one of the finest examples of Russian baroque architecture.

The sky-blue and white facade is decorated with Corinthian columns and crowned with five golden onion domes. The interior is split into two churches: the ornate ceremonial church on the upper floor and the darker church on the lower floor for daily use. Its vaulted interior is beautifully decorated with icons. The cathedral's four-tier bell tower, crowned with a spire, stands in splendid isolation by the river.

Kolomna

The area on the western side of the Kryukov kanal, known as **Kolomna ❾** is one of the oldest, most authentic districts in the city. While there are few outstanding architectural landmarks to speak of, the former workers' district of Kolomna and its faded buildings has something of a rough and ready charm. One significant landmark to look out for is the 19th-

century **Khoralnaya sinagoga ❿** (Choral Synagogue; Lermontovsky prospekt, 2; services daily), built in a neo-Moorish style. It is one of the few houses of worship in the city that was not closed in Soviet times.

New Holland

The triangular island of **Novaya Gollandiya ⓫** (New Holland), bounded by the Moika River, Kryukov kanal and Admiralteysky kanal, was an ideal place for storing flammable ship-building materials (rope, wood, etc.), which were then transported by barge to the naval shipyards. It is named in honour of the Dutch shipbuilders whose techniques were emulated by Peter the Great in the building of his fleet. The austere red-brick buildings, built to store timber vertically, date from the 1760s, while the soaring archway that marks the southern entrance was designed by French architect Vallin de la Mothe. Despite its unkempt appearance, the island presents a romantic picture when viewed from the water. In 2006, British architect Norman Foster won a competition to

Map on page 128

The architect of St Nicholas Cathedral, Chevakinsky, was a pupil of the baroque master Rastrelli (above), creator of many of the city's iconic buildings including the Winter Palace.

BELOW: St Nicholas Cathedral – modelled on Rastrelli's Smolny.

Souvenir shops are stocked with Soviet emblems and memorabilia like this red star badge.

BELOW: playing football under the shadow of St Isaac's.

Map on page 128

redevelop the island and build a hotel complex there.

Three museums

Heading back east towards St Isaac's via the pretty tree-lined **Konnogvardeysky bulvar** (originally a canal which connected New Holland with the Admiralty), there are a handful of museums worth knowing about.

The **Muzey Vodki** ⑫ (Museum of Vodka, Konnogvardeysky bulvar, 5, open daily 11am–10pm) charts the development of Russia's favourite tipple. The collection includes vodka bottles, glasses, posters, medieval decrees on vodka consumption and other memorabilia. The tour of the museum ends with the opportunity to down a shot or two with a snack before braving the cold again.

The **Muzey Istoriya Religiya** ⑬ (Pochshtamskaya ulitsa 14, open Thur–Tues 11am–6pm), which until recently had occupied Kazan Cathedral *(see page 110)* for decades, has a vast collection of artefacts relating to all religions of the world, from ancient Egyptian mummies to pre-

cious icons. The museum also owns a substantial collection of religious art confiscated from Nazi Germany, but which remains hidden in storage. Scholars are only now beginning to study and catalogue these items.

A little further down the street, in a magnificently restored 18th-century mansion, is the **Muzey Svyazi imeni Popova** ⑭ (Popov Telecommunications Museum, Pochtamtskaya ulitsa, 7, open Tues–Sat 10.30am–6pm; tel: 571 0060). Founded in 1924, this is one of the oldest museums of science and technology in the world. It covers the development of telecommunications from the 19th century to the present day with a fascinating and varied collection from horse-drawn postal sleighs and early telegraphic devices, to TVs and mobile phones.

Central to the museum are the exhibits dedicated to Alexander Popov, who Russians consider to be the true inventor of the radio, before Marconi. The museum also has a vast collection of Russian stamps, though access is restricted, so keen philatelists will have to book a tour in advance. ❑

RESTAURANTS

Restaurants

Bliny Domik, $
Kolokolnaya ulitsa, 8
Tel: 315 9915
Open: B, L & D
For a taste of simple but good Russian fare, try Bliny Domik. It has the best bliny in town. Keep your eyes peeled for the entrance which is marked by a very discreet sign. Live piano music and songs every night; great atmosphere.

Cafe Idiot, $$
Naberezhnaya Reki Moiki, 82
Tel: 315 1675
Open: L & D
Café Idiot bills itself as a bohemian hangout for the local intelligentsia, but mostly it's a place for tourists. Serves only vegetarian food, and has the best cappuccino in town. The retro décor is pleasant; books and chess are offered for those wishing to lounge around. Poorly marked and easy to miss unless you go with someone who knows its precise location.

Caravan, $$$
Voznesensky prospekt, 46
Tel: 310 5678
Open: L & D
Caravan offers excellent Central Asian food in an ethnic village interior with music. Shish kebabs are on the menu all year round, and the *chebureki* are

highly recommended. A favourite place for Russian *biznessmen*, Caravan often plays host to a larger-than-life clientele.

Count Suvorov, $$$$
Sodovaya ulitsa, 26
Tel: 315 4328
Open: L & D
One of the few places in St Petersburg to serve exotic tsarist Russian dishes, such as bear stew, made according to recipes recently found in a local archive.

Tres Amigos, $$
Rubinshteina ulitsa, 25
Tel: 340 2685
Open: L & D
Delicious Mexican food, generous portions and excellent value for money make this a popular place to dine.

Krokadil, $$
Kazanskaya ulitsa, 24
Tel: 320 8777
Open: L & D
The menu combines both Latin and Russian dishes. Great spicy chicken wings, and spaghetti. Live music and DJs throughout the week. A popular place with the young fashionable crowd, who clamour for its wide selection of tropical cocktails.

1913, $$$
Voznesensky prospekt, 13/2
Tel: 315 5148
Open: L & D
With more than ten years experience in the business, 1913 is one of the

grand-daddies of the city's restaurant scene and maintains high culinary standards. Fine fish dishes and a good selection of Georgian wines. Live classical music every night.

The Noble Nest, $$$$
Dekabristov ulitsa, 21
Tel: 312 0911
Open: L & D
One of the city's most expensive and elite restaurants, located in a small tsarist-era building belonging to the Yusupov princes, not far from Mariinsky Palace. The Noble Nest has entertained presidents and ministers for over ten years. Excellent cuisine and a wide selection of wines.

Zov Ilicha (Lenin's

Mating Call), $$$
Kazanskaya ulitsa, 34
Tel: 571 8641
Open: L & D
The décor is a tongue-in-cheek nod to the Soviet era, but the fine Russian and French cuisine sell at unabashed capitalist prices. A unique experience that comes highly recommended. Since the interior contains erotic content, no one under 18 will be admitted.

PRICE CATEGORIES

Prices for a three-course dinner per person with a half-bottle of house wine:
$ = under $15
$$ = $15–$35
$$$ = $35–$80
$$$$ = over $80

RIGHT: a traditional dish with a modern twist.

THE RUSSIAN MUSEUM

The Russian Museum, housed in a superb neoclassical palace, has the world's largest collection of Russian art, some 400,000 works in total, ranging from medieval icons to the latest in conceptual art

The Russky muzey (Russian Museum) is housed in **Mikhailovsky Palace** (Inzhenernaya ulitsa 4; open Wed–Sun 10am–5pm, Mon 10am–4pm, last admission one hour before closing time; entrance charge; tel: 595 4248). The palace, one of the city's finest examples of neoclassical architecture, was constructed in 1819–25 by Carlo Rossi.

The driving force behind the museum's foundation was Tsar Alexander III, who actively collected Russian art in the second half of the 19th century in the hope of one day founding the country's first public museum of Russian art. Alexander's dreams were realised after his death when his son, Russia's last tsar Nicholas II, opened the museum in 1898.

The museum's collection grew considerably in the aftermath of the 1917 Revolution, as Bolsheviks expropriated works of art from aristocratic families, and icons and other religious works from churches, to put on display to the public.

Today, with over 400,000 items, the Russian Museum is the world's largest repository of Russian art and illustrates the most important artistic trends in Russian art from its beginning in Byzantine icons to the avant-garde works of the futurists.

The main entrance to the museum is situated on **Ploshchad Iskusstv** (Square of the Arts), but a second entrance to the side of the building, on the Kanala Griboedova, leads directly to the Benois wing, which was added in 1913–9 and hosts 20th-century art and temporary exhibitions. The two buildings are internally connected.

In addition to the main complex, the Russian Museum complex also includes three separate buildings, the **Stroganov Palace** *(see page 109)*, the

Map on Back Cover

LEFT: the *Crowning of Mikhail Romanov.*
BELOW: bust of Peter I.

On the Trail of Rublev

Andrei Rublev was Russia's foremost icon painter in the 14th century and athough few of his works remain today his influence cannot be underestimated – it is visible throughout the religious art that followed him. Any of his original works still in existence are considered invaluable treasures of the nation's cultural heritage. The Russian Museum holds but one of his pieces – the long-robed figures of the Apostles Peter and Paul. Some of his other works still survive in the Tretyakov Gallery and the Annunciation Cathedral, both in Moscow, and the Assumption Cathedral in Vladimir.

Rublev was born into a crucial time in the development of Russian identity. The young nation was struggling against the Mongol yoke and strangling itself through disunity. The Orthodox Church was quickly becoming the only institution that could hope to unite the disparate principalities.

Numerous gaps in the historical documentation of the Russian Middle Ages make it quite difficult to precisely trace Rublev's life. We do know that he was born between 1360 and 1370 in Rus (the chronicles do not say where exactly but experts agree that it was most likely near present-day Moscow). His name hints that he was born into the family of an artisan; *rubel* was the name of a tool used in the processing of leather.

During the late 14th century the Orthodox Church was in a period of monastic revival. One revivalist, Saint Sergius Radonezhsky (1314–92), was dedicated to uniting ancient Rus under the auspices of an all-powerful church in order to put an end to the oppression inflicted by the Mongol yoke. By doing so, Sergius undoubtedly also hoped to end the Mongol habit of raiding monasteries (one of the wealthiest places of the time) for funding.

Saint Sergius founded a monastery based upon more high-minded principles than self preservation: his values were fraternity, peaceful love towards God, and spiritual self improvement. And it is here that the shy Rublev took his vows under Abbot Nikon, a former pupil of and eventual successor to Saint Sergius.

The first account of Rublev's icon work dates back to 1405 when he was asked to help decorate the Annunciation Cathedral in Moscow with Theophanes the Greek – Russia's most celebrated icon painter at the time and Rublev's mentor. Though much of their work was destroyed, the iconostasis still features seven icons painted by Rublev.

In 1408 Rublev collaborated with another icon painter to decorate the Assumption Cathedral in Vladimir. This is the only place where Rublev's large mural work survives today. His most famous work, the *Old Testament Trinity,* illustrates the complicated theological device of the trinity, but it shows his rejection of the contemporary icon style.

Rublev's critics attacked his new style of painting as deviating from the canon and derided his work as too joyful. And where was the fear of the Lord, they asked? Surely icon painting was not meant to be a gentle art which used colours in a subtle way.

But there was no escaping this style for Rublev. Legend has it that he was a shy and gentle man – even for a monk – who when not painting was dedicated to divine service and meditation until his death in 1430. ❑

LEFT: the Russian Museum has the best collection of icons in the world.

Marble Palace *(see page 91)* and the **Engineers' Castle** *(see page 93)*.

Finding your way

Unlike the Hermitage, which tends to overwhelm first-time visitors by its size, one visit to the Russian Museum is enough to do it some degree of justice. Finding your way around the museum is relatively easy and there are signs in both Russian and English to guide you. Tickets are bought in the basement, where there are also toilets, a cloakroom and a café.

The rooms are all numbered – look out for the number at the top of the door frame – in chronological order, starting with medieval icons on the second floor and ending with avant-garde works in the Benois wing.

The audio guides for rent on the ground floor (250 rubles in English, 150 rubles in Russian) follow this order and provide valuable information on a selection of works, the biographies of famous artists and the history of important artistic movements. You may find these particularly useful as many of the artists whose works are displayed are relatively unknown outside of Russia.

The route we suggest below offers a quick chronological tour of the museum focusing on the main artistic movements and some of the museum's most significant works.

Orthodox art

Once in the central hall on the ground floor, climb the stairs to the second floor and go left at the top. In rooms 1 to 4 are displayed the museum's superb collection of icons (about 6,000 in total), the holy images venerated in Orthodox churches and households, dating from the 12th century up to the 17th century.

Icon painters were expected to thoroughly purify their body and mind by fasting and praying before starting work on their painting. Like Byzantine icons, Russian icons seek to convey a spiritual message rather than an image of reality, and are characterised by a lack of perspective and a remote, ethereal quality to the saints they represent.

In room one, a small, early 12th-century icon depicts the Archangel

Andrei Tarkovsky made a film called Andrei Rublev in 1969; far from being a biographical account of the Russian icon painter, the film is essentially a meditation on the search for spiritual and artistic enlightenment in medieval Russia.

BELOW: the Guard Staircase.

Ilya Repin

Ilya Repin, considered by some to be Russia's national painter, was born in 1844 in the small Ukrainian town of Chuguyev. He began work for a local icon painter, and was soon commissioned to paint portraits and religious scenes. This enabled him to earn enough money to enter the Academy of Arts in St Petersburg.

When he arrived, the Academy was experiencing one of its largest rebellions in recent times. Fourteen young artists had decided to leave the Academy rather than use any mythological subjects in their graduation works. To them, such representations were not art. Art, they believed, should be as close to real life as possible. Eventually, Repin would grow to agree with them.

But first he worked to achieve his diploma. Repin's graduation work, *The Raising of Jairus' Daughter* – a stylised work portraying the biblical parable – left the establishment's feathers unruffled and his fellow graduates behind. He received the coveted Gold Medal for which they were all competing and with it a scholarship to study abroad.

Between 1873–6 Repin travelled through Italy and then worked in Paris. He probably witnessed the emergence of another artistic movement – Impressionism. He must have seen the first exhibitions of the new style, but it was not for him.

Instead he gained fame with his work *The Barge-Haulers on the Volga,* which conveys the brutal realities of forced labour and degradation in Russian life. No longer was he painting the idealised past of antiquity; he had joined the Academy rebels.

Back in Russia, Repin lived in his native Ukraine before heading to Moscow and then St Petersburg, where he started teaching at the Academy; here he became involved with the Wanderers (sometimes translated as the Itinerants) – which consisted mostly of the fourteen students who rioted in the 1860s. The group made art for the people and took their exhibitions around villages to reach a greater audience.

In 1900, during another trip to Paris, Repin met Natalia Nordman and moved to her home, Penaty, in Kuokkala, Finland *(see page 213)* – near St Petersburg. Here they organised cultural gatherings that were attended by the cream of Russia's artistic world.

After Nordman's death in 1914, Repin stayed at Penaty, where he had a refurbished house with a studio. He continued to paint, but an atrophy of his right hand greatly hindered his work (he was forced to teach himself to paint with his left hand). He died there in August 1930 at the age of 86. Kuokkala was later renamed Repino.

Repin is often overlooked in the West, as he was no innovator in painting nor was he the leader of a grand artistic movement. But his role as Russia's national artist cannot be overstated. Vladimir Stasov, the prominent Russian art critic, had the following to say about Repin: "Repin is as much a realist as Gogol, and quite as national. It was with a courage unheard-of in our land that he plunged headlong into the depths of folk life, the interests and the pains of the life our people live… Repin is a mighty artist and a thinker". Ilya Repin lived up to these words, and left a legacy of masterpieces, many of which can be seen in rooms 33, 34 and 54 of the Russian Museum. ❑

LEFT: Ilya Repin as a young man.

Gabriel, also referred to as the *Angel with the Golden Hair*, with his head tilted to the side and large, pensive eyes.

In Room 2 you'll find the 14th-century icon *Boris and Gleb*, depicting the young princes of Kiev who were murdered by their brother; in Room 3 are panels by known masters, such as **Andrei Rublev** *(see page 138)*.

18–19th century

The rest of the second floor is devoted to Russian painting, sculpture and tapestries between 1700 and 1860. During this time Russian art began to move away from its Byzantine roots and become heavily influenced by trends in Western Europe. This is most obvious in Russia's new fondness of portrait painting (before Peter the Great, the Orthodox Church had banned even mirrors to prevent people from worshipping their own image). Portraits from this time are on display in rooms 5 and 6.

The highlight of this floor, in Room 15, is *The Last Day of Pompeii* by **Karl Briullov** (1799–1852), who trained at St Petersburg's Academy of the Arts. His painting reflects the influence of Romanticism and neoclassicism in Russia at this time. But his work manages to convey a vitality and drama that set him apart from his contemporaries. *The Last Day of Pompeii* earned him the Grand Prix of the Paris Salon and wide acclaim both in Europe and Russia. Writer Nikolai Gogol billed this dramatic work "one of the most outstanding phenomena of the 19th century", while Alexander Pushkin praised it in his verse.

The Wanderers

Down on the first floor you can see how Russian art came of age in the 19th century. Rooms 18–24 are filled with monumental academic works, landscapes and scenes of rural life. **Vasily Perov**'s *A Meal in the Monastery* shows the hypocrisy of the clergy, juxtaposing rich and poor, false piety and true faith. Then, starting in Room 25, we move on to a new development. In 1863 a group of students led by **Ivan Kramskoi** (1837–87) rebelled

Apart from the main staircase, Room 11 (known as the White Hall) is the finest example of the palace's original white and gold neoclassical decor, designed by the architect Carlo Rossi.

BELOW: *Knight at the Crossroads* by Victor Vasnetsov.

The huge canvases in Room 36 are by Vasily Surikov (1846–1916), who was a leading exponent of historical paintings influenced by Slavic mysticism. Viktor Vasnetsov (1846–1926) painted dramatic compositions (in Room 38) inspired by Russian prehistory, myths and legends (see picture, page 141).

against the conservatism of the Academy of Arts, and spearheaded a new movement known as the Wanderers *(peredvizhniki)* who sought to produce more realistic paintings portraying Russia's common people, nature and folklore.

The Wanderers were also committed to making art more socially relevant and accessible by travelling round the country and taking their art exhibitions to the people.

Repin

Ilya Repin *(see page 140)* is the most famous of the Wanderers, and the Russian Museum owns some of his finest work, particularly *The Barge-Haulers on the Volga* (1870–3) in Room 33, a powerful denunciation of forced labour, and *Zaporozhe Cossacks Writing a Mocking Letter to the Sultan* (1880–91) in Room 34, an exuberant and detailed painting which took over 12 years to complete.

Rossi wing

BELOW: a view of the city's embankments in 1802.

Room 54 in the Rossi wing contains another famous painting by

Repin, the vast *Ceremonial Meeting of the State Council, 7 May 1901*. This wing also has stunning Caucasian landscapes by Arkhip Kuindzhi (1841–1910) in rooms 40 and 41.

If your time is limited, you might want to skip the folk art exhibits on the same floor and head straight to the Benois wing.

BENOIS WING

This wing hosts a dazzling collection of 20th-century Russian art. The permanent collection is on the second floor (rooms 66–79), reached via the corridor off Room 48 and up the stairs of the Rossi wing. Temporary exhibitions are held on the first floor, which has its own entrance on the Griboedov embankment.

World of Art

The first paintings in the Benois wing are from the **World of Art** movement (Mir Iskusstva), founded by **Sergei Diaghilev** and **Alexander Benois** in the 1890s; this movement rejected the concept of utilitarian art, defending instead "art for art's

sake", free of all constraint and focused on self-expression.

Mikhail Nestorov's spiritual paintings, especially the portrait of his daughter Olga, **Nikolai Roerich**'s warm, fairy tale-like paintings, and **Valentin Serov**'s expressive portraits are only a few of the gems displayed in this section.

Keep an eye out for the portrait of Diaghilev with his nanny, through which **Leon Bakst** brilliantly conveys the charisma of the father of the World of Art.

Russian avant-garde

The rest of the Benois wing is devoted to the Russian avant-garde. The Russian Museum has the largest collection of Russian avant-garde paintings in the world, but unfortunately for Russians most of them are either on tour abroad or in museum cellars due to a lack of space. For this reason, we have omitted specific room numbers as exhibitions change very often.

A number of works by **Kuzma Petrov-Vodkin**, whose canvases tend to travel less than some others,

are however likely to be on display. His *Mother* (1905), pictured below, presents strong iconic features despite its modernity. *Mother* is accordingly referred to as "the Village Madonna" and is one of the museum's masterpieces.

The museum is also rich in paintings by **Kazimir Malevich**, known best for his use of bright geometric shapes, including two of the four versions of his world-famous *Black Square*.

Despite being in great demand abroad, some works by leading avant-garde artists such as Natalia Goncharova, who uses folklore as much as industrial themes in her work; **Vasily Kandinsky**, the leading figure of abstract art; and **Alexander Rodchenko**, are also likely to be on display.

Pavel Filonov, although slightly less famous outside of Russia, also deserves attention. Try to find his *Kings' Feast* (1913), a spellbinding painting that features strong geometrical forms representing macabre, bony figures feasting around a table. ❑

Bear in mind that some of the better-known avant-garde paintings may not be on display, as the cash-strapped museum regularly sends them on tour abroad. If there's a particular painting you want to see, check first that it's on view. Tel: 595 4248; www.rusmuseum.ru

BELOW: *Mother* by Kuzma Petrov-Vodkin.

RESTAURANTS

Russian Museum Café, $
Basement
As lovely as it would be for the city's emporium of Russian art to reach equal heights with native cuisine, there is little chance of getting gourmet food at the Russian Museum's only café. It is located in the underground section near the cloakrooms and the ticket office, before the start of the exhibitions. It's nothing special, just a selection of sandwiches and drinks.

●●●●●●●●●●●●●●●●●●
Price includes dinner and a glass of wine, excluding tip. $$$$ $80 and up, $$$ $35–80, $$ $15–35, $ under $15.

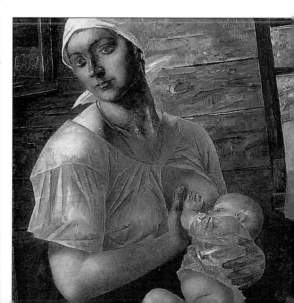

PETER AND PAUL FORTRESS

On this tiny island St Petersburg began, political prisoners met their end and tsars are respectfully buried. The historic buildings make it a prime tourist stop and its beach attracts the locals who take cold dips in the Neva in summer and line up against the fortress walls to bask in the ephemeral sunshine

The **Petropavlovskaya krepost** ❶ (Peter and Paul Fortress; museums are open Thur–Mon 10am–6pm, Tues 10am–5pm, closed Wed and last Tues of each month; cathedral and Prison Museum open daily mid-May–mid-Sept, rest of year opening times as for museums above; grounds open to 10pm; entrance charge) was founded in the summer of 1703 as the core structure in Peter the Great's new capital.

Occupying almost all of Zayachy ostrov, the island opposite the Winter Palace, the fortress has several buildings worth seeing, not least of which is the Peter and Paul Cathedral *(see page 146)* which contains all the tombs of the Russian tsars except two and whose spectacular golden spire is visible throughout the city. The single entrance fee (on sale near the Ivan Gate and at the Boat House outside the cathedral) allows you to see most of the museums and other sites in and around the fortress.

In summer the island becomes a magnet for sunbathers, who pack its pebbly beaches for a feel of the elusive sunshine. In winter, swimmers (known as *morzhi* or walruses) break the ice and swim in the freezing cold water off the Gosudarev Bastion on the south side – you can see a blue walrus symbolising them painted on the outer wall.

A fort at war

Originally known as Fort St Petersburg, the fortress was quickly built in 1704 to secure Russia's hold on the Neva delta at a time when the Northern War with Sweden was in full swing.

The crude earthworks were gradually replaced by brick and stone under the direction of Domenico Trezzini in 1706. Construction proceeded on a section-by-section basis in order not to weaken the military might of the stronghold. In 1740 the

Maps:
Area 154
Plan 146

LEFT: the soaring spire of Peter and Paul Cathedral.
BELOW: fancy dress recreates the atmosphere of the imperial city.

If you look closely at the bas-relief on St Peter's Gate (Petrovskye vorota), you'll see Peter the Great among the onlookers, distinguished by his laurel wreath.

entire fortress was finally dressed in stone; the initial fortifications were doubled around each gate leading to the mainland with a further wall, which explains why you have to pass through two gates to enter the fortress proper. Moats were built between the two walls, which were filled in during the 19th century.

The history of the fort is a gruesome one, since thousands of forced labourers died during its construction, and many political prisoners, including Peter's son Alexis, were tortured within its walls.

Entering the gates

The best way to enter the fortress is by walking across the wooden **Ioannovsky most** Ⓐ (St John's Bridge), on the eastern side of the island. This is the oldest bridge in the city, though the ironwork and lamps only date back to 1953. It underwent a major reconstruction in 2003, so little is left of the original structure.

The bridge leads to the **Ioannovsky vorota** Ⓑ (St John's Gate, 1740), the entrance to the outlying ramparts. As you come through the gate, to your right is (bizarrely) the **Aeronautics Museum**, tracing – in Russian language only – the history of the Soviet space programme. Next you come to the imposing entrance of the main fortress, the **Petrovskye vorota** Ⓒ (St Peter's Gate). Built in 1717–8 in baroque

style by Domenico Trezzini, the wooden bas-relief shows Peter the Great's victory over Charles XII of Sweden – it depicts St Peter casting down the winged sorcerer Simon who is trying to soar above him. The double-headed eagle, symbol of the Romanov dynasty, is above the arch, and in the niches flanking the gates stand Minerva, goddess of wisdom (on the left) and Bellona, goddess of war (on the right).

Old Petersburg Museum

Pass through St Peter's Gate. On your left as you head towards the cathedral, is the **Inzhenerny dom** (Engineers' House), now housing the **Old Petersburg Museum** *(see page 145 for opening times)*. Looking at the 18th- and 19th-century paintings, and the miscellaneous collection of artefacts from old shop fronts and musical instruments to duelling pistols, you get a glimpse of what life was like for the well-heeled in St Petersburg before the Revolution.

Peter and Paul Cathedral

The central passage leads from St Peter's Gate to the majestic **Petropavlovsky sobor** Ⓓ (Peter and Paul Cathedral; *see page 145 for opening times*). The tall golden spire, a city landmark, not only signals defiance and confidence, it also asserts Peter the Great's European influence,

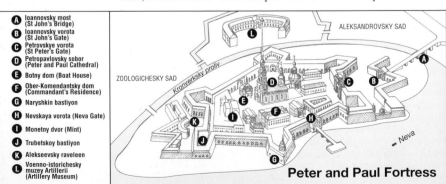

Ⓐ Ioannovsky most (St John's Bridge)
Ⓑ Ioannovsky vorota (St John's Gate)
Ⓒ Petrovskye vorota (St Peter's Gate)
Ⓓ Petropavlovsky sobor (Peter and Paul Cathedral)
Ⓔ Botny dom (Boat House)
Ⓕ Ober-Komendantsky dom (Commandant's Residence)
Ⓖ Naryshkin bastiyon
Ⓗ Nevskaya vorota (Neva Gate)
Ⓘ Monetny dvor (Mint)
Ⓙ Trubetskoy bastiyon
Ⓚ Alekseevsky raveleen
Ⓛ Voenno-istorichesky muzey Artillerii (Artillery Museum)

ALEKSANDROVSKY SAD

ZOOLOGICHESKY SAD

Kronverksky proliv

Neva

Peter and Paul Fortress

being about as far removed from a traditional Russian onion dome as you can get.

The stone cathedral was founded in 1712 in place of the wooden Peter and Paul Church which had been built in 1703. Peter the Great and the architect, Domenico Trezzini, had the belfry built first to ensure the ground would be strong enough to support the rest of the church. Since the belfry was completed earlier than the church, the graves of some members of Peter the Great's family, including his sister, and his son, Alexis, are located at the base of the belfry stairs.

In 1858 the original wooden spire was replaced with a metal one, again crowned with a weathervane in the shape of an angel. With a height of 122.5 metres (402 ft), the cathedral is St Petersburg's second-tallest structure (after the television tower *see page 157*).

Tombs of the Romanovs

The richly decorated interior of the cathedral, with its pink and green Corinthian columns, chandeliers and overarching vaults, is a far cry from a traditional Russian Orthodox church. Dominating the space inside is the baroque iconostasis, a beautiful gilded wood carving created by Moscow craftsmen in the 1720s. It shows the only icons in the church, the archangels Gabriel and Michael.

But the cathedral is best known for its tombs. All the Russian tsars, from Peter the Great to Nicholas II, excluding Peter II and Ivan VI, lie here. The tombs of Peter and Catherine the Great are situated to the right of the iconostasis. Particularly impressive are the tombstones of Alexander II, who was killed by terrorists in 1881, and his wife Maria. Made from 5 tons of Altai jasper and 6.5 tons of rhodonite from the Urals, the stones took 16 years, from 1890 to 1906, to hand polish at Peterhof.

In July 1998 the remains of Nicholas II, the Tsarina Alexandra, three of their children and two servants were buried here. Russian President Boris Yeltsin, as well as the many Romanov descendants living abroad, flew in for the event that also attracted many other top names in Russian politics, business and

The male choir of St Petersburg sings in the Peter and Paul Cathedral twice a week (Mon and Fri at 7pm) in the summer (tel: 230 6431). Other concerts are held during the White Nights *(see page 227)*. Tickets can be bought in the cathedral.

BELOW: the fortress gains its defence from the river it was built to protect.

culture. The remains of two of the children – the Crown Prince, Alexei, and Grand Duchess, Anastasia – have never been found, and stories persist about their supposed escape from execution at the hands of the Bolsheviks.

In 2000 the Russian Orthodox Church canonised the entire family as martyrs for the faith. Today, you may see icons of the imperial family in some Orthodox churches. In 2006, the remains of Tsar Nicholas' mother were reburied alongside the graves of her son and husband.

To the left of the main altar, a special passage leads from the cathedral to the crypt of the Grand Princes, where close relatives of the tsars are buried. The crypt is now under restoration but is open to the public.

Around the cathedral

Opposite the cathedral exit is the elegant **Botny dom** **E** (Boat House, 1760s), which was originally intended for Peter's first sailing boat (known as "the Grandfather of the Russian Fleet"). Today, the original boat is in the Central Naval Museum on Vasilievsky island *(see page 167)* and an exact replica can be seen here in its place.

If you cross back in front of the cathedral, you'll see the two-floored former **Ober-Komendantsky dom** **F** (Commandant's Residence), dating from the 1740s, which now houses an exhibition documenting the history of the fortress.

Southern embattlements

To the south of the Commandant's House, by the river, is the huge **Naryshkin Bastion** **G**, which points its two cannons out over the Neva. According to tradition dating back to the 18th century, when few people had clocks, a single shot is fired daily at noon. On 27 January at 8pm a 24-gun salute is heard to mark the anniversary of the breaking of the Siege of Leningrad *(see page 32)*. You can walk up onto the Naryshkin Bastion for a small fee. It's certainly worth it on a sunny day for the fabulous views over the Neva to the Winter Palace and St Isaac's Cathedral.

St Petersburg is a federal city, with the official status of a "subject of the Federation". It is one of Russia's 89 regions, and the head of the city is called "governor" not "mayor".

BELOW: even in Spring's chilly temperatures, locals come to catch the sun that falls along the fortress walls.

To the east of Naryshkin Bastion is the **Nevskaya vorota** (Neva Gate), leading to the Komendantsky Moorage; this is the spot where the tsars and their court would enter the Peter and Paul Fortress from the water in order to attend official ceremonies in the cathedral. It is also the gate through which prisoners would pass, in the other direction, on their way to the even more notorious Schlüsselburg Fortress *(see page 207)* for capital punishment (hence it used to be called "Death Gate"). Under the arch are plaques that list the years and heights of catastrophic floods that have been the scourge of St Petersburg since it was built on marshes in 1703.

The Mint

Opposite the cathedral is one of the city's oldest enterprises – the **Monetny dvor** ❶ (the Mint; closed to the public). Until Antonio Porto built an edifice specifically designed for the Mint (1798–1806), it was housed in the Naryshkin and Trubetskoy bastions. The world's first lever press for coining money was devised here

in 1811, and gold, silver and copper coins and medals continued to be minted here until the end of the Soviet era; output now is limited to military medals and commemorative medallions, which can be bought in the shop across the courtyard.

Political prisoners

At the southwestern corner of the fortress is the **Trubetskoy Bastion** ❶ (now housing the Prison Museum, *for opening times see page 145*). This was the main interrogation centre and prison for generations of revolutionaries. The first political prisoner to be held here was Peter the Great's son, Alexis, whom it is alleged was tortured and murdered here on the command of his own father. Another famous inmate was Leon Trotsky, held here in the wake of the 1905 Revolution.

In 1917, ministers of the deposed Provisional Government were sent to the prison, as well as four Romanov grand dukes, who were later executed in the courtyard. The Bolsheviks turned the prison into a museum in 1922, highlighting the infamies of

Map on page 146

TIP

The Baltiyskiy dom (Baltic House Theatre) in Alexander Park holds international drama festivals, including the Festival of Russian Theatres.

BELOW: the state seal of the Romanovs.

the tsarist regime while omitting to mention any of the horrors they perpetrated within its walls.

On the ground floor of the museum is a model of the guard room and an exhibition of period photographs and prison uniforms. Upstairs are the isolation cells, restored to their original grim appearance, while downstairs are the punishment cells where prisoners were locked up for 48 hours at a stretch. Once a fortnight prisoners were taken to the Bath House for delousing. Although the cells are stark and damp, they do not convey the full horror of being a prisoner in tsarist times.

Leaving the fortress by its western Vasilievsky Gate, you'll see a U-shaped outbuilding marking the site of the now demolished **Alekseevsky ravelin** ; built by Tsarina Anna in the 1730s, this bastion contained the first long-term prison in the fortress, its maximum security "Secret House", reserved for those who angered Anna's favourite, Count Biron.

Under Nicholas I, the prison held many of the Decembrists *(see

The Artillery Museum has a model of a dog with a mine strapped to its back; the Soviets trained them to run underneath Nazi tanks.

BELOW: taking aim at the Artillery Museum.

pages 27)* and the Petrashevsky Circle, including Dostoevsky.

Around the fortress

In addition to the ramparts and bastions, the Peter and Paul Fortress is further protected by a canal (Kronverksky proliv) on its north side, separating the island from the Petrograd side. You can now take a motorboat along the canal in summer for a half-hour tour of the Neva basin (departure point is on the island side of St John's Bridge).

The huge, horseshoe-shaped building overlooking the water from the Petrograd side is the **Voenno-istorichesky muzey Artillerii** (Artillery Museum; open Wed–Sun 11am–6pm; entrance charge). Built in 1849–60 and originally used as the arsenal, it is now one of the world's largest military museums, with items ranging from medieval swords and muskets to the latest ballistic missiles. It was here that captured German rockets were brought and studied to aid the Soviet's effort to build ballistic missiles. The star exhibit is the armoured car in which

Lenin rode in triumph from Finland Station on 3 April 1917 *(see page 178)*, making speeches from its gun turret. This is one of the few museums in the city that appeals to children, especially the tanks and missile launchers standing in the courtyard.

On a grassy knoll east of the Artillery Museum the **Decembrists' Monument** marks the place where the leading Decembrists were executed *(see page 27)*. It bears a poem by Alexander Pushkin that he wrote to a friend who served a term of hard labour in Siberia:

> *Dear friend, have faith:*
> *The wakeful skies presage a dawn of wonder,*
> *Russia shall from her age-old sleep arise,*
> *And despotism shall be crushed;*
> *Upon its ruins our names incise.*

Garden and zoo

Aleksandrovsky sad ❷ (Alexander Park) dates back to 1845 and is a favourite place for young people to hang out. Here you'll find the **Zoologichesky sad** (Zoo, open May–Oct daily 10am–7pm, Nov–April Tues–Sun 10am–4pm), which is popular with children, and not so popular with the animals; the lack of funds is sadly evident, though St Petersburgers are proud of their zoo, in particular its success in breeding polar bears, and the fact that no animals were eaten during the Seige of Leningrad *(see page 32)*. Also in the park is a Music Hall, built in 1911, which puts on shows and hosts circus troupes from abroad; a planetarium (open Tues–Sun 10.30am–6pm) and an amusement park.

Rising above the treetops east of Kamennoostrovsky prospekt is the dome of St Petersburg's **Sobornaya Mechet ❸** (Great Mosque). Built in 1910–14 and modelled on the 15th-century Gur Emir Mausoleum in Samarkand, the brilliant azure dome and minarets have recently been renovated to striking effect. The interior is stunning too; if you'd like to go in, be sure to respect Muslim tradition: women should have their heads covered and be dressed conservatively, and men should wear long trousers and a collared shirt; footwear should be taken off at the entrance. ❑

Maps:
Area 154
Plan 146

TIP

The beach between the Naryshkin and Trubetskoy bastions hosts an annual festival of sand sculptures in July (open daily 10am–10pm; small entrance charge).

BELOW: an ambitious entrant at the annual sand sculpture competition.

RESTAURANTS

Austeria, $$$
Peter and Paul Fortress, Ioanovsky Ravelin
Tel: 230 0369. Open: L & D.
Set in the fortress, Austeria is one of the few places with an 18th-century atmosphere and ancient Russian recipes rarely found elsewhere.

Troitsky Most, $
Malaya Posadksaya ulitsa, 4
Tel: 232 6693. Open: L & D.
Delicious vegetarian food at prices anyone can afford. Adherents of Hari Khrishna own it. Long lunch-hour lines.

● ● ● ● ● ● ● ● ● ● ● ● ● ● ● ● ● ●

Price includes dinner and a glass of wine, excluding tip. **$$$$** *$80 and up,* **$$$** *$35–80,* **$$** *$15–35, $ under $15.*

PETROGRAD SIDE

This is the area where Peter the Great's dream
of a window to the west began. It was also
here that Russia's greatest poet,
Pushkin, met his end in a duel

Looking at today's **Troitskaya ploshchad ❹** (Trinity Square) it is impossible to tell that it was here, under the protection of the Peter and Paul Fortress, that the capital's first houses were built in the early 18th century. Along the northern side of the square stood the first *Gostiny dvor* (merchants' market), while along its eastern side was the Senate Building. In the centre, there was a church with a spire that rivalled the masts of the ships passing the port, and the houses along the Embankment belonged to powerful officials of the day.

Most of that has now disappeared, and today the square is a park flanked on one side by dull Soviet-era housing and boxy office buildings, and with early 20th-century mansions (not all the money has moved away) on the other. In the square's centre stands a small stone plaque with a crown of thorns – a memorial to the millions who died during Stalin's reign of terror. Here on 30 October – the Day of Victims of the Repression – thousands gather to remember those who disappeared during Stalin's murderous regime.

Peter's cabin

In May 1703, just east of Trinity Square, local carpenters built Peter the Great a small cabin from which

he could supervise the construction of the Peter and Paul Fortress. The cabin, which took three days to build, still stands and is now the **Muzey domik l'etra I ❺** (Museum of the Cabin of Peter I; Petrovskaya naberezhnaya 6; open Wed–Sun 10am–5pm, Mon 10am–4pm, closed last Mon of the month; entrance charge).

The cabin measures 12 by 5.5 by 2.5 metres (39 x 18 x 8 ft) and is a very modest lodging for a tsar. In Peter's time the rooms – study, dining room and bedroom – had neither

Map on page 154

LEFT: two young sailors on the *Aurora* cruiser.
BELOW: a peaceful spot around the Kirov islands.

stoves nor fireplaces, nor even a stone foundation. This is undoubtedly the home of a leader more concerned with grand ambitions than creature comforts.

A look inside the cabin is highly recommended. It features a few original items owned by Peter, as well as many copies of originals, and retains its historic atmosphere. It provides one of the best impressions of life in the city during its first decade.

As soon as his palace in the Summer Garden *(see page 92)* was completed, Peter moved there, leaving the cabin empty and neglected. In 1844, the cabin was encased in a brick outer structure, thus preserving it for future generations. It remains the only wooden building from Peter's time.

Cruiser Aurora

Continue east to the **Kreyser Avrora ❻** (the cruiser *Aurora*; Petrogradskaya naberezhnaya; open 10.30am–4pm, closed Mon and Fri; free admission), anchored at the point where the Bolshaya (Greater) Nevka branches off the River Neva. The ship is famous for firing the signal for the storming of the Winter Palace, where the provisional government was in conference, at precisely 9.40pm on 25 October 1917 *(see page 30)*.

The cruiser's history began in 1903 with a baptism of fire in the Battle of Tsushima – an embarrassing and disastrous defeat during the Russo-Japanese war (1904–5). Its crew was the first in the Baltic Fleet to take the Bolsheviks' side during the 1917 revolution. When the ministers of the provisional government had been safely locked away in the Peter and Paul Fortress, the cruiser broadcast Lenin's address to the citizens of Russia, proclaiming the victory of the proletarian revolution. The *Aurora* then became a training ship.

The guns aboard the Aurora *cruiser fired the shot that signalled the beginning of the Bolshevik Revolution*

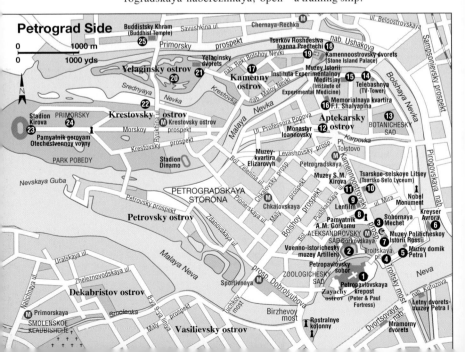

During World War II the battleship's guns were deployed near the front line. In 1956 the ship was repaired and turned over to the Central Naval Museum *(see page 167)*.

Museum of Political History

At the northern end of Troitskaya ploshchad, on the corner of Kuybysheva ulitsa and Kronverksky prospekt, is the **Osobnyak Kshesinskoy** (Kshesinskoy Mansion), an exquisite Art Nouveau building. In Soviet times this housed the Museum of the October Revolution, now the **Muzey Politicheskoy Istorii Rossii ❼** (Museum of Russian Political History; open Fri–Wed 10am–6pm; entrance charge). It provides a relatively balanced view of Russian history, and sometimes hosts chamber concerts in its main hall.

The mansion was originally owned by Matilda Kshesinskaya, a prima ballerina favoured by Tsar Nicholas II. It is thought the mansion was given to her as a love token. As with most grand houses in St Petersburg, the mansion has connections with Lenin and the Bolshevik Revolution. From March to July 1917 it housed the Central and Petrograd city committees of the Bolsheviks, and it was here that Lenin came after his arrival at Finland Station on the night of 4 April *(see page 178)*. In the following weeks he visited the mansion almost daily to write articles and proclamations, address the crowd from the balcony and preside over meetings and party conferences.

Kamennoostrovsky prospekt

Kamennoostrovsky prospekt is the central avenue of the Petrograd side running from Troitsky most (bridge) through Kamenny ostrov *(see page 159)*.

After the completion of Troitsky Bridge across the Neva in the early 20th century, the area underwent a building boom and local property values soared. The area combined the advantage of a central location and proximity to country dachas. Today, it is popular with the intelligentsia and the new rich, many of whom have bought large apartments in the district.

On the corner of Kamennoostrovsky and Kronverksky prospekts, near the apartment building with a semi-circular front, is the **Pamyatnik A.M. Gorkomu ❽** (monument to Gorky), which was unveiled in 1968. Gorky was a proletarian writer who gained fame in tsarist times for his play *At The Bottom*. He was a committed proponent of the Revolution until he became disillusioned with the violent tactics of the Bolsheviks during the civil war.

The Lenfilm Studios

In 1896, the first film was shown in Russia at the Akvarium Hall – part of which still stands in **Lenfilm Studios ❾**. House Nos. 10 and 12 are connected with the industry, having

Not far from Peter's cabin on the bank of the Neva there are two curious sculptures of Shi Chze. These mythological creatures once guarded the entrances to Buddhist temples and crypts in Mongolia, China and Southeast Asia. Russian explorers brought them to the northern capital in 1907.

BELOW:
Kamennoostrovsky prospekt in 1937.

belonged to the studio since 1924. This company developed technology for recording sound on to camera film in the late 1920s, opening the era of soundtrack films in the former USSR. The studio produced such renowned movies as *Chapayev*, *Deputy of the Baltic* and *Peter the Great*.

The studio's days are numbered, however, as President Putin has signed a decree to privatise it. Most people believe investors will purchase the studio, not to make films (these days Russian audiences prefer US films), but for the valuable 4 hectares (10 acres) of city-centre land on which it stands.

Poets and thinkers

Hiding behind the trees further north along Kamennoostrovksy prospekt is a building (No. 21) originally designed for the Aleksandrovsky Orphanage. In 1844, the house was turned over to the **Tsarskoe-selskoye Litsey** ❿ (Tsarskoe Selo Lyceum), whose graduates included Pushkin and his Decembrist friends, Ivan Puschin and Wilhelm Küchel-

beker, and other well-known figures of culture, science, diplomacy and politics.

The Lyceum building is the oldest on the prospekt and is now occupied by a high school. Across the street, Sergei Kirov – the former head of the Leningrad Soviet and rival to Stalin's leadership in the 1930s – lived in apartment 20 of Nos. 26–28 from 1926 until he was murdered at his Smolny office in 1934.

A Russian insurance company originally commissioned this building just before the outbreak of World War I, incorporating the most modern technology and comforts of the era. It seems the proletarian revolutionaries had quite sophisticated tastes and a talent for picking fine housing. Today, only the richest of capitalists in the city can afford to live in this building.

If you have time, step inside the **muzey S.M. Kirova** ⓫ (Kirov Memorial Museum; open Thur–Tues 11am–6pm; entrance charge) to get a sense of the kind of luxury that Sergei Kirov enjoyed. His flat included a dining room, a library (containing

Stained-glass windows at the Museum of Political History.

BELOW:
fishing in the Neva.

more than 20,000 volumes), a study and a guest-room. The museum displays Kirov's personal effects, his telephone hotline to the Kremlin, documents and important historical photographs.

Kirov, who often gained more support from Stalin's politburo than the dictator himself, was a capable organiser and a gifted orator. He remained a committed Bolshevik until his final breath and was convinced only the blood of traitors stained his hands. His speeches contained as many resolute demands to "make short work of the enemies" as Stalin's own. Kirov's assassination in 1934 gave Stalin and his henchmen an excuse to proceed with a campaign of mass terror against alleged enemies.

Bolshoy prospekt

Further up Kamennoostrovsky prospekt is **Ploshchad Lva Tolstovo** (Leo Tolstoy Square), dominated by the neo-Gothic "tower house", as it is known by its residents. **Bolshoy prospekt**, which comes to an end at this square, is one of the city's most fashionable shopping areas, full of expensive clothes shops, as well as clubs and cinemas.

Botanical Gardens

Pioneersky most, a bridge built in 1936, spans the quiet and winding Karpovka reki and leads to **Aptekarsky ostrov** ⑫ (Apothecary island). The name comes from the Apothecary's kitchen garden on the Karpovka, where medicinal herbs were grown by order of Peter the Great to supply the city's needs. In 1823 these kitchen gardens became the **Botanichesky sad** ⑬ (Botanical Gardens; Ulitsa Professora Popova 2, open Sat–Thur 11am–4pm; entrance charge), located just east of Kamennoostrovsky prospekt. The gardens contain over 12,000 different species, but they are in dire

financial straits and surviving each winter is a test of the dedication of the underpaid staff.

In 1931, the Komarov Botanical Institute was founded on the premises. Its pride and joy is the Korolev Night Cactus, whose flowers open on warm summer nights and close at dawn.

The **herbarium**, which is part of the institute's botanical museum (same opening hours as the garden), contains around 5 million samples of plants collected from around the world. The museum is one of the largest of its kind in Europe. On display are medieval treatises on medicine, and various exhibits explaining how to make medicinal potions. A special section is devoted to the extremely diverse flora of the former USSR and to environmental protection.

TV Tower

Just north of the Botanical Gardens, along the Bolshaya Nevka, is the **St Petersburgskaya Telebashnya** ⑭ (St Petersburg TV Tower). The tower was built between 1956 and 1962. In

Map on page 154

The composer Shostakovich lived at No. 14 Malaya Posadskaya and wrote several musical scores for films produced in Lenfilm Studios.

BELOW: I-spy on Petrograd side.

During the reign of Paul, at the end of the 18th century, the Church of the Birth of St John the Baptist was given to the mystical order of the Maltese Knights.

BELOW: getting it picture perfect.

1986 it was given a new antenna and as a result lost 6 metres (19 ft) from its former 316 metres (1,036 ft). This, however, didn't alter the tower's status as the tallest structure in the city. On a windy day, the antenna can sway up to 2 metres (6½ ft) in either direction. The tower has an observation platform, but it is no longer open to the public.

Pavlov's museum

Head west towards Kamennoostrovsky prospekt. Not far from the end of the avenue, at Kamennoostrovsky 69, is the **Muzey Istorii Instituta Experimentalnoy Meditsiny** (Museum of the History of the Institute of Experimental Medicine; open Mon–Fri 11am–5pm; entrance charge), where Ivan Pavlov worked for almost five decades (1890–1936).

He was awarded the Nobel Prize for medicine in 1904. After the Bolshevik revolution, his research was not banned, as might have been supposed. In fact, Lenin considered his theory of reflexes and higher nervous activity an important contribution to materialist philosophy. In 1921 he wrote that Pavlov's achievements had "enormous significance to the working class of the whole world". In a rare example of the Soviet government encouraging science that had no direct military application, Pavlov turned Leningrad into a major international centre of physiology.

The government turned a blind eye to Pavlov's religious activities as an elder of one of the city's Orthodox churches; it would ordinarily have branded him an ignorant and backward enemy of materialism (the official attitude to all believers).

In 1935, Pavlov had a statue of a dog installed in the institute's forecourt as a symbol of human gratitude to the animal that had for so long assisted in his experiments (*see margin, page 159*).

Shaliapin's apartment

Shaliapin, the "great reformer of Russian opera", lived just south of here beyond Chapygina ulitsa, at No. 2b Graftio ulitsa, between 1915 and 1922. Lovers of chamber music come to concerts performed in the hall of

his house. The building also houses the **Memorialnaya kvartira F.I. Shalyapina** (Shaliapin Memorial Apartment; open Wed–Sun noon–6pm, closed last Fri of the month; entrance charge).

Stone island

Heading north, Kamennoostrovsky prospekt leads over the wide Stone Bridge over the Malaya (Little) Nevka. Here lie the **Ostrova** (Islands), a picturesque group of three islands with parks and old mansions. Originally, Peter the Great's comrade-in-arms, Chancellor Gavriil Golovkin, owned Stone island, the island lying between the Bolshaya Nevka and the Malaya Nevka. Ownership then passed to Chancellor Aleksei Bestuzhev-Riumin, who settled thousands of Ukrainian serfs from his estates here. Today the new residential areas built on the site of their settlements preserve the original names – Old Village and New Village.

In the 18th century, canals were dug to guard against catastrophic floods on Stone island. At the same time the construction of luxurious mansions and a park was started and the island soon became the summer dacha area of the Petersburg nobility. By walking along **Kamenny ostrov's** (Stone Island's) lime-tree alley to the eastern side you will reach **Kamennoostrovsky dvorets** (Stone Island Palace; not open to the public) standing over the point where the Malaya and Bolshaya Nevkas meet. The palace was erected between 1776–81 for the son of Catherine the Great, the future Emperor Paul. Today it is a sanatorium for military officers.

Nearby, back on Kamennoostrovsky prospekt, the well-preserved **Tserkov Roshdestva Ioanna Predtechi** (Church of the Birth of John the Baptist) was built between 1776–8. The exterior is decidedly medieval, with a fanciful pointed tower and lancet windows giving the building a Gothic appearance.

Back at Kamenny most (bridge), head west along **Malonevskaya naberezhnaya** (Malaya Nevka Embankment). The domed building at No. 11 was built between 1831 and 1833 by Smaragd Shustov for the

Map on page 154

Pavlov's theory of conditioned reflexes was arrived at accidentally, when he was using his dog in research on saliva and digestion. The professor noted that whereas in the beginning the dog salivated at the sight of food, as the experiment went on it began to salivate every time Pavlov's assistant (who fed the pup) appeared in the room.

BELOW: dacha on Stone island.

The Death of Pushkin

The prelude to the death of Alexander Pushkin (1799–1837) – a duel with D'Anthes, the adopted son of St Petersburg's Dutch Ambassador Heeckeren – was nothing unusual in the life of high society in the beginning of the 19th century.

Pushkin's young wife, Natalia, was beautiful, courteous and clever. Her popularity equalled that of her husband's. D'Anthes, a dashing officer and sought-after guest in St Petersburg salons, fell in love with her.

His insistent attentions placed Pushkin in an uncomfortable position. As rumours were whispered from ear to ear, a hate letter spread among the poet's acquaintants, which pronounced Pushkin "the historiographer of the Order of Horn-Bearers" – a cuckold.

Yet Natalia remained faithful to her husband. She informed Pushkin about D'Anthes' attempts to seduce her, and about Heeckeren's dubious role in the affair. Pushkin concluded that the old ambassador wrote the letter to assist his adopted son.

Meanwhile, more cynical tongue-waggers suspected that Heeckeren was a homosexual and his motives for adopting D'Anthes were less than altruistic. Hence, Heeckeren wrote the letter not to aid D'Anthes's love life, but because the young man's chasing after women infuriated him and he hoped to cause trouble for his ward.

D'Anthes grew more and more insistent in his love for Natalia. He never missed an opportunity to express his admiration to her. Finally, Pushkin could bear it no longer and, following the tradition of the times, challenged D'Anthes to a duel. On this occasion the challenge was not accepted but trouble continued to simmer between the pair.

D'Anthes married Catherine – Natalia's sister, yet his attentions towards Pushkin's wife persisted. Driven to breaking point by jealousy and suspicion, Pushkin sent a letter full of insults to Heeckeren. He wanted a duel and this time the insults were too serious to be avoided. D'Anthes challenged Pushkin.

On 27 January 1837, the duel took place on the bank of Chernaya Rechka. D'Anthes survived, having been shot in the arm, but his aim proved more deadly, as the shot Pushkin sustained proved fatal. The poet was taken to his apartment where friends and the best doctors in town remained at his side. From time to time bulletins about his condition were hung on the front door: crowds of people came to ask about the poet's health, since news of the duel had spread throughout St Petersburg.

Vladimir Dal, the medic and philologist who was Pushkin's friend, remained with him to the last breath: "He seemed to awake, suddenly, with a start. Eyes opened wide, face bright, he said, 'Life is over.' I did not hear, and asked, 'What is over?' 'Life is over!' he said distinctly and positively. 'Can't breathe, something's choking' were his last words… a ghost of a breath – and an impassable, immeasurable chasm separated the living from the dead!"

The pines that grew around the site of the duel have given way to willows and poplars. One hundred years after the event, in what was, for Russia, the far more tragic year of 1937, a 19-metre (62-ft) high stone monument of pink granite with a bas-relief was installed at the site (a 7-minute walk from the Chernaya Rechka metro station) where Pushkin met his untimely end. ❑

LEFT: Alexander Pushkin, Russia's literary hero.

Map on page 154

wealthy Dolgoruky family. Cast-iron sphinxes, made by sculptor Soloviev in 1824, sit on the granite mooring of the Malaya Nevka.

Nearby on Naberezhnaya Reki Krestovki is a memorial to the beginnings of the city. Peter the Great planted an oak tree here in 1714. The oak had to be cut down a few years ago. The city authorities replaced it with a sapling, which, they claim, was grown from an acorn from the original tree.

The dacha where Pushkin spent the last summer of his life in 1836 has not survived. On its site is the neoclassical country retreat of Senator Polovtsev (1911–6, by Ivan Fomin); it houses his extensive art collection.

Yelagin island

The island across the Srednyaya (Middle) Nevka originally belonged to Pyotr Shafirov, a diplomat from Peter's retinue. It then came into the hands of the wealthy aristocrat Yelagin, who gave his name to the island. Yelagin's serfs irrigated the land and built a dam to guard against flood. Soon afterwards **Yelaginsky ostrov ㉒** (open daily during the summer 10am–10pm, winter until 8pm; free) was made the summer residence of the tsars.

Alexander I commissioned Carlo Rossi to build **Yelaginsky dvorets ㉑** (Yelagin Palace; open Wed–Sun 10am–6pm; entrance charge) between 1818 and 1822. Opposite the palace are the two-storey semicircular kitchens, which have a windowless facade to stop cooking odours from drifting into the palace and disturbing the inhabitants. The palace hosts temporary exhibitions and displays of the tsar's furnishings.

Krestovsky island

Cross the Srednaya Nevka to reach **Krestovsky ostrov ㉒**. Before the Bolshevik Revolution this island was not as popular among the nobility as Kamenny and Yelagin islands, probably on account of the greater danger of flooding (Krestovsky island juts out further into the Baltic) and because of the proximity of the workers' quarters on Petrograd and Petrovsky islands. One of the few

Pushkin's wife Natalia – widowed by a foolish duel.

BELOW: *The Duel,* by A. Naumov, depicts Pushkin's demise.

Map on page 154

One of the Egyptian-style statues designed in 1842 at the Bolgorukov Mansion on Stone island.

surviving 19th-century establishments on the island is the Yacht Club, founded in 1860.

On the western half of the island, on a man-made hill in the sea, is the **stadion Kirova** ㉓ (Kirov Stadium). It was built in 1950 and seats 100,000, which makes it the second-largest stadium in Russia. It is built on mud piped from the bottom of the Gulf of Finland and formed into a "volcano" with a very wide crater in which the stadium sits. Unfortunately the stadium is not well managed, and as it has no roof it can only be used during the few months of the year when the weather is warm. It is therefore due to be demolished and replaced by a state-of-the-art stadium designed by a Japanese architect.

Primorsky Park Pobedy

The avenue leading to the stadium bisects **Primorsky Park Pobedy** ㉔ (Seaside Park of Victory; open daily 10am–10pm) which covers 180 hectares (445 acres) of woodland. Though the park was laid out in the 1930s, it was not planted until

one Sunday in October 1945 when the citizens of St Petersburg answered an appeal to plant 45,000 trees in honour of the victims of the Blockade.

Buddhist temple

Cross back over Yelaginsky ostrov to reach the **Novaya Derevny** (New Village District) is the **Buddistsky Khram** ㉕ (Buddhist Temple; Primorsky prospekt 91, open daily noon–7pm; free). Of all the magnificent architectural landmarks in St Petersburg, this is certainly the most exotic and unexpected.

Built between 1909 and 1915 in the face of strong opposition from the Orthodox Church, the temple was the first Buddhist house of worship in Europe. Its construction required a special decree from Nicholas II – as a result of which Russian Buddhists came to honour Nicholas as a holy man. The tsar granted permission in order to accommodate the sensitivities of the growing Buryat and Kalmyk populations in the capital, nearly all of whom are Buddhists. ❑

RESTAURANTS

Restaurants

Aquarel, $$$
Dobrulyubov prospekt, 14a
Tel: 320 8600
Open: L & D daily
Located on a floating barge, Akvarel has great views of the Neva River. It offers fine food prepared by an American cook and is one of the most popular places in the city among the young, fashionable crowd. Live music. Parties and receptions are also held here.

Demyanova Ukha, $$
Kronversky prospekt, 53
Tel: 232 8090
Open: L & D daily
Demyanova Ukha has long been renowned as one of the best places in the city for fish dishes and fish soups. It's more of a place for locals than tourists, and the environment is more relaxing than some of the new trendy upscale restaurants.

Golden Dragon By the Zoo, $$
Kronverksky prospekt, 61
Tel: 232 2643
Open: L & D daily
Golden Dragon was one of the first Chinese restaurants in the city, and is still one of the best even though there are now around 70 in the city. Its tranquil interior makes for a nice get-away from the city's hustle and bustle.

Moskva, $$$
Petrogradskaya naberezhnaya, 18a
(6th floor, City Centre office building)
Tel: 332 0200
Open: L & D daily
www.moskva.su
This is a recent brainchild of Edward Moradyan, the city's leading restaurant developer. It offers a great view, and a wide variety of food (Italian, Indian and Armenian) at prices that are very reasonable considering the quality of the food and the fine interior.

Russkaya Rybalka, $$$$
Primorsky Park Pobeda, Yuzhnaya Doroga, 11
Tel: 323 9813
Open: L & D daily
Russkaya Rybalka not only offers you fine fish, but lets you catch your dinner in the pool. Try the excellent sturgeon or trout. Located on Krestovsky island, it is accessible by car, a 15-minute drive from the centre. President Putin brings guests here.

Salkhino, $$$
Kronverksky prospekt, 25
Tel: 232 7891
Open: L & D daily
Besides offering some of the best Georgian dishes in town, Salkhino also serves as the city's only gallery of Georgian art. The *khachpori* — goat's cheese pie — is highly recommended, as are the stewed meat in tomato sauce and the selection of Georgian soups.

Troitsky Most, $
Malaya Posadksaya ulitsa, 4
Tel: 232 6693
Open: L & D daily
Troitsky Most is one of the best bargains in town, an eatery offering delicious vegetarian food at a price most can afford. The decor is simple with Oriental overtones, since the restaurant is owned by adherents of Hari Khrishna. Expect long queues at lunchtime. No reservations.

Fish & Olives, $$
Petrogradskaya naberezhnaya, 18a
(1st floor, City Centre office building)
Tel: 718 4258
Open: L & D daily
This popular lunch place offers fine Russian and international cuisine at reasonable prices. Offers a lunchtime special during the week for about US$10.

RIGHT: classic Chinese at the Golden Dragon.

VASILIEVSKY ISLAND

Vasilievsky island has played an ever-changing but always vital role in the city, evolving from a busy port and commercial centre into the home of the city's intellectual elite. It is now the domain of students from the University of St Petersburg

Across the river from the Hermitage, **Vasilievsky ostrov** is the largest island in the Neva delta. Its windswept western edge faces the Gulf of Finland while the eastern tip, known as the Strelka, noses into the Neva, splitting it into two branches: the Malaya Neva and the Bolshaya Neva.

Peter the Great had ambitions to turn the island into the administrative centre of his new city. Using Venice as a model, the plan was to carve out a system of canals criss-crossing each other on a grid. But the plans were abandoned, because the island proved too prone to flooding and too isolated from the mainland (the first bridge was not built until the 1850s). The canals were never dug but the original layout remains in the numbered "liniyas" which run north to south, intersecting the three grand avenues – Bolshoy, Sredny and Maly prospekts – which cross the island from east to west.

East-West divide

Despite the island's setbacks after Peter's death, the eastern side of the island became an important economic and educational centre during the 18th century. Prices on the less-fashionable western side were much cheaper and the area attracted German immigrants in the 19th century.

Traces of their past can still be seen in the Lutheran church on Bolshoy prospekt, and at the German Lutheran cemetery on the Smolenka reki across from the Russian Orthodox cemetery.

Nowadays property on the western side is in great demand among wealthy Russians, who are buying apartments with fantastic views onto the Gulf of Finland. The government is launching plans to develop this area and the adjacent seaport, and make it the major point of entry by sea for tourists to St Petersburg.

Map on page 166

LEFT: detail from one of the Rostral Columns.
BELOW: youth comes out to celebrate the city's third century.

The Strelka

The eastern spit of Vasilievsky island, known as the **Strelka**, is the island's focal point. The city's first port was set up here in 1733. It developed into a thriving commercial centre but by the mid-19th century, the increase in traffic and in the size of vessels necessitated the transferral of the port to the open seas of the Gulf of Finland.

But while the port thrived, this area was the most lively (and troublesome) place in town. Merchants and sailors from around the world brought exotic goods – coffee and sugar from South America, tobacco from the United States, and luxury goods from Western Europe – the demand for which quickly grew. As trade increased and generated wealth, makeshift trading posts were replaced by elegant bonded warehouses and customs houses, which now house museums and institutes of learning. Grandest of all these

The days of mud-coated trams disappeared with the Soviets. Now St Petersburg's public transport network is covered in advertising.

neoclassical buildings was the Old Stock Exchange, built in 1810, which is now home to the naval museum (*see opposite*).

The Exchange's construction gave the Spit its present-day appearance. The shores were dressed in granite; stairways led down to the river, where huge stone spheres were installed on pedestals close to the water. The granite-lined paths descending to the Neva were not so much designed for promenading as for loading and unloading ships. Today the bustling area around **Birzhevaya ploshchad ❶** (Stock Exchange Square) is a traditional spot for newlyweds to come and toast their marriage. The views from here across the banks of the Neva are among the finest in the city.

The Rostral Columns

The 32-metre (105-ft) high **Rostralnye kolonny ❷** (Rostral Columns), which stand on the edge of the Spit

were built between 1805–10. Their name is derived from the word "rostrum", which is Latin for ship's prow. The Romans used to decorate their triumphal columns with war trophies, including the sawn-off prows of Carthaginian ships. Here, in similar tradition, mock prows decorate the columns in commemoration of various Russian naval victories. The sculptures at the foot of each column represent the rivers of Russia – all major transport arteries. From left to right (viewed from the Stock Exchange), they are the Dnieper, the Volga, the Volkhov and the Neva.

In the dark winter months, the triumphal columns doubled as lighthouses. After sunset, giant oil lamps on top of each column were lit to guide ships into port. These were later replaced by gas lights. The 7-metre (23-ft) high flaming beacons are still lit on public holidays.

The Naval Museum

In 1940 the disused Stock Exchange was given over to the **Voenno-Morskoy muzey ❸** (Naval Museum; open Wed–Sun 11am–6pm;

closed last Thur of the month; entrance charge), which had been housed in the Admiralty since 1805.

The building is modelled on the Greek temple of Paestum, in southern Italy. It is surrounded by a peristyle with 44 Doric columns and the main interior feature is the exchange hall floor, which measures an impressive 900 sq. metres (9,700 sq. ft). The central statue on the main facade is of Neptune gliding through the waves in his chariot, carried by two rivers – the Neva and the Volkhov. The other statues depict the goddess of navigation and Mercury, the god of trade.

The foundation for the Naval Museum's collection was provided by Peter the Great who started collecting ship models in 1709. Among the 650,000 exhibits are Peter the Great's first boat, the personal effects of Crimean War hero Admiral Pavel Nakhimov, weapons, flags and shipyard blueprints. One of the museums most prized exhibits is an oak boat salavaged from the bottom of the Yuzhny Bug River, which experts date to the first millennium BC.

Map on page 166

The stairs leading to the Stock Exchange building are so wide that they were used as a stage for 2,000 actors in the Soviet era, when mass performances were fashionable.

BELOW: the Naval Museum, modelled on the Greek temple of Paestum.

Zoological Museum

Also part of the Strelka ensemble of buildings are the former bonded warehouses on either side of the old Stock Exchange. They were built between 1826 and 1832 by the architect Giovanni Lucchini, but they were all converted into academic institutions in the early 20th century. The northern warehouse building is dedicated to the study of soil science, while the southern warehouse building has housed the **Zoologichesky muzey** ❹ (Zoological Museum; open Sat–Thur 11am–5pm; entrance charge) since 1900.

This museum has one of the world's largest natural-history collections, which includes more than 10 million insect specimens, 185,000 fish specimens and 88,000 mammals. The star of its famous collection of mammoth remains is the carcass of a mammoth discovered in 1901 preserved in the Siberian permafrost, and thought to be 44,000 years old.

The Literary Museum

The turreted building just behind the northern warehouse that backs onto naberezhnaya Makarova – the northern Embankment – belongs to the Russian Literature Institute. Also known as the **Pushkinsky dom** (Pushkin House), it is one of the foremost centres of Russian literature in the country. Constructed in 1829–82, the old Customs House tower was once used for observation and making signals to ships arriving in port. It was converted into an academic institution in 1905.

Over the years, the institute has gathered manuscripts, archives and first editions of the best-known works of Russian literature, plus collections of pre-revolutionary newspapers. A small proportion of these are exhibited in the **Literatorny muzey** (Literary Museum; viewing by special arrangement only; tel: 328 0502). The collection includes the personal libraries of several writers including Pushkin – the museum's first acquisition in 1905. The museum also owns the manuscript of the Archpriest Avvakum (17th century), spokesman for the so-called Old Believers of Russian Orthodoxy. He opposed reforms which he

A Siberian mammoth, part of the prized mammoth collection at the Zoological Museum.

BELOW: posing for wedding pictures on the frozen Neva.

strongly believed would threaten the purity of the old faith, for which he was tortured and eventually killed. His manuscript is today cherished as a holy relic by the Old Believers. In more recent years the museum has been gathering a fascinating collection of letters from the Gulag camps.

The Kunstkammer

Leaving the Zoological Museum and the Dvortsovy most (bridge), behind you, head west along **Universitetskaya naberezhnaya**. The first building on your right is the elegant sea-green **Kunstkamera** ❺ (the Kunstkammer Museum; open Tues–Sun 11am–6pm, closed last Wed of the month; entrance charge) – from the German *kunst* meaning art and *kammer* meaning room. The Kunstkammer was built between 1718 and 1734, in a restrained baroque style, as Russia's first museum of natural science, and enjoyed the patronage of Peter the Great. It also contained Russia's first public library and first observatory.

To fill the museum, Peter issued a decree ordering all "unusual and curious creations of nature" to be brought to the capital. Before long the tsar had assembled quite a collection of curiosities. Enticed by the offer of free vodka, visitors came to admire the astronomical instruments, maps, rare books, minerals and the tsar's rather freakish collection of anatomical specimens.

Today the Kunstkammer houses two separate establishments: the **Muzey Antropologii i Etnografii** (Museum of Anthropology and Ethnography) and the **Muzey M.V. Lomonosov** (Lomonosov Museum). The latter contains nearly 4,000 items dedicated to the life and times of Russian scientist Mikhail Lomonosov, who worked in the building between 1741 and 1765. Here this extraordinary polymath, born of peasant stock, conducted experiments in chemistry and physics, observed the stars, wrote verse, codified the rules of Russian grammar and studied minerals. Lomonosov was also the first Russian-born member of the Academy of Sciences, which began its life in this building. Prior to his arrival,

A less conventional wedding photo backdrop.

Wedding Spit

Throughout Russia, go to any national monument and you'll see groups of fresh-faced newlyweds and their wedding party posing for pictures. Along with the Field of Mars and the Winter Palace, the most popular backdrop for wedding photos in St Petersburg is by the Rostral Columns on the Strelka. If you go down to the water's edge, you'll not fail to notice the empty champagne bottles scattered about. Local custom dictates that after the photo shoot, the bride and groom make for the Strelka with their wedding guests in tow, where they crack open a bottle of bubbly and toast to their future happiness.

The University of St Petersburg is one of the largest educational centres in the country, with over 20,000 students.

BELOW: sunset on the facades of Vasilievsky Island's houses.

the academy was the exclusive domain of foreign scientists in service to the tsar. The hall where the academicians used to congregate has survived in its original form.

Most people visiting the **Museum of Anthropology** head straight for the eastern gallery which contains the remnants of Peter's grisly collection of pickled anatomical specimens prepared by the Dutch pathologist, Frederik Ruysch. They include Siamese twins, a two-faced man, a two-headed calf, teeth extracted by the tsar himself (he was apparently a keen amateur dentist) and enough assorted body parts to inspire a horror film. Certain objects from the collection (including the unusually long penis of one of the tsar's guards), created so much morbid interest that they were removed from display and transferred to the museum's storerooms.

The Kunstkammer's main collection deserves far more attention than it gets. It's a fascinating assortment of costumes, household utensils, coins, weapons, tools, artefacts and other everyday objects that conjure

the lost worlds of peoples from around the globe: from the Volga, Siberia and the Far East, to Africa, the Americas and Oceania.

Academy of Sciences

By the end of the 18th century, the needs of the Academy of Sciences had outgrown the close confines of the Kunstkammer. So a "new" academy, was built next door. Designed by Quarenghi and built in 1788, during the reign of Catherine the Great, the neoclassical **Akademiya nauk** ❻ is very different in style to its baroque neighbour. The central staircase is decorated with a mosaic of the *Battle of Poltava* by Lomonosov. In 1934 the administrative offices of the academy moved to Moscow, but the scientists got to keep the building, which now belongs to the St Petersburg branch of the academy.

The Twelve Colleges

Just past the Academy of Sciences, running the length of Mendeleyevskaya liniya, is the 440-metre (1,440-ft) facade of the **Dvenadtsat kollegy** ❼ (Twelve Colleges; closed

to the public). Italian architect Domenico Trezzini began work on this baroque building in 1722, but it was finally completed by his son, Giuseppe, in 1742. Behind the uniform facade is a complex of 12 interconnected buildings, designed to house each of the 12 ministries – known as *collegii* – of the tsar's government. By the early 19th century, the Twelve Colleges had outgrown the building, and moved their offices across the river. In 1819 the premises were taken over by the University of St Petersburg (St Petersburgsky Gosudarstvenny Universitet). It turned out many Russian intellectuals and established a reputation as a hotbed of free-thinkers. Among its most famous revolutionary students were Alexander Ulianov (sentenced to death for plotting a terrorist attack on Alexander III) and his brother Vladimir Ulianov, better known by his party pseudonym, Lenin.

Lenin aside, the university's most famous graduate was Dmitry Mendeleev (1834–1907), creator of the periodic table of chemical elements. Mendeleev lived and worked at the museum for 24 years and his old lodgings now house the **Muzey Arkhiv D. I. Mendeleyeva** (Mendeleev Apartment Museum; Mendeleyevskaya liniya 2; open Mon–Fri 11am–4pm; entrance charge), which displays the scientist's personal effects and the laboratory apparatus he designed.

The large grey building at the far end of Mendeleyevskaya liniya is the **Biblioteka akademii nauk** (Academy of Sciences Library), an archive of some 9 million volumes. When Peter the Great founded the library, he purchased copies of all books published in Russia. Fortunately, none of these rare editions was damaged in the fire that ravaged the building in 1988. The library owns *The Apostol*, Russia's first printed book, published in 1564, books from Peter the Great's personal library and the student textbooks of the great polymath and member of the Academy of Sciences, Lomonosov.

Back at the Embankment end of Mendeleyevskaya liniya, overlooking the Neva, stands a bronze statue of Lomonosov – "Russia's Leonardo".

Map on page 166

TIP

From 1am onwards from Apr–Nov, most of St Petersburg's bridges are raised to allow boat traffic through. It's important to bear this in mind if you're planning to stay out late. Otherwise, you may get stranded if you're on the other side of the river from your hotel.

BELOW: the Kunstkammer viewed from Admiralty Embankment.

The Menshikov Palace

The next grand building on the University Embankment is the baroque **Menshikovsky dvorets** ❽ (Menshikov Palace; open Tues–Sun 10.30am–4.30pm; entrance charge), which is part of the Hermitage Museum. The ornate ochre palace was the residence of Peter the Great's closest friend and advisor, and St Petersburg's first governor, Alexander Menshikov (1673–1729). Menshikov had the lavish palace built for himself between 1710 and 1714. It was one of the first stone buildings in St Petersburg and became the centre of the tsar's court, where foreign ambassadors and Russian dignitaries were entertained in style.

When Peter died in 1725, the notoriously extravagant Menshikov managed to hold on to his position as court favourite with Catherine I. But after her death, he fell out of favour and was exiled to Siberia where he died in 1729. His palace was turned over to a military school – the First Cadet Corps. During the Soviet era, the building was given to the Hermitage Museum to house a permanent exhibition on Russian life and culture in the 18th century.

Much of the palace has now been restored to its original form. Roman and Greek statues, which Menshikov imported from Europe, stand in the niches of the main entranceway, and the stairway banister bears the intertwined monograms of Menshikov and Peter. On the first floor, a number of the palace rooms are decorated floor-to-ceiling with exquisite Dutch tiles, which have been meticulously restored. The neoclassical Grand Hall, decorated with gold and stucco, was used for state ceremonies, balls and banquets.

While restorers were working on the Walnut Study (Menshikov's favourite room) they uncovered a full-sized portrait of Peter in military uniform. The mirrors may seem mundane to today's visitors, but owning a mirror in 18th-century Russia was something quite subversive as it went against the strict codes of behaviour laid down by the Russian Orthodox Church, which considered mirrors to be tools of the devil, as they encouraged vanity.

BELOW: the Academy of Arts building.

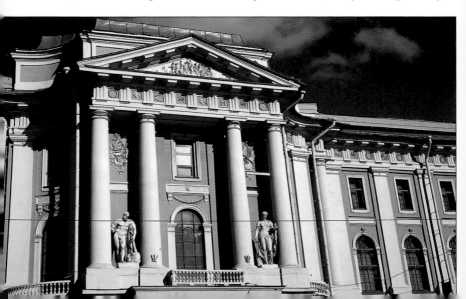

The palace from which Menshikov was chased out after Peter's death soon became too small for the cadets, so another long baroque building was added further down the Embankment in 1758–60. In 1917, the First Russian Congress of Soviets met here.

Beyond the Menshikov Palace, at the centre of a small park stands the **Rumanyantsev obelisk**, which commemorates the victory over the Turks in the Russo-Turkish war of 1768–74. Field Marshal Rumanyantsev, who led the campaign, was a graduate of the nearby military academy.

The Academy of Fine Arts

Last but not least of the grand institutions on University Embankment is the **Akademiya khudozhestv ❾** (Academy of Fine Arts, museum only open Wed–Sun 11am–6pm; tel: 323 6496). Built by Kokorinov and Vallin de la Mothe between 1764–88, the building is considered to be one of the finest examples of 18th-century Russian architecture, and shows the transition from the baroque style to the neoclassical.

"The Academy of the Three Most Noble Arts," – painting, sculpture and architecture – was founded in 1757 and attended by many important painters. Among its most illustrious graduates were Pyotr Klodt (sculptor of the horses on Anchikov Bridge), the painters Dmitry Levitsky (famous for his portraits of aristocrats in the 18th and the early 19th centuries), Karl Bryullov, whose masterpiece *The Last Day of Pompeii*, can be seen in the Russian museum *(see pages 137–143)*, and realist painter Ilya Repin who was also professor of painting here *(see page 140)*. The Ukrainian poet and artist Taras Shevchenko (1814–61) spent the last years of his life at the Academy and a small room, open to the public, is dedicated to his work.

During Stalin's reign the Academy headquarters were moved to Moscow, and St Petersburg became but a branch of the institution, which was renamed the Repin Academy of Arts, which still occupies most of the building.

The museum on the upper floors, run by the Russian Academy of Arts

Map on page 166

In 1707, Peter the Great presented the whole of Vasilievsky Island to Menshikov (above) as a gift. Seven years later, when the tsar set out to create his administrative centre on the island, he took it back.

BELOW: the city's coat of arms.

Don't be afraid to haggle in the city's markets. Prices in tourist areas are often greatly inflated, but will become more reasonable if you make the trader an offer.

BELOW: sun sets over the island.

displays the works of former students collected over the years, including paintings, plaster casts and sketches and models of some of the city's historic buildings. It also has a collection of reproductions of the world's great masterpieces, copied directly from the originals by various artists who were masters in their own right. The work of budding new Russian artists is displayed every September at the Academy's degree show.

The Sphinxes

Outside the academy a wide set of granite steps leads down to one of three mooring posts along the Bolshaya Neva. They are guarded on either side by a pair of imperious **Egyptian sphinxes** ⑩, made of pink granite from the quarries of Aswan. The sphinxes date back to the 14th century BC and study of the hieroglyphics they are inscribed with has led scholars to conclude that their faces are the likeness of Pharaoh Amenhotep III (1417–1379 BC). One inscription reads: "Son of Ra, King of Thebes, Builder of Monuments, Who Rises to the Sky Like Four Pillars Which Hold the Vault of the Heavens."

The sphinxes were discovered in 1820 among the ruins of the ancient Egyptian kingdom of Thebes. They were bought by the Russians in 1831, but it took a year for the pair of 23-ton sculptures to be transported to St Petersburg.

The ornamental girandoles and griffons were added in 1834. What you see are copies of the originals which were stolen.

Bolshoy prospekt

Before continuing along the Embankment, a small detour one block north of the Academy will bring you on to Bolshoy prospekt, a wide avenue that cuts through the middle of the island, which was originally designed to link Menshikov Palace with the Gulf of Finland. The avenue is lined with a mixed bag of elegant and not-so-elegant buildings, but in contrast to the monumental Neva Embankment, there's a real neighbourhood feel about the place.

The prospekt's most distinguished landmark is **Andreyevsky Sobor** ⓫ (Cathedral of St Andrew), the island's main Orthodox church. Part of the original church, built in the 1760s, is incorporated into the main building, which also has a very fine baroque iconostasis.

Across from the church, between liniyas 5 and 6, is the arcaded **Andreyevsky rynok** (St Andrew's Market), dating from the end of the 18th century. It is still the site of a good market, selling produce, clothes and household goods.

Around the corner on liniya 7, the **old pharmacy** in the turreted building at No. 16 is worth a look.

At the western end of Bolshoy prospekt, **Dom Savicheva** (No. 6 liniya 13) reveals the tragic story of a young girl's experience of the Blockade. It was the home of 11-year-old Tanya Savicheva, who kept a diary from 1942–3. It contains the moving account of how she witnessed her entire family die of starvation. Although Tanya survived the Blockade, she died shortly after being evacuated from the city in 1942.

At the opposite end of the prospekt is the **Church of St Catherine**. The former Lutheran church was built for the German community in 1768–71. It now houses a major recording studio.

This is not to be confused with the Orthodox St Catherine's Church **Tserkov Svyatoi Yekaterini**, at the end of Sredny prospekt (one block further north, overlooking the Malaya Neva Embankment and Petrograd side), whose soaring dome is visible from afar. It was built in 1811–23, and was reputed to have one of the most impressive interiors in the city, but it was subsequently destroyed by the communists, who turned the church into a warehouse.

Lt Schmidt Embankment

The **Lieutentant Schmidt bridge** ⓬ marks the beginning of the Embankment of the same name. It was built between 1842 and 1850 by an American engineering company invited from Philadelphia to St Petersburg by Nicholas I (it was originally named the Nicholas Bridge), and was the first permanent bridge to

Map on page 166

The twice-weekly St Petersburg Times is the city's only English-language newspaper. Covering politics, business and culture, it is one of the few independent voices – more than half of its readers are Russian.

LEFT: black-market currency dealer touting for business on the Strelka.
BELOW: Sphinx Quay.

TIP

If you're looking to save money and feel confident negotiating in Russian or sign language, a *chastnik*, or private car, is a much better deal than a normal taxi. Most Russians travel this way, and if you're travelling during the day and in the centre, it is safe and sometimes even interesting, but never get in a car if the driver has a friend or two with him.

BELOW: the Lutheran church of St Catherine's on Bolshoy prospekt.

join Vasilievsky island to the mainland. Both the bridge and Embankment are named in honour of a graduate of St Petersburg Naval College, who became a national hero. As a naval officer on board the battleship *Ochakov*, Lieutenant Schmidt led a mutiny and took control of the tsar's Black Sea Fleet, in the Revolution of 1905–7.

At No. 1 Lt Schmidt Embankment stands the **Dom Akademikov** (Academicians House), built in 1750 as a hall of residence for scholars from the Academy of Sciences. The 26 memorial plaques on the wall commemorate some of the most accomplished among them.

One of the residents at the Academician's House was the Russian physiologist and Nobel Laureate, Ivan Pavlov (1890–1936), best known for his behaviourist theories based on experiments with dogs. Around the corner on the 7th liniya is the entrance to the **Kvartira Pavlova muzey** (Pavlov Memorial Museum, open Mon–Wed and Fri 10am–5pm; must call first, tel: 323 7234) in his former apartment, which contains

books, personal possessions and photographs of Pavlov's experiments *(see also page 158)*.

Naval College

Further down the quay (at the 8th liniya) stands the imposing Naval Cadet Corps building, currently occupied by the **Vysha Voenno-morskaya shkola imeni Petra Velikogo** (The Peter the Great Higher Naval College) – Russia's oldest naval school. The Academy-trained Admiral Fyodor Ushakov, father of the Russian school of navy tactics; Admiral Pavel Nakhimov, hero of Sebastopol in the Crimean war (1854–5); and Admiral Mikhail Lazarev, who accompanied Faddei Bellingshausen on his 1820 Antarctic expedition.

In May 1917, Lenin delivered a public lecture here to the members of the Petrograd Bolshevik Organisation on "War and Revolution"; a plaque recalls the historic event.

On the Embankment outside the naval college stands a statue of Admiral Ivan Krusenstern (1770–1846), another of the Academy's

illustrious graduates. Krusenstern was the commander of the first fleet of Russian ships to circumnavigate the globe in 1803–6. His observations made an outstanding contribution to the advancement of science and navigation.

The Mining Institute

At the far end of the Schmidt Embankment, between liniyas 21 and 23, is the **Gorny institut** ⓭ (Mining Institute), built by Andrei Voronikhin in 1801–11 and fronted by an impressive Doric colonnade. The portico is flanked by two sculpture groups, both by Demut-Malinovsky, which represent man's bond with the earth. The left-hand statues are of the Attack of Proserpina, and on the right Hercules fights with Antaeus.

The institute itself pre-dates the building. It was founded in 1773 by Peter the Great for the training of miners, engineers and the promotion of exploratory missions, particularly to the mineral-rich Urals.

The Institute's **Gorny muzey** (Mining Museum; open Mon–Fri 8.30am–5.15pm; call ahead, tel: 328

8429) is as old as the institute, and has one of the richest collections of minerals, gemstones and fossils in the world, sourced from 60 different countries. Its most precious items include a huge block of Ukrainian malachite weighing 1,054 kg (2,323 lb), a Kazakhstani nugget of copper weighing 842 kg (1,855 lb), a Ukrainian quartz crystal weighing 800 kg (1,800 lb) and a 450-kg (990-lb) meteorite. Look out for the palm tree lovingly fashioned from a strip of iron by blacksmith Alexander Mertsalov.

Moored alongside the institute is the **Icebreaker *Krasin*** (open Tues–Sun 10am–5pm; entrance charge), a floating museum, and the last site of interest on this Embankment. Launched in England in 1917, the ship was part of the international mission to rescue Umberto Nobile's 1928 polar expedition. During World War II, the *Krasin* joined the historic convoy to Murmansk to ensure the safe delivery of supplies to the USSR. The ship's well-restored interior contains displays of navigational instruments and other nautical paraphernalia. ❑

TIP

Cruiseships from London, Helsinki, Copenhagen and even New York now sail to the sea terminal on the western side of Vasilievsky island, at the end of Bolshoy prospekt.

RESTAURANTS

Academia, $$$
Birzhovoy proezd, 2
Tel: 327 8949
Open: L & D daily
Popular with the city's wealthy young crowd, Academia offers fine food, music and dancing. The brick-oven baked pizza is good.

Bellini, $$$$
Universitetskaya naberezhnaya, 13
Tel: 331 1001
Open: B, L & D daily
A favourite haunt among Russia's political and business elite, including

President Putin. The menu offers exquisite European dishes made by a French chef. Stunning views of the Neva and St Isaac's Cathedral.

Kalinka, $$
Syezdovskaya liniya, 9
Tel: 323 3718
Open: D daily
A quaint restaurant with traditional Russian food and folkloric floor shows.

New Island, $$$
moored on the corner of Universitetskaya naberezhnaya and Primerya liniya
Tel: 320 2120

Open: L & D daily
This floating restaurant sails up and down the Neva in summer, but moors here in the colder months when it is closed. The flashing lights and tacky decor may not be to everyone's taste, but the food is good and the views memorable.

Old Customs House, $$$$
Tamozheny pereulok, 1
Tel: 327 8980
Open: L & D daily
The Old Customs House is English-managed and offers fine European and Russian cuisine in a

historic interior. Good caviar and lobster. Live music some weekends.

Restoran, $$$
Tamozheny pereulok, 2
Tel: 327 8979
Open: B, L & D daily
Opposite the Kunstkammer. The sleek and chic interior, combining modern and historic elements, is by leading Russian designer, Andrei Dmitriev. Offers fine Russian cuisine.

● ● ● ● ● ● ● ● ● ● ●
Price for dinner and a glass of wine, excluding tip. **$$$$** *$80 and up,* **$$$** *$35–80,* **$$** *$15–35,* **$** *under $15.*

VYBORG SIDE

This is St Petersburg's industrial area, of great appeal to those interested in Lenin and the history of the revolution, and the seamier side of the city. On the outskirts is a poignant memorial to the hundreds of thousands who died in the siege of Leningrad.

Map on page 180

BELOW: Piskarevsky Cemetery for victims of the Blockade.

The Vyborg side (Vyborgskaya storona) is divided from the Petrograd side by the Bolshaya Nevka channel. It is mostly industrial sprawl, with limited appeal compared to the rest of St Petersburg, but its contribution to the city's history is undeniable. In the second half of the 19th century, industrialists began building huge factories here, and as the slums housing the workers spread northwards, the district became a hotbed of militancy. Locals erupted into revolutionary action in 1905 and 1917, and it was here, appropriately enough, at Finland Station, that Lenin returned from exile.

Today, the factories mostly stand idle and crumbling, but slowly, investors are buying up Vyborg property and turning the buildings into upscale office space.

In the north of the Vyborg side is the Piskarevsky Memorial Cemetery, a stark reminder of the number of people who died during the seige of Leningrad *(see page 32)*.

Revolutionary soil

You can start your tour of the Vyborg side at **Ploshchad Lenina ❶** or Lenin Square, which stands in front of **Finlyandsky vokzal** (Finland Station). This is where Lenin arrived from exile abroad to lead the Bolshevik Revolution.

In the 1950s the Soviet Government replaced the old station with a concrete shed, which hardly does justice to the historic events which took place here.

On 3 April 1917, the train carrying Lenin and other exiles pulled into Finland Station. As he stepped from the train, Lenin was greeted by a host of cheering Bolsheviks; and when he emerged into the square, thousands of people were there to see him.

Lenin climbed onto the now famous armoured car bearing the inscription "Enemy of Capital" (which is in the Artillery Museum – *see page 150–1*), and used it as a podium from which to address the crowds; he gave a short and fiery speech, congratulating the workers for having accomplished the fall of the monarchy *(see page 30)* which, he said, opened the way for a genuine socialist revolution.

If you want to see the station's landmarks, you'll need a platform ticket, as turnstiles have been introduced beyond the entrance hall. The exit by which Lenin left is preserved alongside platform 1, as is the adjacent waiting room. Locomotive No. 293 *(see below)* stands in a special glass pavilion near platform 10. The sculpture of the hammer and wrench beside platform 6/7 commemorates the "Road of Life" convoys that arrived here during the Blockade to provide food and fuel for the starving population.

The monument of Lenin that stands in the square was unveiled on 7 November 1926 and became the prototype for thousands of similar statues and busts throughout the USSR and in many other countries. Ironically, Lenin hated the idea of statues in his honour, saying they were only good for bird droppings.

Bolshoy Sampsonievsky

Head west along the Embankment side of Lenin Square until you reach **Bolshoy Sampsonievsky prospekt ❷**, which leads into Vyborg's industrial area; the sugar factory (No. 24) and the Russky Diezel (Russian Diesel) Factory were built by the Swedish immigrant Emmanuel Nobel in 1824, originally to produce naval mines.

Members of the Nobel family were the most famous residents of the Vyborg side. Towards the end of the 19th century, they built up a vast industrial empire in Russia that was mostly based on oil drilling and refining. Though they were ruthless with their competitors, the Nobel family took care of its workers, voluntarily providing many social benefits that would only be legislated for much later on

Chess is a very popular pastime among Russians. You'll see people of all ages playing it throughout the city.

BELOW: Lenin's statue outside Finland Station.

Locomotive No. 293

One of the most celebrated train engines in the world rests at Finland Station. Near the boarding platform, under a glass cover – just like Lenin's body at the mausoleum in Moscow – is another relic of the revolution: Locomotive No. 293.

Hugo Jalava, a Finnish communist, brought Lenin (disguised as a coal hand) back into Russia on board this engine in October 1917. When Lenin fled the country in August 1917, he'd used the same locomotive.

Finland presented the engine to Russia in 1957. Though far from socialists, Finns retain a fondness for Lenin; he gave their country its independence from Russia in 1918.

in the 20th century. After making his fortune in Russia, Alfred Nobel, son of Emmanuel Nobel, returned to his native Sweden, and went on to greater fame. He invented dynamite and then assuaged his guilt by establishing the Nobel Peace Prize.

Further along Bolshoy Sampsonievsky prospekt is the small but magnificent **Sampsonievsky sobor ❸** (Samson's Cathedral; open Thur–Tues 11am–5pm in winter, 11am–8pm in summer; entrance charge).

Looking incongruous among the chimneys and industrial buildings, this fine sea-green church is one of the oldest structures in the city, built on the orders of Peter the Great in 1709 to commemorate the Russian victory against the Swedes at Poltava. In 1774 the secret wedding of Catherine the Great and Grigory Potemkin allegedly took place here. The interior is notable for its baroque iconostasis.

BELOW: part of Vyborg's industrial landscape.

Kresty Prison

From Lenin Square, if you head east about 800 metres/yards along Arsenalnaya naberezhnaya (Arsenal Embankment), you'll reach **Kresty Prison ❹** (open for tours Sat and Sun; call first to make a reservation, tel: 542 6861, take your passport, and be aware of the appalling conditions and voyeuristic nature of the tour). Built in the 1890s, its name ("crosses") derives from the fact that it is comprised of two buildings in the form of a cross.

Here, Trotsky and other revolutionaries awaited trial in 1905, and the Bolsheviks imprisoned the entire Provisional Government (except Kerensky) in October 1917. The prison became infamous during Soviet times, when thousands of people "disappeared" from here during the mass purges. Today, it is still one of the most notorious prisons in Europe, with gross overcrowding and terrible conditions.

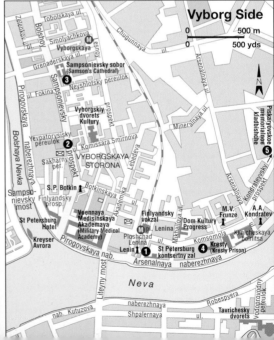

Piskarevsky Cemetery

Situated on Vyborg's outskirts is one of the city's most important sites: the **Piskaryovskoe memorialnoe kladbishche ❺** (Piskarevsky Memorial Cemetery; open daily 10am–6pm), which was opened on 9 May 1960. The cemetery is a memorial to the 670,000 citizens of St Petersburg who died during the Blockade *(see pages 32 and 36–7)*; the extent of the suffering remains an important part of the city's memory to this day. Wreaths are laid every year on 9 May to commemorate Victory Day.

To get to the cemetery take a taxi to the intersection of Piskarevsky and Nepokoryonnykh prospekts. Buried in the long lines of graves, covering 26 hectares (64 acres), are many of the hundreds of thousands of victims of the Blockade: over 600,000 people starved to death and more than 17,000 were killed by shells and air raids.

At the entrance to the cemetery is an eternal flame, and two memorial halls displaying documentary photographs and personal mementos.

One of the documents is the diary of Tanya Savicheva, a schoolgirl who recorded the deaths of her entire family. Tanya herself was evacuated but she too died soon afterwards.

Another exhibit documents the "Road of Life"; this refers to the route across the frozen Lake Ladoga in winter, the only connection Leningrad had with the outside world; this was extremely vulnerable to air strikes, and on one occasion more than 1,000 vehicles and their drivers were lost while attempting to supply the city in the winter of 1941–2.

A bronze, 6-metre (20-ft) tall statue of Mother Russia stands at the far end of the cemetery. On the memorial wall behind is inscribed a poem by Blockade survivor Olga Bergholts, part of which reads:

So many beneath the eternal protection
Of granite here lie, But you, who hearken to these stones, should know
No one is forgotten, nothing is forgotten. ❑

The Piskarevsky Memorial commemorates the victims of the Blockade of 1941–3.

BELOW: many of Vyborg's residents must beg to survive.

RESTAURANTS

Ryba, $$$
5 Akademika Pavlova Ulitsa
Tel: 234 5060
Open: L & D daily
Stylish panoramic restaurant on the top floor of a business centre offering Italian and Asian food.

Fudzhiyama, $$
Petrovsky Fort, Finlandsky proyezd, 4A
Tel: 332 1612
Located in the Petrovsky Ford office centre about a 5-minute walk north of the St Petersburg Hotel along the Pirogivskaya naberezhnaya, this restaurant offers some of the finest sushi in the city.

● ● ● ● ● ● ● ● ● ● ● ● ● ● ● ● ●
Price includes dinner and a glass of wine, excluding tip: **$$** *between $15–35;* **$** *under $15.*

SOUTHERN SUBURBS

The southern suburbs of St Petersburg are a densely populated area – a prime example of the sleeping quarters that dominated Soviet town planning. But there are also some historical gems here – including the Moscow Triumphal Arch and the Chesma Church

Early in the 18th century, who could have imagined that the stretches of forest beyond the canal that served as the town's southern border would give way to huge residential areas? The area had the right credentials for development since the highways that linked St Petersburg with Narva, Moscow and Arkhangelsk, and were vital for the town's budding economy, passed through it.

Originating along these routes, settlements started to grow outwards until the forests that once encircled St Petersburg on the south totally surrendered to Soviet style prefabricated apartment blocks in the second half of the 20th century. Here you get an honest glimpse of daily life.

There are also the triumphal gates of Narvsky and Moskovsky that celebrate Russia's defeat of Napolean and the Turks respectively and Park Pobedy which commemorates the victory over Hitler in World War II.

The Triumphal Gate

In front of Narvskaya metro station stands the only pre 20th-century structure in the square – the **Narvskaya Triumfalnaya vorota** ❶ (Narva Triumphal Gate). Erected in 1814 to celebrate the arrival of the

Russian Guards from vanquished France, the original gates were made of wood. Alexander I loved the arch from the moment he first laid eyes on it. He was very generous to the architect, the Italian Giacomo Quarenghi, bestowing an order and the title of honorary citizen on him.

Quarenghi, by the way, was particularly proud of this honour – and for good reason. In 1811, when Napoleon was preparing to invade Russia, he drafted Italians

Map on page 184

LEFT: selling goods from the kitchen garden.
BELOW: having a ball in the communal courtyard.

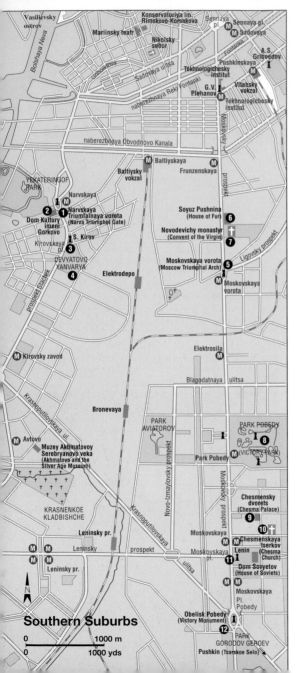

Southern Suburbs

0 _____ 1000 m
0 _____ 1000 yds

into his service. Napoleon's ally, the viceroy of Italy, ordered all Italians who were working in Russia back to Italy. Quarenghi refused – and was sentenced to death in his absence.

Ten years after the victorious return of the Russian Army, the harsh northern climate had all but destroyed the monument. The wooden arch was torn down and replaced by a stone structure (built between 1817 and 1834). It is a pale military green and adorned with military insignia of all sorts that show Russia's might of arms. It was recently restored for the anniversary celebrations in 2003.

Gorky Community Centre

On the west side of the arch is the **Dom Kultury imeni Gorkogo ❷** (Gorky Community Centre). This constructivist piece of architecture was built in 1927 to coincide with the 10th anniversary of the Bolshevik October coup. The centre's main hall, which seats 1,900, is a favourite place for performances by amateur and professional troupes. A little later in 1931, the **Univermag imeni Kirova** (Kirov Department Store), opposite the centre, was opened.

Kirov Square

Further south along prospekt Stachek lies **Kirovskaya ploshchad ❸** (Kirov Square), with its 50-metre (164-ft) high building, once home to the District Soviet of People's Deputies. In the foreground stands the 15-metre (50-ft) Monument to Sergei Kirov, Stalin's henchman and rival *(see pages 156–7)*, erected in 1938.

January 9th Park

The best place to end your tour of the Narvskaya area is in the **Sad Devyatovo Yanvarya ❹** (January 9th Park) just south of the District

Soviet building. Here the downtrodden inhabitants of the workers' quarter gathered on 9 January 1905 (otherwise known as Bloody Sunday, *see page 29)* to march towards the Winter Palace. The demonstration was met by army units near Narva Gate and later in Palace Square in an event that marked the beginning of the end of the tsarist regime.

The sophisticated beauty of the ironwork grille surrounding January 9th Park merited the highest award at the 1901 Paris World Exhibition, after which it was installed at the small park near the Winter Palace. But it blocked the view of the palace front and generally clashed with the ensemble of the square. In 1919, it was removed to the position in which you see it now.

Moscow prospekt

Moskovsky prospekt begins at **Sennaya ploshchad** (Haymarket Square) where the 11-km (7-mile) road runs straight as an arrow along the Pulkovo Meridian.

The avenue branches out when it reaches Ploshchad Pobedy and continues straight to the south as Pulkovskoe shosse – (Pulkovo Highway); this leads to the St Petersburg Observatory, one of the oldest in the world, and on to the Kievskoe shosse (Kiev Highway).

Moskovskoe shosse (Moscow Highway) runs to the southeast, through the town of Pushkin. The avenue was designed in the 18th century as the road to Tsarskoe Selo, as Pushkin was then called, and originally christened Tsarskoselsky prospekt.

Moscow Triumphal Arch

Our tour of Moskovsky prospekt starts at the **Moskovskaya vorota ❺** (Moscow Triumphal Arch). If coming from Narvskaya take the metro back to Teknologichesky

Institut, change lines and continue to Moskovskaya vorota station. The arch was built in 1834–8 to commemorate Russia's victory in the Turkish War of 1828–9, during the reign of Nicholas I. The monument is decorated with statues of Plenty, Glory and Victory.

Parts of the arch are made of cast iron and were used as tank traps to protect the southern approaches to the city in 1941.

House of Fur

Walking north from the arch towards the centre of town, you reach the **Soyuz Pushnina ❻** (House of Fur, No. 98), the only place in Russia where international fur auctions are held. Agents of the world's major fur-buying companies come to these auctions to purchase some of the world's finest furs.

Behind the Soyuz Pushnina, away from Moskovsky prospekt, is the former **Novodevichy monastyr ❼** (Convent of the Virgin), which has been handed over to the Orthodox Church and is slowly being restored to its former appearance.

Map on page 184

The Narva Gate was built to commemorate the defeat of Napoleon's troops in 1812. Over a hundred years later, Hitler's troops didn't fare much better when they tried to take the city.

BELOW: selling watermelons outside the metro station.

In the Avenue of Heroes at Park Pobedy are bronze busts of those locals who were awarded the Gold Star as Heroes of the Soviet Union.

BELOW: the tranquil surroundings of Victory Park.

Park Pobedy

Return to Moskovskaya vorota station and take the train past Elektrosila Station to **Park Pobedy** ❽ (Victory Park). The park was founded to commemorate the end of World War II. The central avenues are unerringly straight, with statues of war heroes flanking each side while the smaller paths wind through trees.

The fountain at the entrance to the park has a pool 25 metres (82 ft) in diameter, and a spring height of 12 metres (39 ft); it is the city's largest (only Peterhof's fountains are bigger). From here there is a view of the huge leisure and sports complex at its eastern end. People flock here not only for sports events: the place is a favourite venue for concerts by Russian and foreign pop groups. It also hosts large conferences, congresses and festivals.

Chesma Palace and Church

Walk south along Moskovsky prospekt towards Pushkin (or taking the metro one stop to Moskovskoy Station), and you find, on the left-hand side, **Chesmensky dvorets** ❾ (Chesma Palace; closed to the public). It was built in 1770 as a stopover where road-weary Catherine the Great could rest on her way between St Petersburg and her out-of-town residence, Pushkin *(see page 200)*.

The palace got its name from a victorious naval battle fought against the Turks in the Aegean Sea's Chesma Bay. The palace was fashioned after a medieval castle with turrets, moat and drawbridges.

The green frog on the palace's coat of arms refers to its site – formerly known as Frog Swamp.

For major receptions, the Green Frog – a set of china – was ordered from the Wedgwood porcelain company. The 592 pieces of the set bear 1,244 landscape scenes of England. Naturally, each piece also bears the symbol of the palace – the green frog. Today the palace is a retirement home for the elderly.

The small, but immensely charming **Chesmenskaya tserkov** ❿ (Chesma Church; open for services

daily at 10am) is one of the few neo-Gothic buildings in the city, and was built between 1777 and 1780.

Moscow Square

Further along to the south on the avenue, not far away from the palace, is **Moskovskaya ploshchad** (Moscow Square). Here the eye is immediately caught by the 220-metre (720-ft) high **Dom Sovyetov** (House of Soviets) and the huge statue of Lenin in the centre of the square.

The House of Soviets was built between 1936–41 with as much pomp as possible to lend every bit of elaboration to the praise of the party. The huge **Monument to Lenin** was erected on the occasion of his 100th anniversary, as the inscription on the pedestal attests. The charismatic leader, with either a cap or a copy of *Pravda* (it is hard to say which) in hand, is depicted delivering one of his speeches.

Pobedy Square

Further to the south along Moskovsky prospekt comes **Ploshchad Pobedy** (Victory Square) with its grandiose **Obelisk Pobedy** (Victory Monument); this was erected in 1975 on the 30th anniversary of the victory against the Nazis, in honour of the heroic defenders of what was then Leningrad.

The 48-metre (157-ft) obelisk stands at the centre of a broken circle that symbolises deliverance from the Blockade *(see pages 32 and 36–37)*. Several groups of sculptures depict sailors, partisans, soldiers and volunteers.

In the memorial hall located under the monument, Shostakovich's 7th Symphony plays to the accompaniment of a metronome. In the centre of the Memorial Hall is the Bronze Book of Memory, a chronicle of the Blockade. The hall displays moving reminders of the privations suffered during the 900-day siege, as well as having screens which continuously show contemporary film footage, vividly recreating the appearance and atmosphere of the city at the time.   ❏

Not far from Haymarket Square along Moscow prospekt, No. 19 houses the Gidromet institut (Meteorological Institute), founded by Dmitry Mendeleev (see page 171). The tower over the building has the largest and, incidentally, most accurate, clock in town.

BELOW: the neo-Gothic facade of Chesma Church.

PETERHOF PALACE

Peter the Great's trips to Western Europe were
an important influence on St Petersburg's
development. His own summer palace, Peterhof,
was to a great extent influenced by Versailles

Russia's imitation of Versailles, Peterhof **❶**, 25 km (16 miles) west of St Petersburg, was the primary country residence of the tsars, especially during the 18th and early 20th centuries. Begun by Peter the Great and expanded by Empress Elizabeth and Catherine the Great, it comprises several dozen buildings, nine of which are now museums. All of these are worth seeing, but Peterhof is best known for its gardens, parks, and magnificent fountains.

The palace is situated on the south coast of the Gulf of Finland and can be reached by hydrofoil from the Dvortsovaya naberezhnaya in front of the Hermitage. Vessels leave twice-hourly and take 20–25 minutes. Opening hours are awkward for visitors as the museums operate at different times and charge separate admission fees (see individual attractions for details). Summer weekends are a good time to visit as everything is open and the fountains are working, but they are also the busiest.

Peter's grand plan

During the Northern War with Sweden (1700–21), Peter the Great often spent his summers on this part of the coast, and in 1705 he had a cottage built here. Like his cabin in the city *(see page 153)*, it was quite small with just two rooms.

After the battle of Poltava (1709) and the naval victories at Gangut (1714) and Grengam (1720), Peter decided to build a summer residence near his new capital to demonstrate the power and wealth of the Russian Empire. His inspiration came from a trip he'd made to France at the end of the 17th century when he'd fallen under the spell of Versailles, Louis XIV's palace outside Paris. He ordered a "palace and kitchen-garden" to be built, "better than the French king's at Versailles."

Maps
on pages
192 & 198

PRECEDING PAGES:
winter at Pushkin.
LEFT: the Hall of
Muses at Peterhof.
BELOW: a golden
moment of
contemplation.

Peterhof was built as a showpiece to stand guard over the Baltic and stoke the jealousy of Sweden, Russia's bitter rival at the time.

Working with the greatest architects of the day, Peter himself sketched out plans and drawings.

The location threw up many challenges. The clay soil had to be drained or removed and fresh earth and fertilisers brought to the site by barge. Tens of thousands of maples, lindens, chestnuts and fruit trees and bushes were imported from Western Europe, but floods and storms often destroyed the newly planted trees and they had to be replaced time and time again. All building materials, fountain parts, statues, paintings and expensive furnishings were brought by ship.

Huge numbers of soldiers and serfs laboured on the palace. Construction of the canal alone took some 4,000 men. Suffering from a lack of food, bitter cold and infectious diseases, many died. In this sense at least, Peterhof succeeded in imitating Versailles, where 15,000 workers died during its construction.

The palace, begun in 1714, was inaugurated in 1723. But work continued on the subsidiary palaces and buildings, including Mon-

plaisir, Marly, the Orangery and the Hermitage Pavilion.

BOLSHOY PALACE

Standing high above the park is the magnificent yellow-and-white **Bolshoy dvorets Ⓐ** (Grand Palace; open Tues–Sun 11am–6pm, closed last Tues of the month; Lower Park open daily 10am–8pm, weekends until 9pm; fountains operate from last week of May to first week of October, 11am–5pm, weekends until 6pm). The Morskoy kanal, backed by the Grand Cascade, offers a dramatic approach to the palace from the hydrofoil terminal on the Gulf of Finland

This is where our tour begins and in some ways where the park's role as a public museum, not a tsar's residence, began. In 1917, by decree of the Bolsheviks, all of Peterhof's monuments were nationalised. In the following May the first workers' excursion passed through the halls of the Grand Palace, carrying a red flag and revolutionary posters.

During World War II the palace was occupied by German forces and

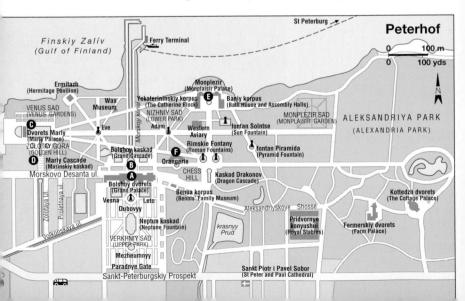

Finskiy Zalív (Gulf of Finland)

St Peterburg →

Peterhof

0 — 100 m
0 — 100 yds

Ferry Terminal

Ermitazh (Hermitage Pavilion)
Wax Museum
VENUS SAD (VENUS GARDENS)
Ⓒ Dvorets Marly (Marly Palace)
ZOLOTAY GORA (GOLDEN HILL)
Ⓓ Marly Cascade (Marlinskiy kaskad)
Morskovo Desanta ul.
Eve
Bolshoy kaskad (Grand Cascade)
Ⓐ Ⓑ
Orangerie

Yekaterininskiy korpus (The Catherine Block)
NIZHNIY SAD (LOWER PARK)
Adam
Western Aviary
Rimskie Fontany (Roman Fountains)
Ⓕ

Monplezir (Monplaisir Palace)
Ⓔ Banïy korpus (Bath House and Assembly Halls)

MONPLEZIR SAD (MONPLAISIR GARDEN)

ALEKSANDRIYA PARK (ALEXANDRIA PARK)

fontan Solntse (Sun Fountain)
fontan Piramida (Pyramid Fountain)

CHESS HILL
Kaskad Drakonov (Dragon Cascade)

Bolshoy dvorets (Grand Palace)
Vesna
Leto
Dubovyy
Benua korpus (Benois' Family Museum)

Aleksandriyskoye Shosse

Kottedzh dvorets (The Cottage Palace)

Neptun kaskad (Neptune Fountain)
VERKHNIY SAD (UPPER PARK)
Mezheumnyy
Paradnye Gate
Sankt-Peterburgskiy Prospekt

krasnyy Prud

Pridvornye konyushni (Royal Stables)
Fermerskiy dvorets (Farm Palace)

Sankt Piotr i Pavel Sobor (St Peter and Paul Cathedral)

Zolotaya Ul.
Proletnaya ul.
Volkonskaya ul.

fell into disrepair. A long period of restoration ensued. It took 10 years just to restore the 2.5-metre (8-ft) gilded urn on the roof of the palace.

Tickets and multilingual tours (obligatory) are available from the lobby of the Great Palace. The **State Rooms** are upstairs and the set tour begins with the splendid **Ceremonial Staircase** by Bartolomeo Rastrelli, who remodelled the palace between 1747–54. The first room is the **Chesma Hall**, named after the Russian naval victory against the Turks at Chesma Bay in 1770. The walls are covered with epic paintings of Russian vessels destroying the Turkish fleet. Next door is the pale-green-and-white **Throne Room**, the largest room in the palace, encrusted with stucco and hung with 12 chandeliers, which was used for official receptions. A portrait of Catherine the Great hangs above the throne while the side walls are hung with portraits of the Romanov dynasty.

Adjoining the Throne Room is the gilded **Audience Hall**, in the baroque style, and then the more restrained **White Dining Room** in classical style, where the table is set with a dinner service made in Staffordshire, England, for Catherine the Great.

Before moving to the drawing rooms and private suites on the eastern side of the palace the tour passes through the central **Picture Hall**, which was the largest room during the Petrine era. It became known as the Picture Hall after Catherine the Great covered its walls in portraits by the Italian artist Pietro Rotari (1707–62). The room is flanked by the flamboyant **Western Chinese Study** and the **Eastern Chinese Study**, dating from the mid-18th century when chinoiseric was popular throughout Europe.

The **Imperial Suite**, containing the domestic quarters of the tsar, are more modest in scale. Peter the Great's **study** is lined in carved oak panels depicting symbols of Peter's military achievements.

Grand Cascade

Peterhof's fountains are a feat of 18th-century engineering second to none. Despite using over 30,000 litres

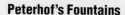

Map on page 192

For two centuries Peterhof's parks were out of bounds to the public. In the 18th century the guard at Peterhof was ordered "in no uncertain terms" to "make absolutely sure that the vulgar masses or, worse, beggars didn't wander around the garden and were not admitted under any circumstances."

LEFT: a view from the Grand Parade.

Peterhof's Fountains

While the architects Peter Yeropkin and Mikhail Zemtsov worked on the construction of Peterhof's palace buildings, the elaborate waterworks – the jewel in Peterhof's crown – were constructed under the supervision of Russia's first hydraulic engineer, Vassili Tuvolkov.

In 1715 Tuvolkov and Vassili Suvorov (father of the future military commander) were sent to France to study the construction of canals, docks and harbours. Returning to Russia in 1720, they set to work at Peterhof, working at such a fast pace that in eight months the first test-run took place.

The intricate gravity-fed system brought water from natural springs in Ropsha Heights, 22 km (14 miles) south of the site. The system was appreciated by specialists as "a masterpiece of hydraulic art of the 18th century". The beauty, grandeur and technical innovation of the fountains were considered to have surpassed the celebrated waterworks at Versailles. Their maintenance required a permanent team of men and boys, the latter to crawl through the pipes and repair leaks.

(6,600 gallons) of water every second, they can work for 10–12 hours a day for up to five months a year.

The **Bolshoy kaskad**  (Grand Cascade; open May–early Oct 11am–5pm) running from the foot of the Grand Palace to the edge of the Nizhniy sad (Lower Park) is the estate's main attraction. Seventeen steps, 39 gilded bronze statues and 29 extravagant bas-reliefs make up the cascade. In the centre at the top are Rastrelli's pair of *Tritons Blowing into Sea Shells*. From here, two descending staircases, adorned with gilded reliefs and sculptures of ancient gods and heroes, representing Russia's victory in the Northern War, lead to the Great Grotto. Several sculptures satirise the defeated Swedish king. One, *The Frightened Actaeon, Running Away from His Own Dogs,* represents Charles XII, abandoned by his allies after his defeat. Another, *Narcissus, Turned into a Flower*, ridicules the king's inflated opinion of himself.

Peterhof's largest fountain is **Fontan Samson** (the Samson Fountain), in the centre of the Great Grotto.

The fountains at Peterhof operate May–Oct. During winter the numerous statues are covered up to prevent damage from the extreme cold.

BELOW: the palatial stables.

The biblical hero Samson tears open the lion's jaws, again symbolising Russia's subjugation of Sweden.

LOWER PARK

Between the Grand Cascade and the Gulf of Finland stretches Peterhof's **Nizhniy park** (Lower Park). Its west end is dominated by Marly Palace, its Golden Hill Cascade and the Hermitage. Towards the Gulf of Finland are the Monplaisir Palace and the Orangerie (containing the Wax Museum).

Marly Palace and Hermitage

In the western end of the Lower Park is the **Dvorets Marly** (Marly Palace; open May–Sept Tues–Sun 10.30am–6pm, Oct–April weekends only 10.30am–5pm; admission charge), built in 1720–4 to accommodate important guests of the tsar. From the middle of the 18th century it was used to house items connected to Peter the Great and still contains relics from the Petrine age, including presents given to Peter, his personal library and items from his wardrobe, such as his naval greatcoat.

Map on page 192

The palace's **Zolotay gora ⓓ** (Golden Hill Cascade) is more modest than the Grand Cascade but still delightful. Water gushes from the mouths of dragons and dolphins and pours from sea shells borne aloft by marine gods. The **Menazherny fontany** (Menagerie Fountain) at the foot of the Golden Hill is noted for its powerful water jets measuring up to 30-cm (12-inch) in diameter. The fact that the jets are hollow gave the fountain its name, *Menagerie,* meaning economic.

To the east of Marly Palace, on the seashore, is the **Hermitage Pavilion**, a two-storey pink and white building enclosed by a moat, built in 1721–5 by Johann Friedrich Braunstein. The reception hall on the upper floor has a large table equipped with its own dumb waiter for carrying plates to and from the kitchen below.

Monplaisir

Morskaya alleya leads to Peter's seafront villa of **Monplezir ⓔ** (Monplaisir; open May–Sept Thur–Tues, closed last Thur of each month, separate admission charge), reputedly Peter's favourite part of Peterhof. The villa's oak panelling is similar to his cabin on the Petrograd side and his study in the Grand Palace.

The walls of the **Lacquer Study** in the palace are lined with intricately decorated lacquered panels. Unfortunately most of the originals were used as firewood during the Nazi occupation of Peterhof, and only three of them, found in a nearby bunker, survived. It turned out that the decorations were not the work of Oriental craftsmen, as was presumed, but rather of Russian icon painters from the village of Palekh. Contemporary Palekh artists were able to recreate the works of their ancestors.

Other interesting rooms include Peter's **Maritime Study** with its sea views of Kronstadt on one side and St Petersburg on the other.

The auxillary buildings of Monplaisir charge separate admission fees and are open at different times. The **Catherine Building** (open May–Sept Fri–Wed), inhabited by the tsarina after her husband was overthrown, is noted for its fine furniture and tableware. Commissioned by Count Dmitry Guryev in 1809, it depicts the multifarious peoples of Russia. On the opposite side of the palace is the **Bath Building** (open May–Sept Thur–Tues), where the tsars took their *banya*.

The Orangerie

Follow the wide avenue that heads back towards the Grand Palace and at the Adam Fountain turn due south to the **Orangerie ⓕ**, now home to a rather dull wax museum. More impressive is the **Triton Fountain** just outside, which shoots jets of water over 8 metres (25 ft) into the air.

South of the fountain is the **Benois Family Museum** displaying the artworks of several generations of the Benois family, who contributed to Peterhof's beautification and restoration for over 300 years.   ❑

In addition to Peterhof's grand fountains, you will come across numerous "trick" fountains, designed to shower unwary passersby. A fountain in the shape of a Chinese parasol, for instance, begins to operate when visitors sit down on the bench below. Trick fountains were all the rage in the late 18th century and remain popular features of Peterhof to this day.

BELOW: the Lower Gardens.

DAY TRIPS FROM ST PETERSBURG

Many of the lavish imperial palaces and beautifully laid-out parks on the outskirts of St Petersburg can easily be reached by train or minibus and make worthwhile day trips

Map on page 198

LEFT: gilded atlantes at the Catherine Palace, Tsarskoe Selo.
BELOW: towers of Catherine Palace, Tsarskoe Selo.

Scattered around the outskirts of St Petersburg are the magnificent imperial palaces of the old tsarist regime. In the west, just beyond Peterhof *(see pages 191–5)*, is Oranienbaum, an extravagant estate built for Peter the Great's sidekick, Menshikov. The buildings are in a sorry state, but the grounds are lovely. To the south of the city is Tsarskoe Selo, the magnificent retreat of Catherine the Great, and the palaces of Pavlosk and Gatchina are not too far away.

To the east, along the banks of Lake Ladoga, is Shlüsselburg, a 14th-century island fortress, one of Russia's oldest northern outposts. The island of Kizhi in Lake Onega is not a day trip away – you'll need at least two days – but is worth a visit for its spectacular wooden architecture.

You can reach these places by minibus or suburban train from St Petersburg, details of which are given under each location.

ORANIENBAUM

Situated about 40 km (25 miles) west of St Petersburg, the palace at **Oranienbaum ❷** (all buildings open Wed–Mon 11am–5pm, closed last Mon of the month; entrance charge) was founded in 1710 by Alexander Menshikov, Peter the Great's closest friend and political advisor. Menshikov wanted to build a palace to rival Peterhof ("Oranienbaum" is German for "orange tree", which Menshikov planted in the Lower Park, the height of extravagance given the northern climate), but the project bankrupted him and the estate was passed into the hands of the crown. It was renamed in 1948 in honour of "the father of Russian science", Mikhail Lomonosov *(see page 169)*, who opened a glass factory here in the middle of the 18th century.

Oranienbaum was the only imperial palace to have escaped occupation by the Nazis.

Since the 1990s, the palace has reverted back to its pre-revolutionary name, while the town has kept Lomonosov's name.

Oranienbaum includes 53 historic buildings, of which 18 are listed, but many of them are in a very poor state of repair. The best feature of the estate is probably the surrounding landscape; the parks and gardens, covering 165 hectares (410 acres), with secluded paths, deciduous woodland, ponds and meadows full of wild flowers.

You can take a suburban train from Baltiysky train station at Baltiyskaya metro (takes about 1 hour), or you can catch a minibus (K-300) from Avtovo metro station.

The Grand Palace

The most important building at Oranienbaum is the baroque **Bolshoy dvorets** (Grand Palace), built on a terrace overlooking the Gulf of Finland between 1710 and 1725. Today this palace, like so many of the estate's buildings, is crumbling away but is still impressive for its sheer size and presence, in particular the two single-storey galleries curving round on either side to domed pavilions. Parts of the palace and the east (Japanese) pavilion are open to the public.

In front of the Grand Palace is the **Lower Park**, built in a geometric formation, which would have been adorned with fountains, statues, greenhouses and menageries. **Peter III's Palace** is in the southeast corner. Peter III, who was given Oranienbaum in 1743, had the two-storey palace built by Antonio Rinaldi before his marriage to Catherine the Great; the lower floor was the servants' quarters so the rooms are relatively bare, while the upper rooms are richly decorated, mostly in Chinese style, with silk

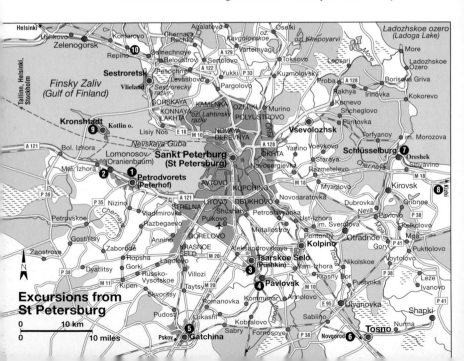

Excursions from St Petersburg

0   10 km

0   10 miles

Map on page 198

hangings, lacquer paintings and dress cabinets; the Picture Hall contains paintings by 18th-century European artists.

The Chinese Palace

At the far end of the **Upper Park** – a pleasantly overgrown stretch of park, with canals, bridges and ponds among the trees – is the **Chinese Palace**, an over-the-top gem commissioned by Catherine the Great and designed by Rinaldi. Built in 1762–8, the palace's exterior is baroque, while the interior is decidedly rococo, with murals and painted panels, ceiling frescoes, delicate stucco work, embroidery and ornate parquet floors. In fact the decor is probably the most sumptuous of all the St Petersburg palaces.

The interiors are mostly in European style; only in the last two rooms of the west wing do Chinese elements really emerge, the most pronounced of these being in the Large Chinese Room, where the walls are covered with Chinese landscapes of wood and walrus-ivory marquetry.

The Glass Study is another masterpiece of extravagance, with panels and door lintels in pearl glass made at Lomonosov's glass factory nearby.

Sliding Hill

Heading back towards the sea through the Upper Park, you come to the ice-blue and white **Sliding Hill Pavilion** (Katalnaya gorka), resembling a misshapen wedding cake. This is all that remains of Catherine's rollercoaster, built around 1770; a long wooden slope descended from the second floor of the pavilion (which was built on a high bank), stretching 500 metres (1,640 ft) down through the Upper Park; people would then whizz down the track in sledges (in winter), or wheeled carts (in summer). It's not surprising that in such a flat landscape this was a very popular form of entertainment.

Sadly Sliding Hill rotted away and collapsed in 1813. You can visit some of the pavilion's rooms though. From the White Study (Beliy kabinet) you get a good view of Kronshtadt island.

The good news for Oranienbaum is that the city government created a

"Sliding hills" were a popular form of entertainment among the Russian nobility in the 18th century, and were the prototype for today's roller coasters.

BELOW: Sliding Hill Pavilion at Oranienbaum.

foundation in early 2004 to raise enough funds to restore this once glorious estate by its 300th anniversary in 2011.

TSARSKOE SELO

The lavish imperial palaces of **Tsarskoe Selo ❸** ("Tsar's Village"), are just 25 km (16 miles) south of St Petersburg. The small town of Pushkin flanks two magnificent palaces, Catherine Palace and Alexander Palace, set among beautiful parkland. In Soviet times the estate was renamed, and Russians still often refer to Tsarskoe Selo by its post-revolutionary name of Pushkin.

From St Petersburg you can catch a train from Vitebsk Station which takes about 30 minutes. Alternatively, you can take a minibus from Moskovskaya metro station (K-286, K-287, K-299 or K-342), which departs every 10–20 minutes and takes about 45 minutes. Either way you will arrive at Detskoe Selo station, from where you can catch bus No. 371 or No. 382, which stops near the palace.

The palaces were very badly damaged during the Nazi occupation, and the process of restoration is long and slow. The palace facades now gleam as new, but many rooms and pavilions are still unrestored.

Catherine Palace

Although primarily associated with Catherine the Great, who loved the place, **Yekaterininsky dvorets** (Catherine Palace; open Wed–Mon 10am–5pm, closed last Mon of the month; entrance charge) was designed by Bartolomeo Rastrelli for Tsarina Elizabeth, who named it after her mother, Catherine I.

The splendid vibrant blue, white and gold baroque facade – an impressive 300 metres (980 ft) in length – is adorned with atlantes, columns, pilasters and ornamental window frames.

Inside, the palace is decorated in a mixture of styles. When Catherine the Great inherited the palace in 1762, she commissioned the Scottish architect Charles Cameron to redesign some of the baroque interiors to suit her more neoclassical taste. While the palace is undergo-

BELOW: detail of the Amber Room.

The Amber Room

The fabulously restored Amber Room at Catherine Palace is made from several tons of amber – the fossilised resin of prehistoric pines. Not only is it the grandest room in the palace, it is also the source of a mystery which has endured for over fifty years. Since the end of World War II when the original Amber Room disappeared, the authorities have been baffled as to where it went and who took it. Speculation has led to sealed mines being dug up and palace vaults being raided throughout Eastern Europe.

The Amber Room, published in 2004 by Catherine Scott-Clark and Adrian Levy, goes a long way to trace the story, if not the location of this sumptuously decorated room.

ing restoration, not all the state rooms will be open.

Highlights of the palace include the ornate **Great Staircase**, installed in 1860; the **Great Hall**, Rastrelli's masterpiece of baroque decor, glittering with mirrors, windows and gilded carvings, above which is a vast ceiling painting entitled *The Triumph of Russia*; the extraordinary **Amber Room** *(see panel opposite)*, which has taken Russian craftsmen over 20 years to restore; Cameron's neoclassical **Green Dining Room**, in sharp contrast to the baroque flamboyance of Rastrelli's work; and the **Blue Dining Room**, with its painted ceiling and delightful silk wall coverings with blue floral motifs.

On the southeast corner of Catherine Palace are the **Agate Rooms**, Charles Cameron's most fabulous creation (1780–7), so-named after the agate, jasper, lapis lazuli and other semi-precious stones used to decorate the interior. Nearby is the elegant neoclassical **Cameron Gallery** (1783–7), one of Catherine the Great's favourite buildings.

Catherine Park

The parks and gardens of Tsarskoe Selo, covering nearly 600 hectares (1,500 acres), were created out of dense forest by thousands of soldiers and labourers. In 1768 Catherine the Great commissioned one of Russia's first landscaped parks, and the result is a delight to explore, dotted with pavilions and follies.

The French-style formal gardens in front of the palace, with radiating avenues and terraces, ponds and statuary, were laid out in the 1740s. The main avenue leads to the baroque Hermitage, built by Rastrelli in 1756 and now in need of restoration.

In contrast, to the west are the more informal gardens in the English style, the focus of which is the **Great Pond**. Dotted around are various interesting structures, including the Pyramid, where Catherine buried her dogs, a marble bridge, Cameron's copy of the one at Wilton House in England, and a poignant statue, *The Girl with the Jug*, which inspired Pushkin to write his poem, *Fountain at Tsarskoe Selo*.

Map on page 198

TIP

Since the reopening of the Amber Room, the Catherine Palace has been inundated with visitors in the summer months. If you can't avoid the busy season, try and arrive early to avoid long queues for tickets.

BELOW: facade of Catherine Palace.

In the summer you can hire a rowing boat to explore the Great Pond. In the middle is a pavilion designed by Giacomo Quarenghi, from where musicians would serenade Catherine and her courtiers as they floated by in gilded gondolas.

Alexander Palace and Park

To the north of Catherine Palace, along Dvortsovaya ulitsa, is **Alexander Palace** (open Wed–Mon 10am–5pm; closed last Wed of month; entrance charge; www.alexander-palace.org), completed in 1796 for Catherine the Great's grandson, future tsar Alexander I. This neoclassical palace, built by Quarenghi, is best known for being the residence of the last tsar, Nicholas II, his wife Alexandra and their children. It was from here that the Romanov family were taken to the Urals by their Bolshevik captors and executed in 1918.

The Empress Alexandra's favourite, Grigory Rasputin *(see page 130)*, was a frequent guest here, and buried in the park, but then removed from his grave by revolutionary soldiers, and his body cremated.

This palace lacks the sumptuous extravagance of Catherine Palace, but it has more intimate appeal. Here you can feel the presence of the last tsar and his family, through displays of personal items such as uniforms the children wore and photographs of them playing. Alexander Park is bigger and wilder than Catherine Park; if you want to explore, there's a gate near the palace.

The Lycée

Across Sadovaya ulitsa from Catherine Palace stands the imperial **Lycée** (open Wed–Mon 10am–5.30pm, closed last Mon of every month; free), from where Alexander Pushkin graduated in 1817.

The Lycée was founded by Alexander I in 1811 to provide a modern education for sons of the nobility. Today you can take a tour to see classrooms and dormitories as they were in Pushkin's day.

Near the Lycée is the **Church of the Sign**, one of the town's oldest buildings, dating to 1734. **Pushkin's dacha** (open Wed–Sun 10am–4.30pm; closed last Fri of month; entrance charge) is on Kuzminskaya ulitsa; it's a delightful wooden house where the poet and his wife spent the summer of 1831.

PAVLOVSK

The superb palace and park ensemble at **Pavlovsk** ❹ (open Sat–Thur

BELOW: winter scene.

10am–5pm, closed last Mon of the month, ceremonial rooms only open on Thur; entrance charge; www. alexanderpalace.org/pavlovs) was built for Catherine the Great's only son, the future tsar Paul I. The neoclassical palace and vast parkland – one of the largest in Europe – lie 30 km (19 miles) south of St Petersburg (5 km/3 miles south of Tsarskoe Selo).

The Nazi occupation left Pavlovsk in an appalling state, but following long and painstaking restoration, the beautiful rooms of the palace are open to visitors.

You can take a suburban train from the city's Vitebsk Station (35 minutes) or a minibus (K-286) from Moskovskaya ploshchad (one hour). From Pavlovsk Station, bus Nos. 370, 383 or 383a go to the Great Palace, or you can walk through the park (about 20 minutes).

Great Palace

The central Palladian mansion of the **Bolshoy dvorets** (Great Palace) was designed by Catherine the Great's favourite architect Charles Cameron (1782–6). Paul did not like his mother's choice, and in 1789 he had the wings added by his preferred architect, Vincenzo Brenna.

The interior of the palace reflects the taste of Paul's German wife, Maria Fyodorovna, who outlived him by 28 years and made many modifications, employing the best architects of the day, such as Voronikhin and Quarenghi.

The treasures on display were acquired by Paul and Maria during their tour of Europe in 1781–2; they bought whatever pleased them, including paintings, furniture, French clocks, Sèvres porcelain, silk and tapestries, and, once their identities became known, were showered with gifts from European royalty.

The palace's elegant suites and halls belong to the best achievements of Russian architecture; they may lack the grandeur of those at Catherine Palace, but their human scale only adds to their charm, as does the fact that relatively few tourists tend to visit.

Map
on page
198

Pushkin was once a model town connected to St Petersburg by Russia's first train line; it was one of the first towns in Europe to have electric lighting, piped water and sewage works.

BELOW:
Pavlovsk during the 18th century.

The park at Pavlovsk

For those not interested in 18th- and 19th-century decor, the main appeal of Pavlovsk is the huge landscaped **park** (open daily 9am–8pm; entrance charge). The architects Charles Cameron and Vincenzo Brenna designed a seemingly natural landscape, with gently sloping hills, winding paths, pavilions, romantic ruins, bridges and woodland, stretching for several kilometres either side of the Slavyanka River. Tolstoy was a frequent visitor.

The best way to see the park is to take a picnic and explore for yourself. Look out for the Temple of Friendship, set in a sharp bend in the river not far from the palace. This temple, designed by Cameron in 1780, was the first building in Russia to use the Doric form.

GATCHINA

The neoclassical palace and park at **Gatchina** ❺ (open Tues–Sun 10am–5pm, closed last Tues of the month; entrance charge; www.alexander-palace.org/gatchina), 45 km (28 miles) south of St Petersburg, date from 1765, when Catherine the Great gave the village to her lover, Grigory Orlov. Antonio Rinaldi built the first palace, which was then altered by Vincenzo Brenna to suit Paul I's militaristic tastes. An additional storey was added, and a moat and drawbridge.

The palace is slowly being restored, but you can visit some of the sumptuously decorated rooms. The grounds are delightful, the most overgrown and wild of all the palace parks, and there's a lake where you can swim in summer or hire a rowing boat.

To get there you can take a train from St Petersburg's Baltisky Station (metro Baltiskaya) to Gatchina-Baltiyskaya train station. Or catch a minibus from Moskovskaya (K-18), Kirovskiy Zavod (K-546) or Prospekt Veteranov (K-631) metro stations, which take about 45 minutes and stop at Gatchina-Baltiyskaya train station, not far from the palace.

Gatchina Palace

Restoration has been confined to the central section of the palace. High-

Like many of the palaces around St Petersburg, this pavilion at Gatchina was badly damaged during World War II.

BELOW: the Grecian Hall, Pavlovsk Palace.

lights include the columned Marble Dining Room, the magnificent White Ballroom, with a parquet floor inlaid with nine types of rare wood, and stucco garlands on the ceiling, and the Throne Hall, adorned with Gobelin tapestries presented by Louis XVI of France.

Gardens

The gardens at Gatchina have grown unkempt, and this is their appeal. Autumn is the best time to visit, when the foliage is at its most vivid. From the formal garden near the palace, paths wend their way across a chain of islands between the White and Silver lakes.

On the far side of the White Lake is a delapidated Temple of Venus dating from 1792–3, standing forlornly on the Island of Love. Nearby is the **Birch Cabin** (open May–Sept Tues–Sun 10am–6pm), from the same period. At first glance the cabin looks like a stack of logs, but inside is a suite of exquisite mirrored rooms.

To the east of the palace, by the Black Lake, is the Priory Palace, built by architect Nicholas Lvov in 1798. Here, Paul held court with his fellow knights from the ancient Maltese Order, of which he appointed himself Grandmaster, after they had been booted out of Malta by Napoleon.

NOVGOROD

Although its name means "New Town", **Novgorod** ❻ is Russia's oldest city, probably founded around 860 AD. Its medieval churches and Kremlin, and its excellent museums, draw tourists (mainly Russian) in their droves. Located about 190 km (120 miles) south of St Petersburg, it's a long way to go for the day – the journey takes about three and a half hours – but many tour companies offer day trips by coach to the city. If you want to stay the night, there are numerous hotels (www. novgorod.ru/english).

Background

From the 9–15th century, Novgorod ruled a vast area, all the way up to the Baltic states and Finland and west to present-day Poland. Its rulers built up

Map on page 198

According to local lore, the full moon wakes the ghosts of the tsar's borzoi hunting dogs, who can be seen relieving themselves on the trees in Gatchina's park.

BELOW: the Throne Hall at Gatchina Palace.

trade links with the Hanseatic League and protected themselves from attack with heavy fortifications. Rich merchants built magnificent churches. Medieval Novgorod was known throughout the world for its architecture, icon painting, jewellery and decorative arts.

The city was all but destroyed during World War II, its population decimated. Many of the buildings you see now have been built from scratch.

The old town

The **Kremlin** Ⓐ (open 6am–midnight; free), on the left bank of the River Volkhov, is at the heart of the old town. The citadel (or *Detinets* as it is known locally) was mentioned in chronicles as early as 1044, but most of it dates from the 15th century. The formidable redbrick walls are interspersed with numerous cone-topped towers, the tallest being the Kukui Tower (open

Tues–Wed and Fri–Sun 11am–7pm); climb it for the splendid panoramic view.

The Kremlin is dominated by the magnificent 11th-century **Sofiysky Sobor** Ⓑ (Cathedral of St Sophia; open daily 10am–6pm), the oldest church in the city. On the west side are beautifully sculpted 12th-century bronze doors, a superb example of Western European Romanesque metalwork tucked away in the heart of Russia. Inside, on the far side of the nave, is a fragment of 11th-century fresco, a portrait of the Byzantine emperor Constantine and his mother Helen. The iconostasis is one of the oldest in Russia and contains icons from the 11–17th century.

Also within the Kremlin is the **Khudozhestveno muzei Novgoroda** Ⓒ (Novgorod Museum of Art; open Wed–Mon 10am–6pm;

BELOW: Cathedral of St Sophia in Novgorod.

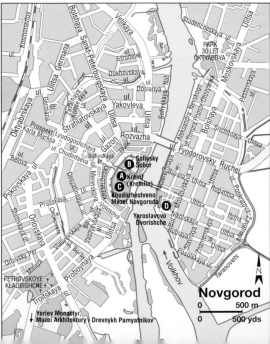

Novgorod

0 _____ 500 m
0 _____ 500 yds

closed last Thur of month), containing an amazing collection of icons from the Novgorod school. Historical artefacts also on display include chronicles and texts scratched on pieces of dried birch bark. The vast, bell-shaped **Millennium Monument** in the Kremlin's central square was unveiled in 1862, commemorating Novgorod's 1,000th anniversary.

On the opposite bank of the river is **Yaroslavovo dvorishche ⓓ** (Yaroslav's Court), where you'll find the greatest concentration of medieval buildings, mainly churches from the 12–16th century.

SCHLÜSSELBURG

Around 70 km (44 miles) to the east of St Petersburg is the island fortress of **Schlüsselburg ❼** (open May–Oct daily 10am–5pm; entrance charge). The island (known to the Russians as Oreshek), is in Lake Ladoga at the point where the Neva flows out of the lake.

You can join a tour agency to get there or take a cruise. Either way the journey takes 3–4 hours. Alternatively you can take a train from Finland Station, which takes about an hour to get to Morozova, from where you have to take a ferry.

History of the fortress

In 1323, the ruler of Novgorod, Russia's first city, built a fortress as defence against attacks by the Swedes. The island was fought for for centuries until Peter the Great recaptured it in 1702, and renamed it Schlüsselburg, (meaning "Key Fortress" in German). Following Peter's victory, it became a prison, and soon became synonymous with tsarist oppression and tyranny.

In the 18th century the prisoners at Schlüsselburg were mostly members of the royal family and the upper classes. The 19th century witnessed the imprisonment of convinced opponents of autocracy. These included certain Decembrists, many members of the People's Will Party and large numbers of revolutionaries. After the February Revolution of 1917 all prisoners were liberated and the prison buildings burnt down.

TIP

The nondescript exterior of the **Chamber of Facets,** backing onto the cathedral, conceals a superb star-vaulted reception hall dating from 1433 in which you'll find a display of ecclesiastical treasures.

BELOW: residents of Novgorod, 1880.

The name of the island of Kizhi in Karelian means "playground." It gained this name from pagan celebrations that once took place here.

BELOW: a wooden church at Kizhi.

The ancient fortress once again acquired military significance during the Siege of Leningrad. Although the town of Schlüsselburg fell to the Nazis in 1941, the fortress held out until the blockade was broken. Lake Ladoga provided the only supply line to the besieged city of Leningrad.

Access to the island

Located about 600 metres/yards offshore, the island is accessible by ferry service, which runs hourly on week days, and every 2–3 hours at weekends between May and October. Boats leave from a jetty not far from the town's bus terminal. Once inside the fortress you will see the prison blocks and mock-ups of the grim cells.

KIZHI

Though certainly not accessible for a day trip, Kizhi is included here for its extraordinary wooden architecture, the finest in Europe. On an island in Lake Onega, **Kizhi ❽** is about 360 km (224 miles) to the northeast of St Petersburg. The nearest city is Petrozavodsk, capital of

the Republic of Karelia, which is 66 km (41 miles) from Kizhi.

In the 16th century, Kizhi was the administrative centre of this region, a land rich in timber, fur and foodstuffs. Though repeatedly invaded by Swedes, Poles and Lithuanians, Russia's victory in the Northern War brought peace, and gave rise to the development of more settlements made entirely of wood.

You can either take a cruise from St Petersburg, or take an overnight train via Petrozavodsk. From here you can catch a hydrofoil (June–Aug) or a boat that operates in the summer months, both of which take about an hour and a half. Beware of return times as you cannot stay on Kizhi, and there are no shops, so bring along your own food and drink.

Folk museum

In 1960 the **Open Air Museum of History, Architecture and Ethnography** (open June–Aug daily 8am–8pm, Sept–mid-Oct 9am–4pm, mid-Oct–mid-May 10am–3pm; 9am–4pm mid-May–end May; entrance charge; http://kizhi.karelia.ru) was created to

preserve the extraordinary buildings and folk culture of the area. Buildings dating from the 14–19th century were brought here from all over Karelia, making a museum-reserve of indigenous and reconstructed villages. The majority of buildings were constructed without nails.

When you enter the museum you will be assigned a guide who speaks either English, French or German. The entrance charge and guide are usually included in the cost if you have taken a cruise.

During the summer you'll see demonstrations of traditional crafts, shows at the Folklore Theatre and other local traditional activities such as bell ringing. In addition to the churches below, you can explore the reconstructed village nearby.

Church of the Transfiguration

Kizhi's main attraction is the 22-domed Church of the Transfiguration, standing 37 metres (120 ft) tall. Built entirely of wood in 1714 to celebrate the victory of the Russian Army in the Northern War, the church has succumbed to the elements over the centuries, and the interior is now supported by a metal cage and is off-limits to visitors while it is being restored.

It has no facade per se – the four side altars are attached to the central octagonal timber structure. To the altars, which correspond to the four points of the compass, five tiers of cupolas are "threaded" together. The cupolas vary in size, giving the church its harmonious proportions.

Legend attributes the construction of the church to a carpenter called Nestor who, the story goes, threw his axe into Lake Onega when he had finished with the words: "This church was built by the master Nestor. There never has been and never will be anything like it evermore."

He was right. Fifty years later the **Church of the Intercession** was built, its nine domes contrasting with and complementing the majestic, pyramidal Church of the Transfiguration. A **bell tower** erected in 1874 completes this well-proportioned ensemble. ❏

Map on page 198

TIP

Try to time your visit to Kizhi to coincide with a festival. The feast of the Church of the Transfiguration is on 19 August, while on 23 August you'll see folk dancing. Feasts are also held at Easter and other religious festivals. For more information, go to http://kizhi.karelia.ru

BELOW: exploring the park grounds.

RESTAURANTS

Podvorye, $$$
Filtrovskoye shosse 16, Pavlovsk
Tel: 466 8544
www.podvorye.ru
Large restaurant with great Russian food, a folk show in the evening and a mini-Russian village theme park. Mostly caters to large groups.

Russian House, $$$
Malaya ulitsa 3, Tsarskoe Selo
Tel: 466 8888
Classic Russian cuisine in a superb location close to the palace.

● ● ● ● ● ● ● ● ● ● ● ● ● ● ● ● ●

Price includes dinner and a glass of wine, excluding tip. **$$$$** *$80 and up,*
$$$ *$35–80,* **$$** *$15–35,* **$** *under $15.*

GULF OF FINLAND

The north coast of the Gulf of Finland was once hotly contested between the Swedish and Russian empires. Now hoteliers and property developers are competing for space in the locale of choice for Russia's extravagantly rich to build summer retreats

Few travellers to St Petersburg make their way to the north shore of the Gulf of Finland. It may lack the glittering tsarist palaces you find on the southern shore, but a visit to the north shore reveals a little known side to the city's leisure life – and one with a truly local character.

The north shore is officially called the "Resort District", and it is still within the St Petersburg city limits. Geographically, the area is part of the Karelian Isthmus, but don't confuse it with Russia's Republic of Karelia much farther to the north.

If the Gulf's south shore was the summer watering hole for the tsarist elite before 1917, the north shore is where today's wealthy Russians, as well as the not-so-wealthy intelligentsia, prefer to spend their summer weekends.

In the past few years, the city's fashionable young crowd has also taken to the Gulf, with the opening of several summer nightclubs and private beaches.

A brief history

For centuries, small Finnish fishing villages mostly populated the north shore of the Gulf, and even though the names of the larger towns have been "Russified", many of the smaller villages still bear Finnish names.

Up until the end of the 17th century, the Swedish empire controlled the area, but after Peter the Great's victory in the Northern War *(see page 20)*, it passed into Russian hands.

In 1812, Alexander I gave the Karelian Isthmus to the autonomous Grand Duchy of Finland, and thanks to its proximity to St Petersburg and the favourable trade relations with the tsarist regime, the

Map on page 198

LEFT: rowing along one of the area's inland lakes.
BELOW: Kronshtadt's impressive Naval Cathedral.

An example of soviet engineering on a grand scale, the Kronshtadt flood barrier keeps St Petersburg's low lying islands from the regular flooding they suffered in the city's beginning.

BELOW: interior of Repin's studio.

area became one of the most developed in Finland.

Today, if you drive along the Primorskoye Shosse, look for the small, fortified positions to your left as you leave Sestroretsk. These are the remnants of the Soviet border posts which stood here before 1939 when the USSR invaded Finland and annexed a large part of the country.

The north shore became a resort in the late 19th century and early 20th century, when St Petersburg's growing class of entrepreneurs and businessmen chose to spend their summers here since they were not part of the official government circles that summered on the south shore. A number of sanatoriums sprung up to offer spa treatments.

If you decide to explore along the Gulf of Finland, it is best to rent a car for the day *(see page 218 for contact information)* so that you can hit all the spots along the coast, but if your budget doesn't allow this, the commuter train runs from the Finland Station to any seaside town along the north shore of the Gulf,

but allow for a 25-minute walk to reach the beach from the station.

Kronshtadt

The resort district is easy to navigate by car since there is only one road from St Petersburg which leads there, the **Primorskoye shosse**. Shortly after you leave the city and pass the access ramp to the St Petersburg ring road, you will see a road on your left leading over the Gulf to the island of **Kotlin**, home to the city of **Kronshtadt** ❾.

The island can now be reached by driving across the **flood protection barrier**, a large earthen dam that ranks as one of the grandest engineering projects in Europe and stretches between the north and south ends of the Gulf of Finland. Construction began in the early 1980s and it is scheduled to be completed in 2010.

Founded by Peter the Great in 1704 as a naval fort to defend St Petersburg from attack by sea, Kronshtadt later served as St Petersburg's main commercial port since large trading ships could not navigate the shallow waters leading to the city.

Before the Bolshevik Revolution it was also the headquarters of the Russian Imperial Navy, and even in Soviet times it was an important naval base and closed to foreigners. The city only opened to outsiders in 1996, and it can now be visited freely.

The **Naval Cathedral** on Anchor Square is the town's main attraction. This neo-byzantine church has been serving the sailing community since 1913 and now houses the **Central Naval Museum** (open Wed–Sun 11am–5pm, entrance charge) which documents the famous sailors' mutiny against Soviet rule in 1921, known as the Kronshtadt Rebellion. Historians say this was a major factor in con-

vincing Lenin that the Russian people would not easily accept Soviet socialism. The result was the enactment of the New Economic Policy (NEP) that allowed for a brief return to capitalism.

Kronshtadt also has a pleasant park. **Petrovsky Park** just southwest of the cathedral makes a good place for a stroll and there's a chance that you'll see warships or submarines in the harbour. If you do, don't take pictures or your camera may be confiscated.

Dachas and mansions

Back on the mainland drive through **Sestroretsk**. During the Soviet period, this town and several of the surrounding villages were famed for dachas (summer cottages) belonging to the Communist Party elite and the intelligentsia, most of whom were in silent opposition to the regime.

As one leaves Sestroretsk, the Shosse forks into the **Nizhny Primorsky shosse**, which runs along the water, and the **Verkhny Primorsky shosse**, which runs parallel to the water about a kilometer (half a mile) inland.

Once you get off either of these main roads, however, travelling is extremely difficult unless you have a guide because rarely is a street sign to be seen, and most roads are narrow and made of dirt.

This lack of development, however, is what gives the area its charm, and you feel transported back into a simpler, more tranquil era, though that is all changing. Since 2000, the area's many pre-1917 and pre-World War II country dachas with their distinctive wooden ornamentation – many of these state protected buildings – have suspiciously burned down as the new rich covet the valuable land on which they can build huge modern mansions.

Repino

The **Muzey Repina** (Repin Museum, Primorskoye shosse, 411; open Wed–Sun 10.30am–5pm, June–Aug; 10.30am–4pm, Sep–May; tel: 432 0834) is situated in **Repino ⑩** – about 50 km (31

Map on page 198

Peter the Great surveys Kronshtadt from Petrovsky Park.

BELOW: Ilya Repin's country estate.

miles) from St Petersburg. The town is named in honour of one of Russia's most famous painters, Ilya Repin *(see page 140)*.

While few foreigners have heard of Repin (1844–1930), Russians nearly deify him. He was a member of the first Russian counter-culture art movement, the Wanderers *(Peredvizhniki)*, in the second half of the 19th century.

Their style eventually came to resemble the French Impressionists. The *Peredvizhniki* rebelled against the Classicism reigning at the St Petersburg Academy of Arts as they strove to create a more realistic art close to the masses.

While most of Repin's most famous artworks hang in the Russian Museum *(see pages 137–43)*, nearly 100 pieces can be found in the Repino museum, where the painter spent the last 30 years of his prolific life. His residence had become a place of pilgrimage for leading Russian cultural figures of his day, including poet Sergei Yesenin, modernist Vladimir Mayakovsky, singer Fyodor Shaliapin, and renowned scientist Ivan Pavlov *(see page 158)*.

The last resorts

The next town down is **Komarovo**, in whose cemetery lies the poet Anna Akhmatova, and the Russian literature professor, Dmitri Likhachev (1906–99), whose opposition to the Soviet regime made him a great spiritual figure and earned him the title, the conscience of Russia. The famous St Petersburg avant-garde underground composer, Sergei Kuryokhin (1954–96), is also buried here.

The last town in the Resort District is **Zelenogorsk**, once known by its Finnish name, Terijoki, before the Soviets conquered the region in 1939. Zelenogorsk boosts a beautiful 19th century Russian Orthodox church built in the old Russian style, and its fine beaches and outdoor cafes attract thousands in the summer.

Bus 213 from metro Chernaya Rechka drops you near the beach of several towns along the coast from St Petersburg to Zelenogorsk, but traffic sometimes makes it slow going.

BELOW: a quiet sunset on the Gulf.

On the beach

There is no point in going to the Gulf if you don't go to one of its beaches. Unfortunately the weather on the Gulf of Finland – even in the hottest of summers – can be cool, and there are few days warm enough to swim. But if the weather permits, the Gulf is famous for its shallow depth and you can walk a long way out into the sea.

Locals often complain about the cleanliness of the water, but it doesn't keep them from taking a dip. The lakes a little further inland are very much worth exploring, and the water there is often pristine and the beaches more secluded.

At the very least a walk on the beaches of the Gulf, especially towards evening, is always romantic. Some places, such as the Golden Beach complex in the seaside town of Zelenogorsk, rent windsurfing gear, jet-skis, and other equipment for fun in the water.

One of the best seaside locations, however, is the Resort District's first private beach, **High Dive**, in **Komarovo**. It has a small amusement park for children, several cafes, and boat and jet ski rentals. The finest feature, however, is its reputation as the cleanest beach on the Gulf.

The younger crowd might want to visit several of the nightclubs and party scenes springing up on the beach.

Next to High Dive in Komarovo is the **Jet Set Beach**, which serves as the summer outdoor party ranch of the trendy city nightclub of the same name.

Such recreational places generally close during the winter and in the past some have changed location, so it's prudent to check the local listings for the most up-to-date information on how to reach them in the summer months.

The holiday season on the Gulf usually runs from the end of May to early September. The weather is not so much cold as it is windy and damp, and even on a summer day you should be careful and always have a sweatshirt on hand because the weather changes from hour to hour, and powerful storms tend to appear quickly, and leave just as unexpectedly. ❑

Map on page 198

HEALTH SPAS, RESORTS & RESTAURANTS

The Old Mill
Solnechnoe Village
2nd Borovaya Ulitsa, 16
Tel: 432 9148
Email: old_mill@smtp.ru
www.oldmillvip.spb.ru
This health spa provides a wide range of services, including traditional Russian baths and Finnish saunas, as well as honey massages. There are three fine restaurants on its premises to take care of your appetite.

Repino Sanatorium
Repino Village
Primorskoye Shosse, 394
Tel: 380 2130
Email: repino@mail.ru
www.repino.ru
This health spa provides a wide range of bath treatments, as well as massage.

Dunes
Zelenorgorsk
Primorskoye Shosse, 38th Kilometre
Tel: 434 0297

Email: dunes@golf.spb.ru
www.golf.spb.ru
Dunes is the most prominent resort and health spa on the Gulf; it owes this status to the fact that besides a wide range of treatments and baths, it has the only professional golf course in the region. Walks in its extensive pine forest are often prescribed for those suffering from respiratory ailments.

Shalyapin Restaurant and Nightclub
Repino Village
Nagornaya Ulitsa, 1
(at the corner of Upper Primorskoye Shosse)
Tel: 432 0775
Shalyapin is one of the best places to eat in the Resort District, with a modern and comfortable interior where Russian classics are served. There is also a selection of international cuisine for those with less sense of adventure. Since it's about a kilometre (half a mile) from the beach, prices are more reasonable and, handily it's directly across from the Repino train station.

T RANSPORT

GETTING THERE AND GETTING AROUND

GETTING THERE

By Air

International airlines connect St Petersburg directly with 16 European countries. There are daily flights from London with British Airways, and two weekly flights with Aeroflot. It is also possible to fly daily with Scandinavian Airlines via Stockholm, or five times a week with Austrian Airlines via Vienna. There is a regular Aeroflot service between Moscow and St Petersburg. There are no direct flights from the US, but numerous connections are available via Europe.

International flights arrive at the Pulkovo 2 Airport, which is 17 km (10½ miles) from the city centre. Pulkovo 2 is just 10 minutes by bus from the domestic airport, Pulkovo 1. A shuttle-bus service to the city centre is available. The St Petersburg Air Terminal is at Nevsky prospekt 7/9; buses for the airports leave from the nearby bus stop at Kirpichny pereulok 3.

Aeroflot operates internal flights linking St Petersburg with 105 cities in the Commonwealth of Independent States (CIS – a loose federation of ex-Soviet states). Fares within the CIS are low, though flights have to be

booked far in advance since there is a far greater demand than capacity. Check-in at Aeroflot counters starts three hours and ends 40 minutes before departure.

By Rail

Within the European part of Russia, railways are the most important means of passenger transport. Railways connect St Petersburg with the largest CIS cities (Moscow, Kiev, Minsk) and Western European capitals. If you can spare the time you can travel in a comfortable first-class sleeping car, the pride of the Russian Railways. From Central Europe the train takes two days to reach St Petersburg, with a change of gauge at the junction with the railway system of the CIS. The Helsinki–St Petersburg route (departure 1pm, arrival 9pm) is the most popular rail route between the West and the CIS.

Travelling time from Berlin: 33 hrs; Paris: 48 hrs; Warsaw: 22 hrs.

If you want to travel within Russia by train, there are transcontinental rail routes, such as those from Moscow to Vladivostok and from Moscow to Beijing, China. They demand an adventurous spirit and a week spent in the train contemplating the endless Siberian and Transsiberian (Baikal) landscapes. Food for the

trip should be taken along since station buffet food often does little to cheer up weary travellers.

St Petersburg has six large stations: Baltic Station with trains to the southern suburbs and Peterhof; Finland Station with trains to Vyborg and Finland; Moscow Station, with trains to Moscow, the northeast and the south of Russia; Vitebsk Station with trains to the Ukraine, Belorussia and Riga, and to Pushkin and Pavlovsk; and Ladoga Station, the most modern in Russia, built for the city's 2003 anniversary, and which services cities to the north and east.
Railway terminal information, tel: 055.

By Car

If you intend to visit St Petersburg by car you should first get in contact with a travel agency as they have worked out a number of routes through the European part of Russia which can easily be negotiated with your own vehicle. The ideal route to St Petersburg is via Helsinki, which can be reached comfortably by car ferry.

If you intend to continue within European Russia you can drive to Moscow, the Caucasus and the Black Sea, ferrying the car across to Yalta or Odessa and crossing the Ukraine to Slovakia or Poland.

AIRLINES

**Airline Offices in
St Petersburg:**
Aeroflot: ulitsa Kazanskaya, 5
Tel: 327 3872
British Airways: Malaya
Konyushennaya ulitsa, 1/3a
Tel: 380 0626
Delta Airlines: Bolshaya
Morskaya, 36
Tel: 571 5819
Finnair: Malaya Konyushennaya 1/3a
Tel: 303 9898
KLM: Malaya Morskaya
ulitsa, 23
Tel: 346 6868
Lufthansa: Nevsky
prospekt, 32
Tel: 320 1000*

CIS Aeroflot Offices:
Kiev: Sak saganskovo
ulitsa, 112a
Tel: +380 44 241 9998
Minsk: Kupaly St, 25
Tel: +375 17 227 2887
Moscow: Eniseiskyaya
ulitsa, 19
Tel: +495 223 5555
Tbilisi: Gamsakh Urdia
prospekt sect 1, bldng 6a
Tel: 99532 943896

**Aeroflot's
International Offices:**
London: 70 Piccadilly
Tel: 020-7355 2233
New York: 10 Rockefeller
Plaza 1015
Tel: 212-944 2300

Details for this and other routes
(across the Baltic States, Belarus,
etc) can be found in the book
*Motorists' Guide to the Soviet
Union*, Pergamon Publishers,
Oxford. It gives details about petrol
stations, repair shops, overnight
stops and emergency procedures.
 Since crossing the border into
Turkey is now possible, you can
also cross via Anatolia. Whether
this route remains open, however,
depends on the changing political
conditions in the Caucasus.
 Sovinterautoservice are the

specialists for car travel in the CIS.
They solve nearly every problem a
foreigner is likely to experience on
Russian roads. Write or phone for
information to Simferopolskoe
shosse, 3, Moscow, tel: 495 411
5433.
 During the past few years
marked changes have taken place
in the quality of services along
Russian roads. St Petersburg now
has new service and repair stations for non-Russian cars. But
you should still be cautious of the
state of the roads. Leaving the
main routes might get you into
some unexpected adventures. It
is now possible to do this at your
own risk, but not necessarily
advisable as accommodation and
fuel supplies are few and far
between. We recommend that you
organise your journey through a
recognised travel agency.
 Entry points to the CIS are:
Brusnichnoe and Torfyanovka from
Finland; Brest and Shegini from
Poland; Chop when coming from
Czech and Slovak rebublics and
Hungary; and Porubnoe and
Leusheny from Romania. You can
ship your car directly to St Peters
burg. Below are the main road
routes to St Petersburg.
From Finland: Torfyanovka–
Vyborg–St Petersburg.
From Western Europe: Brest–
Minsk–Smolensk–Moscow and
Chop–Uzhgorod–Lvov–Kiev–Orel–
Moscow–St Petersburg.

By Cruise Liner and Ferry

St Petersburg can be reached by
cruise liners and ferries from
London, Bremerhaven, Helsinki,
Copenhagen, Gothenburg, Stockholm, Montreal and New York.
Travel agencies will provide
detailed information about sea
routes, schedules and bookings.
 The sea terminal is on Vasilievsky island, as well as on the
English Embankment. There is a
separate port for river transport:
Rechnoy Vokzal, Obukhovskoy
Oborony prospekt, 195, tel: 262
1318 or 262 5511.

GETTING AROUND

From the Airport

If no one can meet you at the
airport, there are cheap options
available to the price-gouging
taxi drivers. By law, a ride to the
city from the airport should not
cost more than US$30. Many
unwitting foreigners end up paying anywhere from US$50 to
$100. If you wish to avoid taxis
altogether, there are a number of
public buses which run frequently just outside the terminal.
Take any one of these for about
10 minutes to the nearest metro
stop, Moskovsky prospekt, and
from there you can continue on
by metro.

Orientation

For a city consisting of islands,
St Petersburg is quite easy to
navigate. Most of the activities
and sights lie along the river
banks. The exception to this is
Nevsky prospekt, which cuts a
swathe from the embankments
to the Alexander Nevsky
Monastery. Moskovsky vokzal,
with trains to Moscow, is found
on Nevsky prospekt.

Taxis

If you're looking to save money and feel confident negotiating in Russian or sign language, a *chastnik*, or private car, is the best deal. Most Russians travel this way, and if you're travelling during the day and in the centre, it is safe and sometimes even interesting should your driver be an aspiring poet or an unemployed nuclear scientist trying to make ends meet. At night and during long trips beyond the city centre, however, most people think twice about whom they hitch a ride from. But if money is not a problem, and one feels uncomfortable doing as the Russians do, there are a number of taxi services to choose from.

Taxi Blues: Tel: 271 8888
Petersburg Taxi: Tel: 068
www.taxi068.spb.ru
Konnyushenny: Konnyushennaya ploshchad, 2, tel: 312 0022; open 24 hours.

Car Hire

Official car-hire agencies can be quite expensive, and many travellers prefer not to drive in a foreign city. Hiring a private car and driver is the best way to get around with the least amount of hassle. Many tourists choose this option.

If you have friends or acquaintances in town, ask them to find a driver; a fee of about US$50–$70 a day is more than enough.

Hertz: Pulkovo 2 Airport
Tel: 326 4505
Malaya Morskaya ulitsa, 23
Tel: 326 4505
Europ Car: Mayakovskaya ulitsa, 3a
Tel: 703 7733
Rolf: Vitebsky prospekt, 17
Tel: 320 0020

Petrol and Parking

In St Petersburg, service stations are not common in the city centre, but are mostly located towards the outskirts. They are all self-service.

Parking is free where there is no prohibiting sign. Protected parking is available at Isaakiyevskaya ploshchad, next to the Astoria Hotel, and at the city's only public parking centre, just off the River Moika on Volynsky pereulok.

Rules Of The Road

Russia is a signatory to the International Traffic Convention. Rules of the road and road signs correspond in general to international standards. The basic rules,

however, are worth mentioning.
● Traffic drives on the right, and when you come to an intersection without a traffic light, the car to the right has the priority.
● It is prohibited to drive a car after consuming even the smallest amount of alcohol. If the driver shows a positive alcohol test, the consequences may be very serious. It is also prohibited to drive a car under the effect of drugs or strong medicines.
● Drivers must have an international driving licence and documents verifying their right to drive the car. These papers must be in Russian and are issued by the Russian Auto Inspection (GIBDD).
● Vehicles must carry the national registration code. All must have a national licence plate.
● Using the horn is prohibited in city limits except in emergencies.
● The speed limit in populated areas (marked by blue-coloured signs indicating "town") is 60 kph (37 mph); on most arterial roads the limit is 90 kph (55 mph). On motorways different limits apply and are shown on road signs.
● You can insure your car in Russia through Ingosstrakh, the state-owned insurance company, or any other private insurer.

The Metro

The most convenient local transport is St Petersburg's metro. Construction started before World War II and was completed in 1955. All the major hotels have metro stations marked "M" nearby.

BRIDGE CLOSING TIMES

One of St Petersburg's most original and beautiful sights is the raising of the bridges. In the early hours of the morning the bridges are raised to let boat traffic through. You should schedule your night life around the bridges if you don't wish to be stuck in one part of town. If you are, and need to cross the river, the city

has allowed Dvortsovy Bridge to open for about 30 minutes to let road traffic pass. The sight of the 3am bumper-to-bumper traffic jam of cars trying to cross the bridge is also something to see. Bridge closing hours are:
Lt Schmidt 1.40–4.55am
Liteyny 1.50–4.40am
Troitsky 1.50–4.50am

Dvortsovy 1.35–2.55am and then again from 3.15–4.50am
Okhitinsky Bolshoy 2–5am
Volodarsky 2–3.45am and then again 4.15–5.45am
Volodarsky 2.00–3.45 and 4.15–5.45
Birzhevoy 2.10–4.50am
Tuchkov 2–2.55am and then again 3.35–4.45am

On 15 November 1955, the first metro line was opened from Uprising Square (now ploshchad Vosstaniya) to Avtovo, covering some 11 km (7 miles). Now the lines total 60 km (38 miles), and trains run at 40 kph (25 mph); during the rush hours, trains arrive every 2 minutes.

The signs and underground maps with lighted routes make it possible to find the right direction quickly, as long as you read Cyrillic. The cost of a one-way ticket is 12 rubles, or a little more than 50 US cents/24 British pence. Tokens are bought at the ticket office and fed into the automatic barriers. You can buy a range of metro cards for various time periods, which offer a slight saving. The metro runs from 5.45 to 12.30am.

There are four lines in operation: the Moskovsko–Petrogradskaya liniya, the Kirovsko– Vyborgskaya liniya, the Nevsko– Vasileostovskaya liniya and the Pravoberezhnaya liniya.

The stations were built in many architectural styles. Some of the most impressive are: Avtovo, Kirovsky Zavod, Narvskaya, Baltiskaya, ploshchad Vosstaniya and ploshchad Muzhestva on the Kirovsko-Vyborgskaya liniya.

Nevsky prospekt and Petrogradskaya are impressive for their use of space. The Nevsko-Vasileostrovskaya liniya brings you from the Pribaltiyskaya Hotel to Nevsky prospekt. At Gostiny Dvor station there is no surface station; the exits lead directly into the department store. At ploshchad Alexandra Nevskovo the exit leads into the Moskva Hotel.

The transfer stations, where you can change from one line to another, are Gostiny Dvor, ploshchad Vosstaniya, Tekhnologichesky Institut, Sadovaya/ Sennaya ploshchad, Vladimirskaya/ Dostoyevskaya and ploshchad Alexandra Nevskovo.

By Bus, Tram & Minibus

Bus and **tram** services run from 5.30am–midnight. Prices are about 12 rubles, or 50 US cents.

Minibuses follow a specific route but can be flagged down at any point along it; they are not usually overcrowded like buses or trams so are more comfortable. Services run every 10–20 minutes and you buy your ticket on board.

By Boat

From May to October it is possible to view the city from a steamer on the Neva (departure point: Senate's Square, the Winter Palace or the Embankment by the Summer Garden) or take a river trip to Peterhof (departure point: Palace naberezhnaya at the Hermitage). This is a highly recommended way to pass the time, especially in the evening during the White Nights *(see pages 227)*. Many groups throw parties on these ships.

On Foot

Anyone lucky enough to be in St Petersburg for the White Nights *(see page 227)* should walk from

- *ulitsa (Ul.)* = street
- *ploshchad (Pl.)* = square
- *pereulok (Per.)* = lane, small street
- *naberezhnaya (Nab.)* = embankment
- *most* = bridge
- *ostrov* = island
- *Vasilievsky ostrov* = Vasilievsky island
- *Petrogradskaya Storona* = Petrograd side

Dvortsovaya ploshchad (Palace Square) along Millionnaya ulitsa (Millionaire's Street) to Zimnyaya kanavka (Winter Canal), then left to Dvortsovaya Naberezhnaya (Palace Embankment), along to Dvortsovy most (Palace Bridge) and across the Neva to Birzhevaya ploshchad (Stock Exchange Square) on the Strelka spit.

Thanks to the unique lighting provided by the White Nights, from this spot, the breathtaking view over one of the most beautiful parts of the city is doubly impressive.

Another bonus of walking is that it gives visitors an opportunity to take in the detail of the city's outstanding architecture.

A CCOMMODATION

HOTEL ROOMS, HOMESTAYS, YOUTH HOSTELS AND CAMPSITES

CHOOSING A HOTEL

Ten years ago, an independent traveller to St Petersburg had two options: a ridiculously priced luxury hotel or the ludicrously dismal hotels which served travelling Russian businessmen. The city's 300th anniversary, however, stimulated a boom in hotel construction, especially of mini-hotels, small guest-houses and B&Bs. While the majority of visitors to St Petersburg

HOMESTAYS

Interchange, a UK-based tour company specialising in travel to Central and Eastern Europe, offers the opportunity to stay with English-speaking Russian families in St Petersburg. You are provided with your own room, breakfast and dinner and use of shared family facilities. Home stays are a wonderful opportunity to experience Russian domesticity and home cooking. For more details, contact: Interchange, Interchange House, 27 Stafford Road, Croydon, Surrey CR0 4NG, United Kingdom. Tel: 020 8681 3612; email: interchange@interchange.uk.com

have their accommodation pre-arranged as part of a package tour, the increasing number of options available means that more visitors are booking their hotels direct.

The Astoria and the Grand Hotel Europe are the hotels of choice for those on an unlimited budget. One notch down the luxury scale, the four-star Angleterre and three-star Hotel Dostoyevsky are good, central choices.

Mini-hotels are a welcome addition to the accommodation scene. They have filled the gap in the market for Western tourists looking for clean but affordable rooms. These typically small establishments fall somewhere between US chain-style hotels and European pensions. They offer all the basics you need: clean rooms, simple breakfasts and friendly staff (by Russian standards). If you're lucky, the building or location will have a charm of its own.

For something clean and pleasant, but with an eye on budget, the best bet is the American-owned and operated B&B chain, Rand House, and its neighbouring competitor, Comfort Hotel.

The cheapest option of all is to stay at one of the city's youth hostels or campsites. These are listed below. Our selection of the best hotels from five-star to B&B, arranged by district, is listed on the following pages.

Youth Hostels

Sleep Cheap
Mokhovaya ulitsa, 18/32
Tel: 715 1304
Email: hostel@sleepcheap.spb.ru
www.sleepcheap.spb.ru
This hostel is the best buy for the budget traveller. Located in the heart of the historic centre near the Fontanka River and the Summer Gardens, it offers clean and recently renovated dorm rooms. A small breakfast is included.

St Petersburg International Youth Hostel
3rd Sovietskaya ulitsa, 28
Tel: 329-8018; Fax: 329-8019
E-mail: ryh@rh.ru; www.ryh.ru
Located in a historic working-class neighbourhood not far from the Moscow train station, this American-owned hostel offers single-sex dorms in a 19th-century building. Accommodation is basic but clean.

Campsites

Retur Motel-Camping
Bolshaya Kupalnaya ulitsa, 28, Sestroretsk
Tel: 437-7533; www.retur.ru
Located in a wood near Sestroretsk on the Gulf of Finland, this peaceful campsite is a good summer option. Facilities include swimming pool, sauna, tennis courts and horse-riding. It also has chalets for rent.

AROUND THE HERMITAGE

FIVE-STAR

Astoria Hotel $$$$
Bolshaya Morskaya ulitsa, 39
Tel: 494 5757
Fax: 494 5059
E-mail: reserve@astoria.spb.ru
www.roccofortehotels.com
Overlooking St Isaac's Square, the elegant Astoria is one of the best and most central places to stay in St Petersburg. The historic hotel opened its doors in December 1912, and much of the original Art Nouveau styling remains. The rooms have been refurbished and many have views over the square and St Isaac's Cathedral. Service can be brusque. Most tourist sites and theatres are within walking distance. The Davidov restaurant serves good Russian cuisine.

Renaissance
St Petersburg
Baltic Hotel $$$$
Pochtamskaya ulitsa, 4
Tel: 380-4000
Fax: 380-4001

Email: Petersburg.info@renaissancehotels.com
www.marriot.com/ledbr
Located in the heart of St Petersburg directly across from St Isaac's Cathedral, this hotel is managed by the Marriot chain. It has over 100 rooms and a 24-hour business centre. The top floor rooms offer good views of the city centre, but they were illegally built, violating city zoning laws that ban construction higher than neighbouring buildings.

FOUR-STAR

Alexander House $$$
Krukov Kanal naberezhnaya, 27
Tel: 334 3540
E-mail: info@a-house.ru
www.a-house.ru
Close to the Mariinsky Theatre, Alexander House has some of the best luxury apartments in the city, which are relatively well priced. Rooms are spacious with high ceilings, and the interior of each is uniquely decorated according to a major international style. Apartments sleep up to three, and there is a bridal suite. Well suited for guests on an extended visit.

Angleterre Hotel $$$
Malaya Morskaya ulitsa, 24
Tel: 494 5666
Fax. 494 5125
E-mail: reservations@angleterrehotel.spb.ru
www.angleterrehotel.com
Cheaper sister hotel to the Astoria next door. The Angleterre has excellent business services, a fitness centre and a pool, as well as a casino and nightclub on the ground floor. Since it shares the same prime St Isaac's Square location, the same views and the same facilities as the Astoria, many travellers have come to realise that the Angletere, though more modern than its historic neighbour, is better value for money.

Matisov Domik $$
Naberezhnaya Reki Pryazhky, 3/1
Tel: 495 1439 or 495 0242
Fax: 495 2419
Email: matisov@lek.ru
www.matisov.com
Opened in 1993, this is one of St Petersburg's first budget hotels. It offers modern, clean rooms, some of which have a good view onto the canal. The downside is its location on a small island at the edge of

the city's historic centre. The Marinsky Iheatre is about a 15-minute walk, but most other places of interest are a bus- or car-ride away.

MINI-HOTELS

Comfort Hotel $
Bolshaya Morskaya ulitsa, 25
Tel: 314-6523
E-mail: info@comfort-hotel.spb.ru
www.comfort hotcl.spb.ru
The price and central location of this mini-hotel, makes it a much sought after place to stay. Within walking distance of the Hermitage, St Isaac's and other key sights around Nevsky Prospekt. Rooms are well furnished and comfortable.

Pushka Inn $
Reki Moika naberezhnaya, 14
Tel/fax: 312-0913
E-mail: pushka@pushkainn.ru
www.pushkainn.ru

PRICE CATEGORIES

Price categories are for a double room without breakfast:
$ = $40–$79
$$ = $80–$199
$$$ = $200–$259
$$$$ = more than $260

BELOW: Davidov restaurant, Astoria hotel.

This hotel occupies an 18th-century building in one of the most prestigious and picturesque bends in the Moika Canal – a stone's throw from the Hermitage and Palace Square, and near Pushkin's apartment. Rooms are elegant and do justice to the enchanting allure of old St Petersburg. Facilities include satellite TV and internet access. On the ground floor below is one of the city's most popular watering holes – the Pushka Inn.

Rand House $
Bolshaya Morskaya ulitsa, 25
Flat 17 (3rd floor)
Tel: 314 6333

Grivtsova pereulok, 11
Flat 83 (4th floor)
Tel: 310 7005
Malaya Morskaya ulitsa, 7 flat 1
Tel: 570 4597
Sadovaya ulitsa, 11, Flat 50
(3rd floor)
Tel: 315 1037
www.randhouse.ru
American-owned and managed, this chain of B&Bs offers comfort-able and modern rooms in historic city centre buildings. The Grivtsova pereulok location is more for budget travellers, while the Admiral-teyskaya naberezhnaya provides the high standards that are preferred by Western business travellers.

AROUND NEVSKY PROSPEKT

FIVE-STAR

Corinthia Nevskij Palace Hotel $$$$
Nevsky prospekt, 57
Tel: 380 2001
Fax: 380 1937
E-mail: reservation@corinthia.ru
www.corinthia.ru
Commonly called the Nevsky Palace, this is the preferred accommodation for upscale business travellers, and it does an excellent job of providing conference services. Its location at the far end of Nevsky prospekt, means major sites are a bit of a walk and in many cases a bus- or car-ride away. There's a wonderful Sunday brunch at the Imperial restaurant, while the rooftop Landskrona is ranked as one of the best places to eat in the city with great views.

Grand Hotel Europe $$$$
Mikhailovskaya ulitsa, 1/7
Tel: 329 6000; Fax: 329 6001
E-mail: res@grandhoteleurope.com
www.grandhoteleurope.com
Commonly referred to as the "Europa" by locals, this was Russia's first five-star

hotel in the post-Soviet period, and continues to attract the city's most illustrious visitors, which have included Bill Clinton and Paul McCartney. The rooms are spacious and finely decorated with period furniture. The hotel offers fine dining with seven restaurants to choose from, including Chinese, Italian, European and Russian cuisines.

Radisson SAS Royal Hotel $$$$
Nevsky prospekt, 49
Tel: 322 5000
Fax: 322 5002
E-mail: reservations.led@radissonsas.com
www.radissonsas.com
The 18th-century building was entirely gutted and renovated several years ago, and today the Radisson offers all mod cons. The rooms are on the small side and service is not up to the standard you would expect from a five-star hotel, but the atmosphere is lively. The ground-floor Cannelle bar and café overlooking busy Nevsky prospekt is one of the best places in the city to have a drink and watch the world go by.

FOUR-STAR

Grand Hotel Emerald $$$
Suvorovsky prospekt, 18
Tel: 740 5000
Fax: 740 5006
Email: reservation@grandhotelemerald.com
www.grandhotelemerald.com
Built in 2003, this is one of St Petersburg's most modern hotels, and it is working hard to prove its worth. Rooms are spacious and comfortable. The sleek and steely modern exterior contrasts with the more distinguished classical interior, inspired by imperial palace architecture. It has a health spa that includes a Russian bath and a Turkish sauna. While it is close to City Hall, the main tourist destinations are further than walking distance.

THREE-STAR

Arbat Nord Hotel $$
Artilleriiskaya ulitsa, 4
Tel: 703 1899
Fax: 703 1898
Email: info@arbat-nord.ru
www.arbat-nord.ru

Located in a district that is home to many foreign consulates, this hotel offers good modern accommodation at a reasonable price. Staff are attentive, and there is a nice restaurant on the ground floor. Rooms offer wireless internet access and satellite TV. The Letny Sad (Summer Garden) and Nevsky prospekt are a short walk away.

Helvetia Hotel Suites $$
Marata ulitsa, 11
Tel: 326 5353
Fax: 326 2009
Email: info@helvetia-suites.ru
www.helvetia-suites.ru
This quiet and private apartment hotel is located in a courtyard just next to the Swiss Embassy, so you can feel safe in the knowledge that security is strict. Apartments are tastefully decorated and

ABOVE: The historic Astoria Hotel on St Isaac's Square.

serviced, and overall it is considered one of the best value-for-money establishments in town. The neighbouring area also has a number of good restaurants, and Nevsky prospekt is a short walk away.

Hotel Dostoyevsky $$
Vladimirsky prospekt, 19
Tel: 331-3200
Fax: 331-3201
E-mail: info@dostoevsky-hotel.ru
www.dostoevsky-hotel.ru
The main attractions of the city's newest hotel are its fabulous view of St Vladimir Cathedral, one of the most beautiful churches in St Petersburg, and the friendly and attentive staff who make you feel very welcome. The hotel occupies the top three floors of the building. The lower floors are taken up by a shopping arcade which has a

good choice of shops (including a late night supermarket where you can buy bottled water) restaurants and cafés. Facilities include a fitness club, sauna, and nightclub.

Hotel Moskva $$
Alexandra Nevskovo ploshchad, 2
Tel: 274-0022
Fax: 274-2130
E-mail: servis@hotel-moscow.ru
www.hotel-moscow.ru
Just across from the soaring domes and spires of the Alexander Nevsky Lavra, this Soviet-era hotel stands in stark contrast. It is located at the very end of Nevsky prospekt, and overlooks the Neva on its north side. Rooms vary; some are modern and comfortable, while others retain a somewhat spartan Soviet air. Popular with groups.

Rachmaninov Hotel $$
Kazanskaya ulitsa, 5
Tel: 571-7618
www.kazansky5.com
A small, but lovely upscale hotel in the very heart of the city, just behind the Kazansky sobor (Kazan Cathedral). Partly furnished with genuine antique furniture, it exudes the atmosphere of old St Petersburg. The hotel is family-run and you are made to feel very much at home. The entrance is on the third floor, however, and there is no lift. Rooms also tend to be on the small side, and two people sharing a standard room may feel cramped.

Oktyabrysky Hotel $$
Ligovsky prospekt, 10
Tel: 578-1515
Fax: 315-7501
E-mail: reservation@oktober.spb.ru
www.oktober-hotel.spb.ru

Built in the mid-19th century, this hotel, with its large windows and high ceilings, retains the airy charm of a by-gone era. In the 1860s, Imam Shamil, the legendary Chechen warlord, was held under house arrest here while the tsarist government decided his fate. Considered a luxury hotel in tsarist times, today it is comfortable but could not be considered upscale. Situated on Vosstaniya ploshchad across from Moskovsky vokzal

PRICE CATEGORIES

Price categories are for a double room without breakfast:
$ = $40–$79
$$ = $80–$199
$$$ = $200–$259
$$$$ = more than $260

ABOVE: many hotels have their own souvenir shops.

(Moscow Station), it's in a good position for those arriving by train from Moscow.

Rus $$
Artilleriiskaya ulitsa, 1
Tel: 273 4683
Fax: 579 3600

Email: admin@hotelruss.spb.ru
www.hotelruss.spb.ru
The architecture of this Soviet-era hotel clashes with the surrounding 19th-century facades, but rooms are decent. Service, however, leaves much to be desired. Most travellers tend to be businessmen from provincial Russian cities and other republics of the former Soviet Unions.

MINI-HOTELS

Five Corners Hotel $
Zagorodny prospekt, 13
Tel or Fax: 380 8181
Email: booking@5ugol.ru
www.5ugol.ru
This mini-hotel is located on the second and third floors above one of the city centre's most famous landmark intersections. Rooms are well designed, comfortable and clean. The

staff are very helpful, and the hotel offers a 24-hour room service, for hot drinks and snacks (but not full meals). The entrance is next to an electronics store on Zagorodny prospekt.

Korona Guest Centre $
Malaya Konnyushennaya Ulitsa, 7
Tel: 571 0086
Fax: 314 3865
E-mail: korona-spb@peterlink.ru
www.korona-spb.com
This hotel's main advantage is its location on one of the city centre's few pedestrianised streets, and a quiet one at that. Rooms are nicely furnished and the hotel offers a range of services usually reserved for the more upscale hotels, such as satellite TV, heated floors, safe, internet access, and free tea around the clock.

PETROGRAD SIDE

THREE-STAR

Eurasia Hotel $$
Gatchinskaya ulitsa, 5
Tel: 498 0800
Fax: 230 4432
E-mail: eurasia@eurasia-hotel.ru
www.eurasia-hotel.ru
This hotel, occupying an early 20th-century building in the backstreets of the Petrograd Side, is one of the city's few European-style inns. It is a little far from the sites, but conveniently situated for shopping, being just off the Bolshoy prospekt – the dis-

trict's main street for fashionable boutiques and cafés. It has a choice of 18 newly refurbished rooms. Breakfast is included and the service is very friendly.

Hotel St Petersburg $$
Pirogovskaya naberezhnaya, 5/2
Tel: 380 1919
Fax: 380 1920
E-mail: reservation@hotel-spb.ru
www.hotel-spb.ru
While this dreary Soviet structure is the city centre's worst eyesore, it has one of the best views onto the Neva River and the *Aurora*

battleship. It offers both modernised and non-modernised rooms, but the service leaves much to be desired. Its location across the river from the centre makes getting around difficult, and you are dependent on the exorbitant hotel taxis or your own hired car.

Hotel Regina $$
Podrezova ulitsa, 21
Tel: 237 1653
Fax: 230 3565
E-mail: regina@eurasia-hotels.ru
http://regina.eurasia-hotel.ru
Only five minutes from the metro station, Regina is a bargain for

those on a budget. There are 28 rooms of varying sizes, but all have been refurbished and offer satellite TV and telephones. The hotel occupies the whole building, with underground parking and proper security.

FURTHER AFIELD

GULF OF FINLAND

Baltic Star Hotel $$$
Beriozovaya alley, 3 Strelna
Tel: 438 5700; Fax: 438 5888
E-mail: info@balticstarhotel.ru
www.balticstar-hotel.ru
The Baltic Star is the best option for travellers wishing to get away from the noise and pollution of the busy city centre. It is located on the Gulf of Finland in the magnificent grounds of the recently renovated Konstantin Palace, an official residence of the Russian government. The rooms tend to be on the small side, but the service is excellent. Also available are 20 cottages that comfortably fit up to 10 people. The city centre is about a 45-minute drive away.

Pribaltiiskaya Hotel $$
Korablestroiteley ulitsa, 14
Tel: 740 3979 or 900 6288
E-mail: market@pribaltiyskaya.com
www.pribaltiyskaya.com
At the western end of Vasilievsky Island, the 'Hotel by the Baltic' lives up to its name, offering impressive views of the Gulf of Finland from many of its rooms. It is one of the largest hotels in the city, and is the perfect place for large groups. Transport needs to be booked in advance at reception since the city centre is a 20 to 45-minute drive away, depending on the traffic. Most rooms retain their Soviet-style decor, but they are nonetheless comfortable.

ELSEWHERE

Three-star

Best Western Neptun Hotel $$
Obvodnovo Kanala naberezhnaya, 93a
Tel: 324 4600
Fax: 315 6625
Email: bc@neptun.spb.ru
www.neptun.spb.ru
While it is located in one of the worst places in the city centre – along the dismal industrial Obvodny Canal that is slowly being modernised – the hotel provides a host of services for the business traveller, including three conference halls. It has one of the city's best fitness centres and a swimming pool, as well as an eight-lane bowling alley.

Hotel Okhtinskaya $$
Bolsheokhtinsky prospekt, 4
Tel: 222 8601
Фах: 227 2618
Email: info@okhtinskaya.spb.ru
www.okhtinskaya.spb.ru
This hotel across the Neva River from the Smolny Cathedral offers a breathtaking view from some of its rooms, but it's not that conveniently placed for the centre. You will be dependent on the hotel's free hourly shuttles to Nevsky prospekt – or the unscrupulous taxi drivers who lurk outside. Rooms are comfortable and clean, and staff are generally quite helpful.

Nautilus Inn $$
Rizhskaya ulitsa , 3
Tel: 449-9000
Fax: 449-9009

Email: info@nautilus-inn.ru
www.nautilus-inn.ru
This hotel, just across the Neva River from the Alexander Nevsky Lavra, offers bright and clean rooms. It caters to business travellers and provides conference and work facilities. The city centre is a 15–20 minute ride if traffic is not heavy.

Pulkovskaya Park Inn $$
Pobedy ploshchad, 1
Tel: 740 3900
Fax: 740 3913
E-mail: info@pulkovskaya.spb.ru
www.rezidorparkinn.com
Conveniently located about ten minutes from the airport on one of the city's main thoroughfares, this hotel provides easy access to the city centre. The metro is a short walk away. The hotel certainly has a Soviet feel to it, but rooms are comfortable. There is a congress hall that seats 600, and a nice Bavarian restaurant. In the summer, it hosts Cossack dancing shows.

Mini-Hotels

Austrian Yard $
Furshtatskaya ulitsa, 45
Tel or Fax: 579 8235
Email: natali@austrianyard.com
www.austrianyard.com
This hotel next to the Austrian Embassy has very high security. Rooms live up to the Austrian reputation for efficiency and cleanliness, and guests can also use a sauna and play billiards. One of the city centre's few parks, the Tauride Gardens (Taurichesky sad), is just down

the block.

Marshal Hotel $
Shpalernaya ulitsa, 41
Tel: 579 9955
Email: reserv.hotel@tpark.spb.ru
www.marshal-hotel.spb.ru
Clean and comfortable hotel, not far from the Taurichesky sad (Tauride Gardens) and the Smolny Cathedral. The building dating from 1806 was once the headquarters of one of the tsar's cavalry regiments. Rooms are basic but clean, and are equipped for internet access. Other facilities include three conference rooms and a sauna.

Prestige Hotel $
3 liniya, 52; Vasilevsky ostrov
Tel: 328 5338; Fax: 328 4228
Email: reservations@prestige-hotels.com
www.prestige-hotels.com
For something central but away from the hustle and bustle, try this hotel in the historic centre of Vasilevsky Island, a short drive from the Hermitage. Rooms are basic but clean and modern – some have jacuzzis.

PRICE CATEGORIES

Price categories are for a double room without breakfast:
$ = $40–$79
$$ = $80–$199
$$$= $200–$259
$$$$ = more than $260

ACTIVITIES

THE ARTS, FESTIVALS, NIGHTLIFE, SHOPPING AND SPORTS

THE ARTS

Classical Music and Theatre Venues

Theatre shows and concerts almost always begin at 7pm, unless it's a matinee or special event. It is customary and considered good manners to hand in your coat when visiting museums or the theatre. Don't be surprised when audiences start clapping before the performance has even begun.

The Alexindrinsky Theatre
Ostrovskovo ploshchad, 2
Tel: 710 4103
Ticket office open 11am–8pm.

Ballet and Opera Conservatory
Teatralnaya ploshchad, 3
Tel: 312 2519
Ticket office open 11am–7pm.

Baltiysky Dom Theatre
Alexandrovsky Park, 4
Tel: 232 6244
Ticket office open noon–7pm.

The Bolshoy Drama Theatre
Fontanka naberezhnaya 65
Tel: 310 0401
Ticket office open 11am–6pm.

The Bolshoy Puppet Theatre
Nekrasova ulitsa, 10
Tel: 272 8215
Ticket office open 11am–7pm. Performances at 11.30am and 2pm.

Capella

Moika River naberezhnaya, 20
Tel: 314 1153
Ticket office open noon–7pm.

Hermitage Theatre
(ballet, opera and chamber music)
Hermitage Museum
Dvortsovaya naberezhnaya, 34
Tel: 710 9030
Ticket office open 11am–6pm.

Komissarzhevskaya Drama Theatre
Italianskaya ulitsa, 19
Tel: 571 0849
Ticket office open noon–7pm.

The Maly Drama Theatre
Rubinshteyna ulitsa, 18
Tel: 713 2078
Ticket office open noon–7pm.

Mariinsky Opera and Ballet Theatre
Teatralnaya ploshchad, 1
Tel: 326 4141
Ticket office open 11am–8pm.

Mironov Russian Enterprise Theatre
Bolshoy prospekt, 75
Tel: 346 1675
Ticket office open noon–7pm.

Mussorgsky Opera and Ballet Theatre
Iskusstv ploshchad, 1
Tel: 595 4284
Ticket office open 11am–8pm.

Nikolaevsky Art Centre
Nikolayevsky Palace
Truda ploshchad, 4
Tel: 312 5500
Ticket office open 11am–6pm.
Performances at 7pm and 9pm.

Russian folk dance and music shows.

The Saint Petersburg State Philharmonic
Mikhailovskaya ulitsa, 13
Tel: 312 9871
Ticket office open 11am–8pm.

The State Circus
Fontanka naberezhnaya, 3
Tel: 313 4260
Ticket office open 11am–7pm.
Matinee begins at 11am and 3pm; evening performances at 7pm.

Galleries and Museums

Borei Art Gallery
Liteiny prospekt, 58
Tel: 275 3837
Exhibitions of local and foreign painting, graphics, photographs and installations. Open noon–8pm.

D137
Nevsky prospekt, 90–92
Tel: 275 6011
www.d137.ru
Open Tues–Sat noon–7pm.

Marina Gisich Gallery
Fontanka, 121
Tel: 314 4380
www.gisich.com

Mikhailov Gallery
Liteyny prospekt, 53
Tel: 272 4848
Open 11am–8pm.

Palitra Gallery
Malaya Morskaya, 5

CINEMA

Cinemas open at 9am or 10am and show films all day long. The entrance fee is the ruble equivalent of US$3–$12/ £1.60–£6. Up to 4pm tickets are sold at half price. All shows are dubbed into Russian, except for some films at Mirazh and Aurora cinemas.

Avrora, Nevsky prospekt, 60
Khudozhestuenny, Nevsky prospekt 67
Mirazh, Bolshoy prospekt, 35, Petrograd side.
Jam Hall, Kammenoostrovsky, 42. Luxury cinema with soft couches and waiter service during show.
Crystal Palace, Nevsky prospekt, 72
Dom Kino, Karavannaya ulitsa, 12

Tel: 272 4880
Open 11am–7pm.
SPAS
Moika Reki naberezhnaya, 93
Tel: 571 4260
Open 11am–7pm. Exhibitions of paintings.

FESTIVALS

St Petersburg spends a good part of the year in cold and darkness, so when the short summer comes with its radiant White Nights, the locals let loose with an intensity rarely seen elsewhere in Europe. In June, the city centre throbs around the clock as people rush to take part in dozens of cultural events in palaces, theatres and museums.

Since the fall of the Soviet Union, St Petersburg has witnessed a cultural boom, with an explosion of festivals from art and music to film.

The central attraction of the White Nights is the Stars of the White Nights Festival, sponsored by the Mariinsky Theatre, which

every June features a host of Russian and international stars in opera and ballet. Tickets cost US$50–$100/£26–£50 and reservations can be made online at the theatre's website: www.mariinsky.ru, but you must go in person to the theatre box office at Teatralnaya ploshchad to purchase them.

Little sister to the Mariinsky's White Nights festival is the Annual Chamber Music Festival, "Palaces of St Petersburg", organised by the chief conductor of the Moscow Chamber Orchestra, Konstantin Orbelian, and violinist Mariya Safariants. Featuring international and Russian singers and musicians, among which are those from the Mariinsky Theatre and the St Petersburg Philharmonic, it also runs the entire month of June but is organised on a much smaller scale, with quartets and soloists performing in the close and intimate quarters of small palace theatres, such as the State Hermitage Theatre, which was the personal theatre of the tsars and tsarinas; the State Russian Museum's Mikhailovksy Palace; the Yusupovsky Palace; the Marble Palace; as well as the Catherine, Peterhof and Gatchina palaces, all three located on the outskirts of the city.

St Petersburg's cultural life is certainly steeped in classical arts and culture, but it continues to develop on the popular level. On 27 May, City Day, the city commemorates its official founding by Peter the Great in 1703. A flood of parade floats and revellers dressed in costume stream down Nevsky prospekt, the city's main avenue, to Palace Square next to the Hermitage.

Summer is not the only time for festivals. During the Christmas and New Year season, the St Petersburg Philharmonic (The Shostakovich Philharmonic) organises the annual International Arts Square Winter Festival, which brings together leading classical musicians and opera singers from around the world.

NIGHTLIFE

Nightclubs

Clubs usually have a cover charge, which varies between US$3 and US$20 (£1.60–£10) depending on the day and whether or not a top group may be playing.
City Bar
Furshtatskaya ulitsa 20
www.citybar.ru
Friendly American bar with good hamburgers.
Central Station
Lomonosova ulitsa, 1/28
Tel: 312 3600
www.centralstation.ru
The city's most recent gay club has four floors.
Datscha
Dumskaya ulitsa, 9
Small bar with various DJs that is popular with Russians and foreigners alike.
Griboedov
Voronezhskaya ulitsa, 2a
Tel: 973 7273
www.griboedovclub.ru
Housed in a former bomb shelter, Griboedov attracts an arty crowd with its cheap drinks.
Golden Dolls
Nevsky prospekt, 60
Tel: 571 3343
Erotic nightclub with topless waitresses who do almost whatever you want – for money, of course.

Jet Set
Furshtatskaya ulitsa, 58b
Tel: 275 9288
Face-control and club cards.
Sumptuous Eastern-style interior
and resident European DJs.
Konyushney Dvor
Griboedova Canal, 5
Tel: 315 7607
Swinging scene for students and
tourists; strip shows daily.
Luna
Voznesensky prospekt, 46
Tel: 310 1616
Upscale; rich crowd.
Magrib
Nevsky prospekt, 84
Tel: 275 1255

CASINOS

Plaza
Admiral Makarov
naberezhnaya, 2
Tel: 323 9090
City's top casino with a popular
nightclub and upscale, glam-
orous crowd; cover US$10–20.
Astoria
Malaya Morskaya ulitsa, 20
Tel: 313 5020
Conti
Kondratyevsky prospekt, 44
Tel: 321 6565
Premier
Nevsky prospekt, 47
Tel: 703 5370
Taleon Club
Moika River naberezhnaya, 59
Tel: 315 7645

Sexy and upscale.
Metro
Ligovsky prospekt, 174
Tel: 766 0204
www.metroclub.ru
Large popular dance club with
three floors.
Pin Up
Mokhovaya ulitsa, 37a
Tel: 273 9789
www.pinupclub.ru
A trendy place popular with young
people.
Plaza
Admiral Makarov naberezhnaya, 2
Tel: 323 9090
www.plazaclub.ru
Popular nightclub across from
the Hermitage.
Purga
Fontanka naberezhnaya, 13
Tel: 313 4123
New Year's Eve is celebrated
every night.
Red Lion
Dekabristov ploshchad, 1
Tel: 571 4526
Nice mix of Russian and ex-pat
crowd; one of the few fine pubs.
Rossi's
Zodchevo Rossi ulitsa, 1/3
Tel: 710 4016
www.rossis.ru
Large and fun club which plays
pop music and sometimes has
live bands.
Sinners (Greshniki)
Griboedova kanala, 28
Tel: 570 4291
www.greshniki.ru
Gay club.

Jazz Clubs

St Petersburg has had Russia's
most vibrant jazz scene, and jazz
clubs open every year.
Che Café and Club
Poltavskaya ulitsa, 3
Tel: 717 7600
Fashionable yet easygoing crowd.
Jazz Philharmonic Hall
Zagorodny prospekt, 27
Tel: 764 8565
Sophisticated venue with main-
stream and Dixieland jazz.
JFC Jazz Club
Shpalernaya ulitsa, 33
Tel: 272 9850
Relaxed venue with all forms of
jazz and Latin nights.
Jimi Hendrix Club
Liteyny prospekt, 33
Tel: 579 8813
Live bands every night.

Cabarets

Chaplin Club
Ulitsa Tchaikovskovo, 59
Tel: 272 6649
City's best comedy club. Some
shows are mime, but most in
Russian.
Comic Trust
Venueless underground comedy
theatre that uses no language,
but music, gestures and mimicry.
This is the "other" St Petersburg,
far from the high culture of the
Mariinksy Theatre. Check their
website for shows:
www.comic-trust.com
Caberet
Naberezhnaya Obvodnovo
kanala, 181
Tel: 714 5056
Famous gay club that can hold up
to 500 people. Features colourful
transvestite shows from 2am that
offer the audience the chance to
dance with the drag queens.

SHOPPING

What To Buy

Though the city economy is
growing and has greatly diversi-

fied since Soviet times when it was entirely dependent on the military-industrial complex, there are few high-quality, speciality items for tourists to buy. Many visitors take advantage of the fact that pirated CDs and DVDs sell in Russia for as little as US$3 (£1.60), and can be found at video and audio stores that seem to be everywhere.

If you want something besides the usual trinkets of Russian dolls and lacquer boxes, try the Lomonosov Porcelain Factory (LFZ), Europe's third-oldest such factory. Founded in 1743 as the Imperial Porcelain Factory by Empress Elizabeth to provide the tsarist court with high-quality porcelain, the factory makes fine china at prices much lower than major European manufacturers.

LFZ has stores at:
Yefimova ulitsa, 3
Tel: 740 4757
Open daily 10am–8pm.
Kondratyevsky prospekt, 32
Tel: 542 3055
Open Mon–Sat 10am–7pm.
Visits to the factory and its wonderful museum can also be arranged, but by appointment only.

St Petersburg Doll Museum
Kamskaya ulitsa, 8
Tel: 327 7224
Has an exhibition and sale of handmade dolls and doll-making materials.

Where To Buy

Retro Antiques
Hotel Astoria
Bolshaya Morskaya ulitsa, 39
Tel: 315 9673
Fine antiques from a reputable dealer.

Babushka Souvenirs
Lt Schmidt Embankment, 33
Tel: 321 7952
Truly one of the finest assortments of quality Russian souvenirs, in contrast to the sometimes dubious trinkets sold at outdoor markets such as the one near the Church on the Spilled Blood.

Heritage
Malaya Sadovaya, 4
Tel: 570 4397
Standard Russian souvenirs.

Nevsky Souvenir
Nevsky prospekt, 58
Tel: 312 3201
Standard Russian souvenirs.

Mexx
Nevsky prospekt, 46
Tel: 449 2745
European clothing store.

Gostiny Dvor
Nevsky prospekt, 35
The city's largest department store containing dozens of small boutiques where you can find everything from food to clothing and appliances. Open every day 10am–10pm.

DLT
Bolshaya Morskaya, 19
Large department store with nearly everything on sale. Open every day 10am–9pm.

Gianni Versace
Nevsky prospekt, 39
Tel: 314 1492
Designer clothing.

Tatyana Parfionova
Nevsky prospekt, 51
Tel: 713 3669
www.parfionova.ru
Clothing by a top St Petersburg fashion designer.

Passazh Shopping Mall
Nevsky prospekt, 48
Tel: 315 5209

Larusse
Stremyanaya ulitsa, 3
Open 11am–8pm

BUYING ANTIQUES

Antiques (items produced before 1945) and pieces of contemporary art can only be taken out of Russia with an export licence from the Ministry of Culture. Call City Culture Committee, Nevsky prospekt, 40, tel: 312 2187.

Larusse is the world's only antiques shop that specialises in Russian rural antiques. www.larusse.ru

Grand Palace
Nevsky prospekt, 44
Open 11am–9pm
City's most elite shopping mall.
Tel: 710 5504

Yeliseyevsky Gastronom
Nevsky prospekt, 56
Open 10am–9pm
Fine delicacies and caviar.

Markets

There are 16 so-called collective markets where farmers sell fruit, vegetables and other food products from different regions in Russia. The biggest and best include: **Kuznechny**, Kuznechny pereulok, 3; **Andreyevsky**, Vasilievsky ostrov, 18, Bolshoy prospekt; **Maltevsky**, ulitsa Nekrasova, 52; **Sytny**, Petrogradskaya storona, Sytninskaya ploshchad, 3/5; **Sennoi**, Moskovsky prospekt, 4b.

Fur Shops

Lena
Nevsky prospekt, 50
Tel: 907 1047
Open daily 10am–9pm.
Laplandia
Bolshaya Konnyshenaya ulitsa,
10
Tel: 570 0669
**Soyuz Pushnina
(House of Fur)**
Moskovsky prospekt, 98
Tel: 388 4543
www.soyuzpushnina.ru
Open Mon–Fri 10am–8pm,
Sat–Sun 11am–5pm.

SPORT

Participant Sports

Sports Centres

St Petersburg, like most Russian
cities, has few public sports centres where you can play basket-
ball, tennis or go for a swim.
Russian men prefer to sit with
friends to drink and smoke. It is
such habits that contribute to the
average male mortality rate of 59
years. Still, the city is in the midst
of a fitness boom as young successful professionals are more
and more concerned about their
appearance and health. Most turn
to fitness centres to lift weights
and attend aerobic classes. Since
most work on monthly member-

ships, if you're in the city for a
short visit, it might be best to
enquire at any of the major hotels.
Galaxy Sport Club
Petrovsky Stadium,
Petrovsky ostrov
Tel: 328 8941
Small but upscale fitness centre
that sells monthly passes only for
about US$60.
Planet Fitness (10 branches)
Kazanskaya ulitsa, 37
Tel: 315 7175
www.spb.fitness.ru
Grand Hotel Europe,
Mikhailovskaya, 1
Tel: 329 6597
Robespera naberezhnaya, 12
Tel: 275 6201
Gloria Tennis Club
Kuznetsovksaya ulitsa, 25
Tel: 388 3410
www.spb-tennis.ru
Open daily 8am–11pm. Two tennis
courts in pleasant atmosphere.
SKA Swimming Pool
Litovskaya ulitsa, 3
Tel: 295 8608
Open daily 6.30am–10.30pm.
A 50-metre swimming pool. For a
swim, you need a certificate of
good health to get in.
Mini Golf in the Park
Lunacharskovo prospekt
Mini-golf course. Open 6am–6pm.
Dunes Country Club
38 km, Primorskoe Shosse
Tel: 434 0297
Elite golf club *(see page 215)*
Diving Empire
Pravdy ulitsa, 11
Tel: 937 0289

St Petersburg Shooting Range
Sredny prospekt, 83
Tel: 321 3014
Carting Centre
Krasno putilovskaya ulitsa, 69
Tel: 703 1493

Spectator Sport

Football

Petrovsky Stadium is home to the
local club, Zenit. Games start at
7pm; call the club for fixtures,
tel: 315 6202 or see www.fc-
zenit.ru. Things sometimes get out
of hand and public disorder is
quite common after matches.
Police are out in full force.

OTHER ACTIVITIES

Banyas

The Russian sauna, or *banya*,
is a rite of passage for foreigners
visiting Russia. Unfortunately,
the city is often not the best
place to do it, and St Petersburg
has few saunas whose hygienic
standards correspond to what
foreign travellers might find
acceptable. If you are lucky
enough to have a friend with a
dacha, go to the countryside
where you get the real thing,
especially in winter when you
alternate between the scorching
steam of 45°C (113°F) and diving
in the snow.
**Kazachaya Banya (Cossacks
Baths)**
Bolshoi Kazachy pereulok, 11
Tel: 315 0734
One and a half hours in a private
cabin is 1,000 rubles.
Open 24 hours.

City Walks

Walking tours of the city are
offered by **Peter's Walking
Tours**: www.peterswalk.com. Since
1996, this small company has
offered a selection of routes
that best give the feel of the real
St Petersburg.

BUYING ART

The past decade has seen a
boom in art which never had
anything to do with "socialist
realism". Theatre and especially
painting has just emerged from
the underground. Artists who
were banned are now openly
exhibited; on Nevsky there are
dozens of painters selling their
work or willing to draw your portrait. Some artists have already
found a way to sell their works
in the West, others will gladly

sell their paintings for US$100.
Bear in mind that such paintings
may cost several thousand
dollars in Western Europe.
Naturally, the streets are full of
cheap stuff – moons over
ponds, imitation icons, portraits
of rock stars and naked women
– but you may also run into
something interesting. Most of
what the artists sell on Nevsky
prospekt tends to be mass produced for broader appeal.

A–Z

A HANDY SUMMARY OF PRACTICAL INFORMATION, ARRANGED ALPHABETICALLY

A dmission Charges

Most major museums in Russia charge foreigners from between five and ten times more than they do Russian visitors. This economic discrimination has been the bane of travellers for decades, and in the 1990s when foreigners began to live in Russia en masse, some brave souls took the Russians to court, citing the Russian Constitution that forbids discrimination on the basis of race or nationality. The good news is that they won, and many Russian organisations began to change their policies. The bad news is that some still insist on price discrimination, and have found a clever loophole – everyone must pay the high price, but if you are a citizen of Russia, you are entitled to a "discount". The worst offenders are the Hermitage Museum, the Mariinsky Theatre, Peterhof and the Russian Museum. If you wish to spare your nerves, just pay. Still, some visitors try to sneak in as Russians.

Peterhof and the Hermitage are the most expensive museums in St Petersburg, costing about US$14/£7. Tickets at the Mariinsky for a foreigner however, can cost at least US$30/£16 and much more, especially if you buy through your hotel, which tacks on a hefty charge.

Most museums, however, are reasonably priced, and if it's any consolation, just remember that the higher price you pay goes towards the upkeep of a museum that is most certainly in dire financial straits.

B udgeting for your Trip

Do not be put off by horror stories in the press that St Petersburg is one of the most expensive cities in the world. An enjoyable trip on a low budget is certainly possible.

However, there are a lot of inflated prices in the city. So if someone quotes you a high price, say for a taxi ride, just ask someone else – eventually you'll get a good price. A taxi anywhere in the city centre should not cost a foreigner more than the ruble equivalent of US$5, though some drivers will say US$20. It's recommended to take a private car, and not a regular taxi, since the latter are notorious for ripping off tourists.

In the past year, the city has seen the opening of more quality restaurants that cater to the bud-

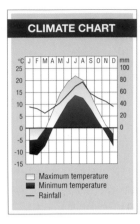

CLIMATE CHART

- ☐ Maximum temperature
- ■ Minimum temperature
- — Rainfall

get market. If you wanted to, you could keep your daily food budget under US$20/£11.

Likewise, the city has seen the arrival of inexpensive mini-hotels and private apartments for rent. If you don't need fine service or large accommodation, finding a place for under US$80/£45 a night isn't difficult.

Business Hours

Most shops open 10am–8pm, though in the city centre there are 24-hour convenience food stores. More and more businesses are working the entire day, foregoing closure at lunchtime. But many organisations, such as banks, do close for one hour, either between 1–2pm or 2–3pm.

C hildren

Unless your children are interested in high culture, there is not much for them to do. Even locals bemoan the fact that on weekends there are few places to take children except for a walk in the park, or in the forest when the weather is warm. Amusement parks are often small and decrepit, though there is the highly regarded Bolshoy Puppet Theatre *(see page 226)*. Few travellers bring children under 18.

Customs

Migration cards and registration

When arriving you will have to fill in a migration card (available on the plane or on arrival) and give it to your hotel or travel agency who sent your visa invitation to get registered. Registration is compulsory if you will be in Russia for more than three working days. Keep the card safe as you will have to give it in when leaving – if you can not show one you will not be allowed to leave.

Customs regulations have been revised several times in the past few years. Customs authorities want to find a compromise between conforming to international customs regulations and preventing the export of large batches of goods bought cheaply in Russian shops for resale in other countries.

The latest edition of the customs regulations prohibits the import and export of weapons and ammunition (excluding weapons for shooting fowl and hunting tackle), and of drugs and devices for their use. It is prohibited to export antiquities and art objects dating from before 1945 except for those which the visitor imported into the country and declared on entry. You may leave the country with contemporary art work, but do ask the vendor for a certificate stating that the work is not a protected item in the cultural heritage. Any respectable art vendor should have the proper forms from the Ministry of Culture.

Duty-Free Export
● Articles imported by the visitor.
● Foodstuffs in small amounts.
● Alcohol (over 21). Spirits 1.5 litres, wine 2 litres per person.
● Tobacco (over 16). 100 cigarettes or 100 grammes of tobacco.

Some of the customs officers are indeed quite severe in their observation of these regulations. While St Petersburg's Pulkovo 2

Airport has recently instituted a "green line" for those with nothing to declare, don't be surprised if officers ask to make a careful examination of your luggage.

D isabled Travellers

It is strongly recommended that disabled travellers do not travel alone. In general, Russian society is not sympathetic to the plight of the disabled, and has a long way to go to improve their ability to be active members of society.

The city is quite difficult for disabled travellers to get around, though progress is slowly being made. The Russian Museum and the Hermitage, for instance, recently installed equipment to allow those in wheelchairs to go upstairs. But most places do not have the means to accommodate wheelchair users. Likewise, the transport system provides no assistance, and it is even difficult to rent a car or van that would have such capacity.

E lectricity

The electrical current in St Petersburg tourist hotels is normally 220 volts AC. Sockets require a continental-type, two-pin plug. It is best to have a set of adaptors with you. If your gadgets depend on a supply of unique batteries, bring plenty with you, since they might not be available in Russia.

Embassies

Russian Missions Abroad
Australia: Griffith, 70 Canberra Ave, Canberra, tel: 6295 9474.
Canada: 285 Charlotte St, Ottawa, tel: 235 4341.
Ireland: 186 Orwell Road, Dublin, tel: 492 3492.
New Zealand: Karori, 57 Messines Rd, Wellington, tel: 476 6113.
Singapore: 51 Nassim Road, Singapore 258439, tel: 6235 1834.

United Kingdom: 5 Kensington Palace Gardens, London, tel: (020) 7229 8027.
USA: Embassy: 2650 Wisconsin Ave NW, Washington DC, tel: 202 298 5735.
Consulate: 2790 Green Street, San Francisco, tel: 415 928 6878.

Emergencies

Security & Crime

In the aftermath of the disintegration of the Soviet Union and the communist planned economy, newly won freedoms have combined with economic decline to produce a drastic increase in crime. This is particularly the case in Russian cities.

Avoid private taxis at train stations and the international airport. While these locations tend to attract scoundrels, most Russians take private cabs to get around, and as long as you are travelling in the centre, there is little reason to worry. The centre is well policed, by both traffic officers and those on foot. It's not advised to take a private cab on the outskirts of town, however.

Be wary of the ladies of the night – many of them are just waiting for you to fall asleep. When you wake up, your possessions and money may be gone.

Do not open your door to people you do not know. Most apartment break-ins occur when the unwitting tenant opens the door to criminals posing as either police officers or service personnel.

Police Problems

The threat of crime, however, extends mostly to corrupt police officers, who are probably the only major worry a visitor to St Petersburg will have. Best to stay away from them if you see them coming, and do not get drunk and appear in public places: most foreigners victimised by the police are drunk, and indeed corrupt police target the inebriated.

In the past few years, street crime has become a big problem in the centre, ranging from pickpockets that work main arteries, such as Nevsky prospekt, to violent muggings in broad daylight. The most violent of crimes, such as murder, are mostly connected to conflicts in the rough world of Russian business, and if you are only in the city for pleasure, there is little reason to worry about your physical safety.

Women should be aware that often what is considered to be sexual harrassment in Anglo-American countries, is considered a normal way to meet a woman in Russia.

Russian women, on the other hand, tend to be demure and rarely take the initiative to meet a man. If a woman in a restaurant or bar comes across as forward, there is a good chance she is a prostitute.

Medical Services

Visitors from the USA, Canada, European countries and Japan need no health certificate. It is a good idea to take your own medicines, although there are chemists selling foreign medicines and you can find most things you need.

The most common ailment is a mild stomach upset, but there is a more serious illness that can be picked up from drinking contaminated water containing the parasite Giardia lamblia. It is thus advisable to drink either boiled tap water or bottled mineral water.

The following are clinics which also stock foreign medicines:

American Medical Clinic

Naberezhnaya Reki Moiki, 78
Tel: 740 2090
www.amclinic.com
English-speaking doctors; open 24 hours; overpriced medical care from Russian doctors.

Euromed Clinic

Suvorovksy prospekt, 60
Tel: 327 0301
www.euromed.ru
Quality medical care at reasonable prices.

Medem International Clinic

Marata ulitsa, 6
Tel: 336 3333
Quality medical care at reasonable prices.

Medi

Nevsky prospekt, 82
Tel: 777 0000
www.emedi.ru
The city's best dental clinic. Open 24 hours.

Etiquette

Don't be surprised by the brisk manner or even rudeness of Russians, and don't expect a Russian to apologise if he happens to bump into you accidentally on the street. Also, car drivers can be one of the most dangerous encounters for a foot-bound traveller. Even if you have a green light, they may not stop and may beep and shout at you to get out of the way.

Don't worry about Russian mood swings. Despite their public rudeness, Russians can be extremely nice.

If you are invited into a Russian's home, you should take off your shoes and put on slippers when entering the house. Failure to eat and drink what your host offers may be taken as a grave offence.

Russians don't like small talk, as is common in the West, and don't be surprised if they ask you some questions Westerners find quite personal, as well as make comments in that vein. For instance, a young woman, aged 27, might be questioned as to why she isn't married with children. Likewise, feel free to act the same way towards your Russian acquaintance or friend. They won't be offended, but will rather enjoy the chance to talk in depth, and not just about the weather.

G ay Travellers

Since the change in Russia's legal system in the mid-1990s that abolished Soviet-era prohibition of homosexuality, the city's gay community has come out and gained more acceptance. There are several gay and lesbian clubs, and society is more tolerant. Some say that a gay lifestyle is even fashionable in

TRANSPORT

ACCOMMODATION

ACTIVITIES

A – Z

LANGUAGE

the city and common among prominent government officials and business leaders. Still, as Russia sees a rise in neo-Nazi groups, beatings of visitors to gay establishments are becoming more frequent.

I nternet

Most internet cafés are open 24 hours, and are centrally located. Rates are reasonable, a little more than US$2/£1.10 an hour.
Café Max
Nevsky prospekt, 90; www.cafemax.ru; Popular with student video-game players.
Quo Vadis
Nevsky prospekt, 76; www.quovadis.ru; Hip café; great place to hang out, centrally located.

M aps

Unlike Soviet times, when a good map, in any language, was impossible to find, today you can find excellent English-language maps in your hotel, or in any bookshops. Street name-changing, which was a big issue in the 1990s, has pretty much come to an end, so maps don't change as often as before.

Media

Under President Putin, Russia's media freedom has been curtailed since its heyday during the Yeltsin era in the 1990s. Today, all TV stations are under tight state control, and news reports are censored.

Only published media is allowed a modicum of freedom, but even then, the Kremlin is not afraid to sack an editor from one of the major "independent" dailies when it sees fit. The last remaining credible papers are *Izvestiya*, which is something like the *Times*, as well as the business dailies, *Kommersant* and *Vedomosti*. Weekly Magazines, such as *Itogi* and *Gorod*, are also informative. The most reliable

source of news remains the *St Petersburg Times*.

The best bi-weekly and monthly guide to what's on is *Pulse* (in Russian and English).

Money

There is no restriction on the amount of money you can bring in to the country. However, currency taken out of the country must not exceed the amount shown on the import declaration.
Exchange
All major hotels have an official exchange counter where you can buy rubles with hard currency cash, travellers' cheques and credit cards. There are bureaux de change in many of the larger shops. You will be asked to present your passport when exchanging money. Keep these forms given to you by the bank, since you might have to present them to customs when leaving the country.
Credit Cards
Most tourist-related businesses accept credit cards. But it's a good idea to always have enough cash on hand since Russian credit-card machines often break down. Also, since credit-card fraud is common, think twice about whether a place is respectable before giving them your card.
Local Currency
Rubles come in both banknotes and coins. One ruble is equal to 100 kopeks. The smallest bank note is five rubles, while the largest is 1,000 rubles, though the government might soon institute a 5,000-ruble banknote. Be careful about being slipped old bills that are no longer valid. The last major currency reform was in 1997, and bills before then are no longer valid.
The Black Market
As everyone knows, dealing in convertible currency is against the law. It is true to say that no foreign national has yet been punished for violating currency regulations. As for the speculators, they do not even attempt to hide – in part because they know that their crime

is difficult to prove. Even so, think twice before you agree to do business. Foreigners are often conned with money that has been withdrawn from circulation or through sleight of hand (money is counted as you watch, but only half of the agreed sum – at best – will make its way into your pocket).

P ostal Services

Main post office (Glavny Pochtamt): Pochtamtskaya ulitsa, 9 (24 hour).

Every large hotel has facilities for basic postal services at reception, usually open 8am–10pm. Other post offices usually open at 10am. The regular Russian postal service is unreliable at worst, and slow at best. If you value what you are sending, better to use any of the private services listed below. Note: because of Russian customs, even the express mail companies can not promise overnight international delivery. Usually it takes two days to destinations abroad.
Westpost: Nevsky prospekt, 86, tel: 327 3092; open Mon–Fri 9.30am–8pm. US-owned postal service that delivers to Europe and America in three to seven working days for US$3–5 for a standard letter. If it doesn't have to be there overnight, this service is the best buy.
Fedex: Grivtsova Pereulok, 6, tel: 325 8825; open 8am–8pm, Sat 9am–7pm, closed Sun.
TNT: Sofiiskaya ulitsa, 14, tel: 718 3330; open 8am–8pm, Sat 10am–2pm, closed Sun.
Pony Express: 27 Kamennoostrovsky, Parkovaya ulitsa, 4 Tel: 449 7752
www.ponyexpress.ru
DHL: Izmailovsky prospekt, 4, tel: 326 6400 (24 hours); open Mon–Fri 8am–8pm, Sat 10–4pm, closed Sun.

Public Holidays

Besides the official state holidays below, Russians celebrate many other holidays. For instance, Russians celebrate the "Old" New Year on 13 January, which is the New Year according to the pre-Revolution Gregorian calendar. On 27 May, St Petersburg celebrates City Day, which marks the foundation of the city by Peter the Great.

Also in May, because of the proximity of three official days off, many people take a 10-day holiday, going to their country house to prepare for summer.

On 21–22 June, the city celebrates White Nights, and crowds take to strolling the city streets until morning.

In August, it seems the whole country shuts down, and it's difficult to find anyone at his or her place of work. Many go to their country house, or visit relatives elsewhere in Russia.

● 1–7 Jan inclusive: New Year and Orthodox Christmas
● 23 Feb: Armed Forces' Day
● 8 March: Women's Day
● April: Easter
● 1–2 May: Labour/Spring Holidays
● 9 May: Victory Day
● 12 June: Independence Day
● 4 Nov: National Unity Day

T elecommunications

Central telephone and telegraph office: Pochtamtskaya ulitsa, 9. In a pay phone the token must be inserted before dialling. If you hear a bip-bip tone during the conversation insert another token.

In the past, visitors had to book international calls in advance. Now, if you don't enlist the services of a hotel, it is possible to call abroad direct from a private phone. Dial 8 +10 + the international code: Australia 61; France 33; Germany 49; Japan 81; Netherlands 31; Spain 34; United Kingdom 44; US and Canada 1. If calling St Petersburg from abroad be warned that the lines are not always good and are sometimes

busy. The international direct-dial code for St Petersburg is 7-812.

Still, the cheapest way to call home is to buy a phone card that uses an internet-based system. These cards are usually sold at internet cafés, or at stores and kiosks that sell music CDs. Internet cafés, such as Quo Vadis *(see page 234),* also offer their own web-based telephone system, and rates are very cheap when compared to hotels.

Time Zone

St Petersburg time is GMT plus 3 hours. The same time is adopted nearly everywhere west of the Urals, although western Ukrainians and the people of the Baltic States prefer to use the Mean European Time (GMT plus 2 hours) in their daily life to demonstrate their independence.

Tipping

Although the former Soviet Union was a socialist state for 70 years, tipping, one of the capitalist sins, was always an accepted practice. Waiters, porters, guides and interpreters, especially in Moscow and St Petersburg, have always appreciated tips. As in most European countries, 10 percent is the accepted rule.

Tour Companies

Local Tour Companies
ADM: Ulitsa Marata, 9, office 30, tel: 325 2233, www.adm.ru
Arctur Travel: Goncharnaya ulitsa, 13, tel: 717 7184
Baltic Tours: Pereulok Sergeya Tyelenina, 4, Tel: 320 6663
Dassi: Bolshaya Moskovskaya ulitsa, 1–3, tel: 315 3559
Eclectica Guide: Nevsky prospekt, 44, tel: 710 5579, e-mail: gid@eclectica.spb.ru, www.eclectica-guide.ru.
Specialises in tours of St Petersburg and its suburbs.
Infinity Travel: Angleterre Hotel,

RELIGIOUS SERVICES

Russian Orthodox: Cathedral of the Trinity, Alexandra Nevskovo ploshchad; Cathedral of St Nicholas, Kommunarov ploshchad; Cathedral of the Transfiguration, Radischeva ploshchad; Vladimir Church, Vladimirskaya ploshchad.
Catholic: The Catholic Church, Kovensky pereulok, 7, and St. Catherine's at Nevsky prospekt, 32
Baptist: The Baptist Church, Bolshaya Ozernaya ulitsa, 29a.
Mosque: Mechet, Kronversky prospekt, 7.
Synagogue: The Synagogue, Lermontovsky prospekt, 2.

St Isaac's Square, tel: 494 5085, www.infinity.ru
Intourbureau: Galemoya ulitsa, 22, tel: 315 7876. Tours around Russia including river cruises. Available in English.
Lenart Tours: Nevsky prospekt, 40, tel: 312 6553
Pilgrim: tel: 275 5936. Tours to the south of Russia, Sochi, Akhazia and also to retreats in the Leningrad region.
Russian Cruises: Nevsky prospekt, 51, tel: 325 6120, www.russian-cruises.com. Specialises in boat tours on Russia's rivers, as well as to the islands of Valaam and Kizhi.
West Travel: Griboedov Canal, 12, tel: 325 8200
Wild Russia: Naberezhnaya Reki Fontanki, 59, tel: 494 8060, www.wildrussia.spb.ru. Specialises in tourism to wilderness areas.

Travel agencies can send out invitations for individual visas, arrange hotel and private accommodation, and make out-of-the-way travel arrangements. They have interpreters, hire out cars with or without drivers and can organise symposiums.

In St Petersburg they arrange for theatre tickets, restaurant reservations and individually guided city and museum tours.

Tourist Information

Russian National Tourist Offices Abroad

London: 70 Piccadilly, London W1J 8HP, tel: (020) 7495 7555, www.visitrussia.org.uk
New York: 224 West 30th Street, Suite 701, New York NY 10001, tel: 877 221 7120.

Other Travel Agents
United States
Free Wind Travel, 165 Broad St, Lynn, MA 01901.
A & S Travel, 350 Fifth Ave, New York 16118.
Russian Travel Bureau Inc, 245 E. 44th St, New York, NY 10017.

United Kingdom
onthegotours.com, tel: 020-7371 1113. Cultural and adventure tours around Russia.
rus-tours.com, Package tours from $650 for a 5-night trip.
russia-tour.net, Tours to Moscow, St Petersburg and Velikiy Novgorod with full visa support.
Scotts Tours, 141 Whitfield Street, London W1T 5ER, tel: 020-7383 5353
visitrussia.com, Comprehensive and flexible tours around different Russian cities. Fully arranged, including visa support.
Voyages Jules Verne, 21 Dorset Square, London NW1 6QG, tel: 020-7616 1000

V isas

A visitor to Russia must have a valid passport and a visa. The easiest way to obtain a visa is through a travel agent. A tourist visa is valid for between 10 and 90 days and varies in price, depending on how quickly it is needed. On the visa are the date and place of arrival and departure as well as the length of the trip. Changes are possible by approaching a travel agency. It is only possible to extend a trip to St Petersburg after arrival. In order to obtain a visa, the travel agency will require a valid passport, visa application form, three

passport photographs and, if you do not have an invitation from relatives or friends *(see below)*, confirmation of hotel reservations. If you apply individually from an embassy or consulate, rather than through a travel agency, you should allow ample time, as it might take up to a month or so to check your papers.

According to the new regulations, this term can be shortened to 48 hours if an applicant is a business traveller or if he has a written invitation (telex and fax are also accepted) from a Russian host. However, it might take the Russian counterpart some time to have the invitation stamped by the local authority. If you go to Russia at the invitation of relatives or friends, you can get a visa for a private journey which presupposes that no hotel reservation is needed. Still, this process is long and cumbersome, and you'd do better to go through an agency in order to save your Russian friends the hassle of getting an official invitation from the police. Individual tourists should have their trip organised through their Russian hosts or a travel agency.

According to Russian law, everyone should carry his or her passport (Russians have an internal one) at all times. Foreigners also need to carry a visa. Some choose to carry photocopies of these in case they go missing, as indeed it is extremely difficult to replace your visa if lost or stolen. But police don't always accept photocopies as valid. Be careful of the police, especially at night, as they often swindle citizens and tourists, claiming their documents are not in order.

W ebsites

To best prepare for your trip, here are some good websites:
St Petersburg Times:
www.sptimes.ru
List of hotels: www.hotels.spb.ru
Hermitage Museum:
www.hermitagemuseum.org

Russian Museum:
www.rusmuseum.ru
Yellow Pages: www.yell.ru/eng/
City News (in Russian):
www.cityspb.ru
City portal:
http://petersburgcity.com
Russian and city history:
www.alexanderpalace.org

What to Wear

Today, St Petersburg is visited by many people who demonstrate all the caprices of fashion. Therefore the old guide book phrase, "when going to Russia, follow a modest and classic style of clothes" is outdated. You may dress as you would at home.

Visiting St Petersburg in the cold months (November to March), you should not be surprised to encounter temperatures as low as $-30°C$ ($-22°F$). Waterproof shoes are a necessity in winter, since the traditional Russian frost is not as frosty anymore and is often interrupted by periods of thaw. For business meetings formal dress is obligatory. The dress code is as rigorously enforced as in the West and compliance with it is an important matter of status.

Women Travellers

Women are much safer in Russia than in the 1990s. Still, be aware than many Russian men tend to be rude and aggressive. Be careful if walking alone late in the evening; if you are on a main street, you may be mistaken for a prostitute. Women are strongly advised not to take private cabs when alone, especially at night.

At the same time, as if proving the split nature of the Russian character, Russian men can also be chivalrous, often giving flowers, opening a car door for you, and extending a hand when going up or down stairs.

Unlike a decade ago, shops are stocked with goods to meet women's needs.

LANGUAGE

UNDERSTANDING THE LANGUAGE

Language Tips

Modern Russian has no established and universally used forms of salutation. You can address a man as *gospodin* (sir), and a woman as *gospozha* (madam). If you know the name of the father of the person you are talking to, the best and the most neutral way of addressing them is to use either *gospodin/gospozha* together with the relevant paternal name. English forms of address – Mister/Sir or Madam/Miss are also acceptable.

Transliteration

To transliterate some Russian letters, English letter combinations are used:

ж = zh, х = kh, ц = ts, ч = ch, ш =sh, щ = shch, ю = yu, я = ya, ё = yo. The Russian letter combination кс is transliterated both as *ks* and as *x* Russian letters are transliterated (with a few exceptions) in a similar way: й, ы = y, е, ё = e.

To transliterate Russian soft sign between the consonants and before no-vowel, the apostrophe is used, or the soft sign is ignored, as before vowels. The transliteration of nominal inflections has a number of peculiarities: ый, ий = y, ие, ье = ie, ия = ia.

If the traditional English spelling in names differs from their letter-by-letter transliteration they are mostly translated in their English form: Moscow (city), but river Moskva. The genetive inflections in the names of streets and other objects are translated according to their pronunciation, and not their spelling: площадь Горького, *(ploshchad' Gór'kogo)* = pl. Gorkovo in this book. The transliteration in this section shows the way to pronounce Russian words and therefore does not correspond exactly with their spelling.

The city maps and their captions use Russian words and abbreviations: ul. *(úlitsa)* means street; per. *(pereúlok)* – lane; prosp. *(prospékt)* – avenue; pl. *(plóshchad´)* – square; alléya – alley; bul'vár – boulevard; mag-istrál – main line; proézd – passage; shossé – highway; spusk – slope.

The Russian system of writing out house numbers is *prosp. Kalinina 28 (28 Kalinin Avenue).*

English/Russian

It is important when speaking Russian that you reproduce the accent (marked here before each stressed vowel with the sign ') correctly to be understood well.

Modern Russian has absorbed a considerable number of foreign words. Few tourists will be puzzled by Russian words such as *telefon, televizor, teatr, otel, restoran, kafe, taxi, metro, eroport.*

An understanding of the Russian alphabet permits one to make out the names of the streets and the shop signs.

The Alphabet

The first two columns printed below show the printed letter in Russian upper and lower case. The third column shows how the Russian letters sound and the fourth column shows the name of the letter in Russian.

А	а	**a**, archaeology **a**
Б	б	**b**, buddy **be**
В	в	**v**, vow **v**
Г	г	**g**, glad **ge**
Д	д	**d**, dot (tip of the tongue close to the teeth) **de**
Е	е	**e**, get **ye**
Ё	ё	**yo**, yoke **yo**
Ж	ж	**zh**, composure **zhe**
З	з	**z**, zest **ze**
И	и	**i**, ink **i**
Й	й	**j**, yes **jot**
К	к	**k**, kind **ka**
Л	л	**l**, life (but a bit harder) **el'**
М	м	**m**, memory **em**
Н	н	**n**, nut **en**
О	о	**o**, optimum **o**
П	п	**p**, party **pe**
Р	р	**r** (as in Italian, the tip of the tongue is vibrating) **er**

С	с	**s**, sound **es**
Т	т	**t**, title (tip of the tongue close to the teeth) **te**
У	у	**u**, nook **u**
Ф	ф	**f**, flower **ef**
Х	х	**kh**, hawk **ha**
Ц	ц	**ts**, (pronounced conjointly) **tse**
Ч	ч	**ch**, charter **che**
Ш	ш	**sh**, shy **sha**
Щ	щ	**shch**, (pronounced conjointly) **shcha**
	ъ	(the hard sign)
Ы	ы	**y** (pronounced with the same position of a tongue as when pro nouncing G, K) **y**
	ь	(the soft sign)
Э	э	**e**, ensign **e**
Ю	ю	**yu**, you **yu**
Я	я	**ya**, yard **ya**

Numbers

1	*adín*	один
2	*dva*	два
3	*tri*	три
4	*chityri*	четыре
5	*pyat'*	пят́
6	*shes't'*	шесть
7	*sem*	семь
8	*vósim*	восемь
9	*d'évit'*	девять
10	*d'ésit'*	десять
11	*adínatsat'*	одиннадцать
12	*dvinátsat'*	двенадцать
13	*trinátsat'*	тринадцать
14	*chityrnatsat'*	четырнадцать
15	*pitnátsat'*	пятнадцат́
16	*shysnátsat'*	шестнадцать
17	*simnátsat'*	семнадцать
18	*vasimnátsat'*	восемнадцать
19	*divitnátsat'*	девятнадцать
20	*dvátsat'*	двадцать
21	*dvatsat' adin*	двадцать один
30	*trítsat'*	тридцать
40	*sórak*	сорок
50	*pidisyat*	пятьдесят
60	*shyz'disyat*	шестьдесят
70	*s'émdisyat*	семьдесят
80	*vósimdisyat*	восемьдесят
90	*divinósta*	девяносто
100	*sto*	сто
200	*dv'és'ti*	двести

300	*trísta*	триста
400	*chityrista*	четыреста
500	*pitsót*	пятьсот
600	*shyssót*	шестьсот
700	*simsót*	семьсот
800	*vasimsót*	восемьсот
900	*divitsót*	девятьсот
1,000	*tysicha*	тысяча

Greetings

Hello!
zdrástvuti (neutral)
Здравствуйте!
zdrástvuj (informal)
Здравствуй!

Good afternoon/Good evening
dóbry den'/dobry véchir
Добрый день/Добрый вечер

Good morning/Good night
dobrae útra/dobraj nóchi
(Sleep well)
Доброе утро/Доброй ночи

Goodbye
dasvidán'ye (neutral)
До свиданья
paká! (informal, literally "until")
Пока!

What is your name?
kak vas (tibya) zavút?/kak váshe ímya ótchistva? (formal)
Как вас (тебя) зовут?/Как ваше имя отчество?

My name is…/I am…
minya zavut…/ya…
Меня зовут…/Я…

Good/excellent
kharashó/otlichna
хорошо/отлично

Do you speak English?
vy gavaríti pa anglíski?
Вы говорите по-английски?

I don't understand
ya ni panimáyu/ya ni pónyal
Я не понимаю/Я не понял

**Please/
Thank you (very much)**
pazhálsta/(bal'shóe) spasíba
Пожалуйста/
(бальшоэ) спасибо

Exchanging Money

I want to exchange currency
ya khachyu abmin'át' val'yutu
Я хочу обменять валюту

Do you accept credit cards?
vy prinimáiti kridítnyi kártachki?
Вы принимаете кредитные карточки ?

Do you cash traveller's cheques?
vy mózhyti razminyat' darózhnyj chek?
Вы можете разменять дорожный чек?

What is the exchange rate?
kakój kurs?
Какой курс?

Useful Words & Phrases

Where is the…?
gd'e (nakhóditsa)…?
Где находится…?

bathroom
vánnaya
ванная

bus station
aftóbusnaya stántsyja
автобусная станция

airport
airapórt
аэропорт

railway station
vakzál/stántsyja (in small towns)
вокзал/станция

post office
póchta
почта

police station
milítsyja
милиция

ticket office
bil'étnaya kássa
билетная касса

embassy/consulate
pasól'stva/kónsul'stva
посольство/консульство

Where is there a...?
gd'e z'd'es'...?
Где здесь...?

pharmacy
apt'éka
аптека

(good) hotel
(kharóshyj) atél'
(хороший) отель

Metro station
mitró
метро

public telephone
tilifón
телефон

hospital
bal'nílsa
больница

Do you have...?
u vas jes't'...?
У вас есть...?

I (don't) want...
ya (ni) khachyu...
Я (не) хочу...

I want to buy...
ya khachyu kupít'...
Я хочу купить...

Where can I buy...
gd'e ya magú kupít'...
Где я могу купить...

film
fotoplyonku
отоплёнку

a ticket for...
bilét na...
билет на...

I need...
mn'e núzhna...
Мне нужно...

I need a doctor
mn'e núzhyn dóktar
Мне нужен доктор

I need help
mn'e nuzhná pómashch'
Мне нужна помощь

Car/plane/trains/ship
mashyna/samal'yot/póist/karábl'
машина/самолёт/поезд/
корабль

Please, take me to...
pazhalsta atvizíti minya...
Пожалуйста, отвезите
меня...

Where are we?
gd'e my?
Где мы?

Stop here
astanavíti z'd'es'
Остановите здесь

Where does this bus go?
kudá id'yot état aftóbus?
Куда идёт этот автобус?

At the Hotel

I have a reservation
u minya zakázana m'esta
У меня заказана места

A single (double) room
*adnam'éstnuyu (dvukhmestnuyu)
kómnatu*
одноместную (двухместную)
комнату

I want to see the room
ya khachyu pasmatrét' nómer
Я хочу посмотреть номер

Eating Out

Waiter/menu
afitsyánt/minyu
официант/меню

I want to order...
ya khachyu zakazat'...
Я хочу заказать

Breakfast/lunch/supper
záftrak/ab'ét/úzhyn
завтрак/обед/ужин

Mineral water/juice
minirál'naya vadá/sok
минеральная вода/сок

Coffee/tea/beer
kófe/chai/píva
кофе/чай/пиво

**What do you have to drink
(alcoholic)?**
shto u vas jes't' vypit'?
Что у вас есть выпить?

Beef/pork/chicken/fish
gavyadina/svinína/kúritsa/ryba
говядина/свинина/курица/
рыба

Vegetables/rice/potatoes
óvashchi/ris/kartófil'
овощи/рис/картофель

Soup/salad/sandwich/pizza
sup/salát/butyrbrót/pitsa
суп/салат/бутерброд/пицца

The bill, please
shchyot pazhalsta
Счёт, пожалуйста

I want my change, please
zdáchu pazhalsta
Сдачу, пожалуйста

Time

What time is it?
katóryj chas?
Который час?

How long does it take?
skól'ka vrémini éta zanımáit?
Сколько времени это
занимает?

At what time?
f kakóe vrémya?
В какое время?

SHOPPING

How much does it cost?
skól'ka eta stóit?
Сколько это стоит?

That's very expensive
eta óchin' dóraga
Это очень дорого

A lot, many/A little, few
mnóga/mála
много/мало

It (doesn't) fits me
eta mn'e (ni) padkhódit
Это мне (не) подходит

Further Reading

History

Catherine the Great, by J.T. Alexander. Oxford University Press, 1989.
Stalin, Man of Contradiction, by K.N. Cameron. Strong Oak Press, 1989.
A History of the Soviet Union, by G. Hosking. Fontana/Collins, 1990.
The Blackwell Encyclopaedia of the Russian Revolution, ed. by H. Shukman. Blackwell, 1989.
St Petersburg, by Solomon Volkov, Simon & Schuster, 1995.
From Leningrad to St Petersburg, Robert Ortung, 1996.
Sunlight at Midnight, by W. Bruce Lincoln, Basic Books, 2000.

Politics

Voices of Glasnost, by S. Cohen and K. van den Heuvel. Norton, 1989.
The Other Russia, by Michael Glenny and Norman Stone. Faber & Faber, 1990.
Perestroika, by M.S. Gorbachev. Fontana, 1987.
Black Earth: a Journey Through Russia After the Fall, by Andrew Meier. Perinnial, 2004.
Putin's Russia, by Anna Poliakovskaya. Harvil Press, 2004.
Darkness at Dawn: the Rise of the Russian Criminal State, by David Satter. Yale University Press, 2004.
Against the Grain, by Boris Yeltsin. Jonathan Cape, 1990.

Biography & Memoirs

The Making of Andrei Sakharov, by G. Bailey. Insight Penguin, 1990.
Alone Together, by Elena Bonner. Collins Harvill, 1986.
An English Lady at the Court of Catherine the Great, ed. by A.G. Gross. Crest Publications, 1989.
On the Estate: Memoirs of Russia Before the Revolution, Olga Davyd-off Bax. Thames&Hudson, 1986.
Into the Whirlwind and Within a Whirlwind, by Eugenia Ginzburg. Collins Harvill, 1989.
In the Beginning, by Irina Ratushinskaya. Hodder&Stoughton, 1990.
Ten Days that Shook the World, by John Reed. Penguin, first published 1919.
The Gulag Archipelago, by Alexander Solzhenitsyn. Collins Harvill, 1988.
Russia: Despatches from the Guardian Correspondent in Moscow, by Martin Walker. Abacus, 1989.

Art

A History of Russian Painting, by A. Bird. Phaidon, 1987.
Russian Art of the Avant Garde, by J.E. Bowlt. Thames&Hudson, 1988.
New Worlds: Russian Art and Society 1900–37, by D. Elliot. Thames & Hudson, 1986.
The Kremlin and its Treasures, by Raimann. Phaidon, 1989.
Russian Art from Neoclassicism to the Avant Garde, by D.V. Sarabianov. Thames & Hudson, 1990.
Street Art of the Revolution, by V. Tolstoy, I. Bibikova and C. Cooke. Thames & Hudson, 1990.
The Art of Central Asia. Aurora Art Publishers, 1988.
Folk Art in the Soviet Union. Abrams/Aurora, 1990.
The Hermitage. Aurora, 1987.
Masterworks of Russian Painting in Soviet Museums. Aurora, 1989.

Travel, Geography & Natural History

First Russia, Then Tibet, by Robert Byron. Penguin, first published 1905.
Caucasian Journey, by Negley Farson. Penguin, first published 1951.
Sailing to St Petersburg, by Roger Foxall. Grafton, 1990.
The Natural History of the USSR, by Algirdas Kynstautas. Century Hutchinson, 1987.
Portrait of the Soviet Union, by Fitzroy McLean. Wwidenfeld and Nicolson, 1988.
Atlas of Russia and the Soviet Union, by R. Millner-Gulland with N. Dejevsky. Phaidon, 1989.
The Big Red Train, by Eric Newby. Picador, 1989.
Journey into Russia, by Laurens van der Post. Penguin, first published 1964.
Among the Russians, by Colin Thubron. Penguin, first published 1983.
Ustinov in Russia, by Peter Ustinov. Michael O'Mara Books, 1987.

Literature

The Russia House, by John le Carré. Coronet, 1990.
The Brothers Karamazov; The Idiot, by F. Dostoevsky.
Doctor Zhivago, by Boris Pasternak.
Eugene Onegin, by Pushkin.
Children of the Arbat, by A. Rybakov. Hutchinson, 1988.
And Quiet Flows the Don; The Don Flows Home to the Sea, by Mikhail Sholokov.
War and Peace; Anna Karenina, by Leo Tolstoy.

Other Insight Guides

Insight Guide Russia, Belarus and Ukraine is a recently updated edition of our largest guide to Russia and its neighbours, packed with information and great photography. Insight FlexiMap St Petersburg is a large fold-out map of the city, laminated for easy folding and durability. As well as clear cartography, it includes useful travel information and contacts.

St Petersburg Street Atlas

The key map shows the area of the city covered by the atlas
section. An index of street names and places of interest
shown on the maps can be found on the following pages.
For each entry there is a page number and grid reference.

Map Legend

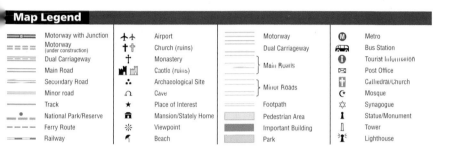

Motorway with Junction	✈	Airport		Motorway	Ⓜ Metro
Motorway (under construction)	✝	Church (ruins)		Dual Carriageway	🚌 Bus Station
Dual Carriageway	✝	Monastery		Main Roads	❶ Tourist Information
Main Road	🏰🏠	Castle (ruins)			✉ Post Office
Secondary Road	∴	Archaeological Site		Minor Roads	✞ Cathedral/Church
Minor road	∩	Cave			☾ Mosque
Track	★	Place of Interest		Footpath	✡ Synagogue
National Park/Reserve	🏛	Mansion/Stately Home		Pedestrian Area	⚥ Statue/Monument
Ferry Route	※	Viewpoint		Important Building	� Tower
Railway	⚲	Beach		Park	⚑ Lighthouse

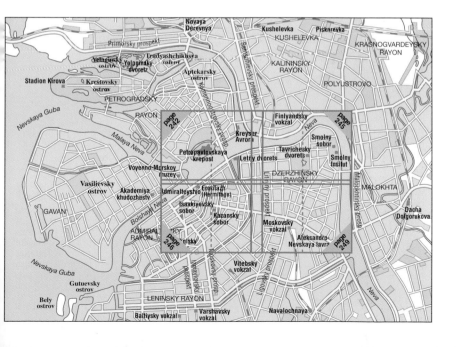

Chkalovskaya

ul. Bol. Zelenina

Oranienbaumskaya ul.

ul. Shamsheva

ul. Gatchinskaya

ul. Lenina

Muzey SM Kirova

PETROGRADSKAYA
STORONA

Bolshaya Monetnaya ul.

Kamennoostrovski pr.

Lenfilm

ul. Mira

Kolpinskaya ul.

Bolshaya Pushkarskaya

Malaya Pushkarskaya

Kropotkina

Ropsinskaya ul.

Rybakskaya ul.

Bol. Zelenina

Bol. Raznocinnaya ul.

Malyi prospekt

Bolshoy prospekt

Sablinskaya

ul. Voskova

Kronverkskaya ul.

Mal. Raznocinnaya ul.

Monchegorskaya ul.

Sytninskaya ploshchad

Sytny
rynok

A.M. Gorko
(Go

Pionerskaya ul.

Vvedenskaya

ul. Voskova

Sytninskaya ul.

Kronverksky prospekt

GORKOVSKAYA

Mal. Grebeskaya ul.

Bolshaya Pushkarskaya

Institut Tochnoy
mehaniki optiki

Markina

Teatr im.
Leninskovo
Komsomola

ALEKSANDRO
SAD

ul. Krasnovo Kurssanta

Bolshoy prospekt

Maliy prospekt

ul.

Planetary

Kronversky Kana

Blagoyeva

Tchaikinnoy Lizi

Voenno-
istoricheksy
muzey
Artillerii

Syezzhinskaya ul.

Tatarsky pereulok

Zverinskaya ul.

Kronversky Karal

Kronverkskaya

ul. Blokhina

Mytninsky per.

ZOOLOGICHESKY
SAD

Kronversky Proliv

Sportivnaya

Mytninskaya

ul. Yablochkova

Kronversky prospekt

Petropavlovky
sobor

Py

dvorets sporta
Yubileyny

pr. Dobrolyubova

Kronverkskaya naberezhnaya

Monetny dvor

Petropavlov
kr

naberezhnaya

Malaya Neva

Birzhevoy most

naberezhnaya Makarova

Volkhovsky
pereulok

Birzhevoy
pereulok

Biblioteka
Akademii nauk

Literaturny muzey
(Pushkinsky dom)

Rostralnye
kolonny

Birzhevaya
ploshchad

Ermita
teat

Tuchkov
pereulok

Birzhevaya liniya

Tiflisskaya

proezd

Voenno-Morskoy
muzey

Vasilievsky ostrov

Dvenadtsat
kollegy

Mendeleyevskaya liniya

Birzhevoy proezd

Birzhevoy

Zoologichesky
muzey

Ermitazh
(Hermitage)

Millionna

Gosudarstvenny
universitet

Kunstkamera
(Muzey Antropologii
im. Petra Velikovo)

Neva

Dvortsovaya naberezhnaya

0   400 m

0   400 yards

M.V.
Lomonosov

Akademiya
nauk

Bolshaya

D   E

Malaya
Pevchesky

Pinsky per.

Bolshaya Nevka

Sakharny pereulok

ul. Chapaeva

Bolshaya Posadskaya

Bolshaya Posadskaya ul.

Petrogradskaya naberezhnaya

Sampsonievsky
most

Pirogovskaya naberezhnaya

Orenburgskaya

Il.n eksysburh.n

Astrakhanskaya ul.

Saratovskaya ul.

S.P. Botkin

Botkinskaya
ul.

1

Pei.

Malaya Posadskaya ul.

Finlyandsky prosp.

Ya. V. Viltie

Monetnaya

Posadskaya ul.

Mchurinskaya

Bol. Sampsonievsky prosp.

Klinicheskaya ul.

Kamennoostrovsky

Mestyansky

Kronverksky prospekt

Konny pereulok

**Sobornaya
Mechet**

Penkovaya ul.

**Kreyser
Avrora**

Pirogovskaya naberezhnaya

**Muzey Politicheskoi
Istorii Rossii**

ul. Kuybysheva

**Akademiya
Nakhimova**

2

**Troitskaya
ploshchad**

prospekt

**Muzey
domik Petra I**

Petrovskaya naberezhnaya

**Ioannovsky
vorota**

Neva

Litevny most

naberezhnaya Kutuzova

**Dom pisatelya
im. Mayakovskovo**

ul.

3

Troitsky most

naberezhnaya Kutuzova

ul. Shpalernaya

naberezhnaya Reki Fontanki

ul. Gagarina

Litevny prospekt

**Letny dvorets-
muzey Petra I**

**I.A.
Krylov**

**Institut Kultury
im. Krupskoy**

ul.

Tchaikovskovo

naberezhnaya

**A.V.
Suvorov**

Millionnaya ul.

Fontanka

Oruzheynike Fedorova ul.

Mokhovaya
ul.

**Mramorny
dvorets**

LETNY SAD

Gangutskaya ul.

ul. Gagarina

Litevny prospekt

vortsovaya

**MARSOVO
POLO**

naberezhnaya Lebyazhyevo kanala

Solyanoy pereulok

**Muzey
Gangutsky**

Aptekarsky pereulok

**Bortsam
revolutsii**

Lebyazhy kanal

**Panteleymonskaya
tserkov**

Pestelya ul.

4

naya

Reki Moika

Pestelya ul.

Mokhovaya

Litevny prospekt

Korolenko ul.

naberezhnaya

Naberezhnaya Reki Moika

Pestelya ul.

nab. Reki Fontanki

**Muzey-kvartira
Pushkina**

Naberezhnaya Reki Moika

Moika

nab. Reki Fontank

**Institut teatra,
muziki i
kinematografii**

ovaya
lla im.
inki

**MIKHAILOVSKY
SAD**

**Mikhailovsky
zamok**

Mokhovaya

**Uchebny
teatr**

**Khram
Spas-na-krovi**

D   E

VYBORGSKAY STORONA

A

B

S.P. Botkin

Botkinskaya ul.

Lesnoy prospekt

Akademika Lebedeva

1

Botkinskaya ul.

Ya. V. Villie

Finskiy pereulok

Klinicheskaya ul.

ul. Komsomola

Akademika Lebedeva

Finlyandsky vokzal

Dom Kultury Progress

M.V. Frunze

Arsenalnaya ul.

Kondraty

A Kon.

PL. LENINA

ul.

Mikhaylova

ul. Komsomola

Klinicheskaya bolnitsa

ploshchad Lenina

Lenin

ul. Komsomola

Pirogovskaya nabr.

2

Arsenalnaya naberezhnaya

St Petersburg kontsertny zal

Mikhaylova ul.

Kresty (Kresty Prison)

Arsenalnaya naberezhnaya

Liteyny most

Neva

naberezhnaya Robespyera

naberezhnaya Robespyera

nab. Kutuzova

Shpalernaya ul.

Shpalernaya ul.

Liteyny prospekt

prospekt

3

Dom pisatelya im. Mayakovskovo

Zakharyevskaya ul.

Zakharyevskaya ul.

Tavrichesky dvorets

ul. Tchaikovskovo

ul. Tchaikovskovo

Chernyshevskovo

Potemkinskaya

Y geroyam ob

Furshtadtskaya ul.

Furshtadtskaya ul.

TAVRICHESKY SAD

Mokhovaya ul.

Liteyny prospekt

Kirochnaya ul.

CHERNYSHEVSKAYA

Kirochnaya ul.

Kirochna

Spaso-Preobrazhensky sobor

ploshchad Preobrazhenskaya

Manezhny pereulok

ul. Vosstaniya

4

Pestelya ul.

ul. Ryleyeva

ul.

Ryleyeva

Radishcheva ul.

Paradnaya ul.

Korolenko ul.

Artilleriyskaya ul.

Grodnensky pereulok

Saperny pereulok

Krasnoy Svyazi

Kirochna

0 ____ 400 m

0 ____ 400 yards

A

B

D

E

bul. Vaulina

Sverdlovskaya naberezhnaya

Feodosiyskaya ul.

Gorodskaya
bolnitsa

Piskarevsky
prospekt

1

Neva

Smolnaya naberezhnaya

lovskaya naberezhnaya

Orlovskaya ul.

bespyera

Smolnaya naberezhnaya

Urlovskaya ul.

Smolnaya naberezhnaya

2

Smolnovo ul.

Stavropolskaya

Orlovskaya

ul.

Tavricheskaya ul.

Tavricheskiy
pereulok

Chesmenskaya ul.

Diktatury ul.

Smolnovo ul.

Smolny
monastyr

Smolny
sobor

F.E. Dzerzinskom

ploshchad
Rastrelli

Shpalernaya ul.

Kontserlno-Vystavochny
kompleks

Stavropolskaya

Kavalergardskaya

pereulok

Kvarengi

SAD
SMOLNOVO

3

Tverskaya ul.

ploshchad
Proletarskoy
Diktatury

F. Èngels

Smolny

Tverskaya ul.

Kaluzhsky pereulok

Odesskaya ul.

Tverskaya ul.

Smolnovo alleya

V.I. Lenin

Smolny
Insitut

Ochakovskaya ul.

Karl
Marks

Proletarskoy

ul.

Muzey-kvartira
Kozlova

Smolny
proyezd

proezd

Suvorovsky prospekt

Tulskaya ul.

Smolny prospekt

Martinisky

Kavalergardskaya

Bonch-Buev ul.

emorialny muzey
V. Suvorova

Tulskaya ul.

most Petra Velikova

Sinopskaya naberezhnaya

Sverdlovskaya nab.

4

Tavricheskaya ul.

Suvorovsky prospekt

Yaroslavskaya

Bolnitsa

Krasnovo-Tekstilshika

Maloohktinsky
prospekt

Kirochnaya ul.

Novgorodskaya

D

E

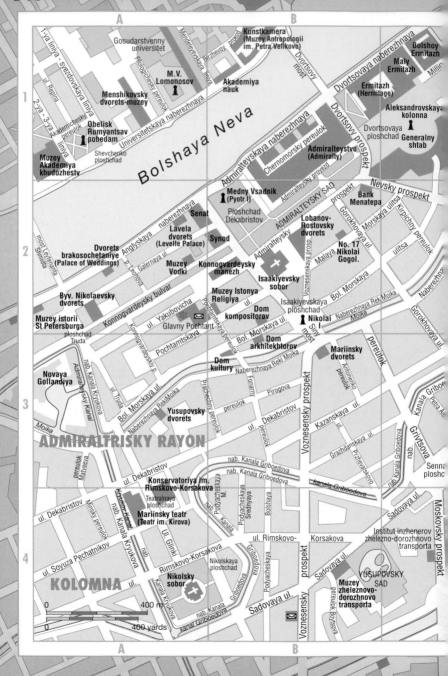

A · B

1
2
3
4

1-ya liniya - sredlovskaya liniya

ul. Repina

2-ya · 3-ya liniya

Akademichesky pereulok

Filologichesky pereulok

Mendeleyevskaya liniya

Birzhevoy proezd

Gosudarstvenny universitet

Kunstkamera (Muzey Antropologii im. Petra Velikovo)

M.V. Lomonosov

Akademiya nauk

Menshikovsky dvorets-muzey

Obelisk Rumyantsav pobedam

Universitetskaya naberezhnaya

Shevchenko ploshchad

Muzey Akademiya khudozhesty

Bolshaya Neva

Dvortsovy most

Dvortsovaya naberezhnaya

Admiralteyskaya naberezhnaya

Chernomorsky pereulok

Dvortsovy prospekt

Ermitazh (Hermitage)

Bolshoy Ermitazh

Maly Ermitazh

Milli

Aleksandrovskaya kolonna

Dvortsovaya ploshchad

Generalny shtab

Admiralteystvo (Admiralty)

Admiralteysky proezd

Nevsky prospekt

naberezhnaya

Angliyskaya

Senat

Lavela dvorets (Levelle Palace)

Synod

Medny Vsadnik (Pyotr I)

Ploshchad Dekabristov

ADMIRALTEYSKY SAD

prospekt

Admiralteysky

Lobanov-Rostovsky dvorets

Gorokhovaya ul.

Morskaya ulitsa

Kirpichny pereulok

Bank Menatepa

ulitsa

No. 17 Nikolai Gogol.

Voznesensky prosp.

Malaya

Isaakiyevsky sobor

Bol. Morskaya.

d. Lednova

d. Galernaya

Dvorets brakosochetaniye (Palace of Weddings)

Muzey Vodki

Konnogvardeysky manezh

Muzey Istonya Religiya

Isaakiyevskaya ploshchad

Naberezhnaya

Naberezhnaya Rek Moika

Gorokhovaya ul.

Naberezhn

Byv. Nikolaevsky dvorets

Muzey istorii St Petersburga

ploshchad Truda

Konnogvardeysky bulvar

Konnogvardeysky p.

ul. Yakubovicha

Pochtamtskaya ul.

Pochtamtskaya ul.

Glavny Pochtamt

Pochtamtskaya

Dom kompozitorov

Nikolai I

Moika

Dom arkhitektorov

Siny most

pereulok

Mariinsky dvorets

Novaya Gollandiya

Admiralteysky Kanal

Moika

ul. Truda

Bol. Morskaya ul.

Naberezhnaya ReKMoika

Pochtamtsky pereulok

Pirogova

ul. Dekabristov

Dom kultury

Naberezhnaya Reki Moika

Glinki

pereulok

Kazanskaya ul.

Grazhdanskaya ul.

Przhevalskovo

Antonenko pereulok

Kanala Gribo

Grivtsova

Petra Ale

ADMIRALTEYSKY RAYON

pereulok Matveeva

Yusupovsky dvorets

nab. Kanala Griboedova

Voznesensky prospekt

Kanala Gribo

nab

Senna ploshc

ul. Dekabristov

Kryukov Kanal

nab. Kanala Kryukova

Minsky pereulok

Konservatoriya im. Rimskovo-Korsakova

Teatralnaya ploshchad

Mariinsky teatr (Teatr im. Kirova)

nab. Kanala Griboedova

Podyacheskaya M.

Podyacheskaya Srednyaya

Bolshaya

Kanala Griboedova

ul. Rimskovo-Korsakova

Sadovaya ul.

Moskovsky prospekt

Institut inzhenerov zhelezno-dorozhnovo transporta

KOLOMNA

ul. Soyuza Pechatnikov

ul. Dekabristov

Rimskovo-Korsakova

Nikolsky sobor

Nikolskaya ploshchad

Kanala Kryukova

nab. Kanala Kryukova

kanal Griboedova

Sadovaya ul.

Podyacheskaya Bolshaya

Voznesensky prospekt

Sadovaya ul.

YUSUPOVSKY SAD

Muzey zhelezno-dorozhnovo transporta

pereulok Bolsha

0 ———— 400 m
0 ———— 400 yards

A · B

SENTRALNY RAYON

Muzey-kvartira Pushkina

Naberezhnaya Reki Moika
Moika

Pestelya ul.

MIKHAILOVSKY SAD

Mikhailovsky zamok

Uchebny teatr

Institut teatra, muziki i kinematografii

Mokhovaya ul.

Korolenko ul.

Khram Spas-na-krovi (Church of the Saviour on the Spilled Blood)

Zamkovaya ul.

Sadovaya ul.

naberezhnaya Reki Fontanki

Fontanka

Pyotr I

Simeonievskaya tserkov

Liteyny prospekt

Russky muzey

Tsirk

Klenovaya ul.

Shvedsky pereulok

Bol. Konyushennaya

nab. Kanala Griboedova

Kanala Griboedova

Mussorgsky teatr

Muzey ètnografii

Inzhenernaya ul.

Inzhenernaya

A.S. Pushkina

Teatr na Liteyny

ul. Belinskovo

naberezhnaya Reki Fontanki

Muzey Akmatovov

Bol. Konyushennaya

Ploshchad Iskusstv

Teatr muzykalnoy komedii

Zimny stadion

Manezhnaya ploshchad

Dvorets Sheremetyevykh

Philarmoniya

Italianskaya

NEVSKY PROSP.

Mikhailovskaya ul.

Armyanskaya tserkov

Paoooozh

Muzey zdravookhraneniya

Dom Druzhby i Mira

Kazansky sobor

Teatr kokol-marionetok

Karavannaya

Skulpturniye gruppy na Anichkovom mostu

Kazanskaya ploshchad

pereulok Tyulenina

GOSTINY DVOR

Rossiskaya Natsionalnaya Biblioteka

Anichkov most

Dom Zhurnalista

Beloselsky-Belozersky dvorets

Liteyny prospekt

Dumskaya ul.

Gostiny dvor

pereulok Krylova

Yekaterine Velikoi

Kabinet

Anichkov dvorets

ul. Lomonosova

Sadovaya ul.

Ploshchad Ostrovskovo

Bibl. im. Mayakovskovo

Teatr dramy im. Pushkina

Bankovsky per.

Moskatelny per.

Muchnoy pereulok

Vorontsovsky dvorets

ul. Zodchevo Rossi

Teatralny muzey

naberezhnaya Reki Fontanki

Fontanka

naberezhnaya Reki Fontanki

Grafsky

Teatr im. Lensoveta

Dimrrovsky pereulok

Vladimirsky prospekt

Apraksin dvor

ul. Lomonosova

Ploshchad Lomonosova

M.V. Lomonosov

Shcherbakov pereulok

Maliy dramatichesky teatr

Teatr Narodn. tvorchestva

Vladimirskaya Sobor

Apraksin pereulok

Torgovy pereulok

Vorontsovsky dvorets

Vladimirskaya ploshchad

DOSTOEVSKAYA

Kuznechny rynok

AYA PL.

SADOVAYA

Teatr im. Gorkovo

naberezhnaya Reki Fontanki

ul. Lomonosova

ul. Rubinshteyna

Zagorodny prospekt

VLADIMIRSKAYA

Bolsh. Moskovskaya

Razyezzhaya ul.

pereulok Svechnoy

Dostoyevskovo ul.

Gorokhovaya ul.

Borodinskaya ul.

Dzhambula

Muzey-kvartira Rimskovo-Korsakovo

Sotsialisticheskaya ul.

ul. Pravdy

Sotsialisticheskaya

Dostoyevskovo

ul. Marata

Borovaya

naberezhnaya Reki Fontanki

Fontanka

nab. Vedenskovo Kanala

Kazachy pereulok

Muzey Revolutsionno dvizheniya

Gorokhovaya ul.

Zagorodny prospekt

Zvenigorodskaya ul.

A.S. Griboedov

ul. Pravdy

A   B

Artilleriyskaya ul.

Grodnensky pereulok

ul. Mokhovaya

Liteyny prospekt

Korolenko ul.

Saperny   pereulok

Institut teatra, muziki i kinematografii

ul.

Radishcheva ul.

Krasnoy Svyazi

1

Muzey-kvartira Nekrasova

Bolsoy teatr kukol

Baskov

pereulok

Fontannaya ul.

Maltsevsky rynok

Paradnaya ul.

9 Sovetskaya ul.

ul. Nekrasova

ul. Nekrasova

ul. Nekrasova

8 Sovetskaya ul.

Simeonievskaya tserkov

V.V. Mayakovskomy

Ozernoy pereulok

N.A. Nekrasov

7 Sovetskaya ul.

Suvorovsky prospekt

ul. Belinskovo

Chekhova ul.

Mayakovskovo ul.

Vosstaniya

Ligovsky prospekt

pereulok

6 Sov

Teatr na Liteyny

Kovensky

Radishcheva ul.

6 Sovetskaya ul.

5 Sove

Muzey Akhmatovoy

Kostel

Kontsertny zal Oktyabrsky

Grechesky prospekt

5 Sovetskaya ul.

5 Sov

Dvorets Sheremetyevykh

ul. Zhukovskovo

ul. Zhukovskovo

4 Sovetskaya ul.

4 Sov

Gorodskaya Bolnitsa

Bolnitsa im. Rauhfusa

3 Sovetskaya ul.

2

Liteyny prospekt

ul. Mayakovskovo

ul. Vosstaniya

Ulyany Gromovoy pereulok

Orlovsky pereulok

Suvorovsky prospekt

3 Sovetskaya ul.

4 Sov

Dom Zhurnalista

Muzey Okyabrskoy zheleznoy dorogi

2 Sovetskaya ul.

3 Sovetskaya ul.

Degtyarnaya ul.

Dom Akterov

1 Sovetskaya ul.

2 Sovetskaya ul.

Beloselsky-Belozersky dvorets

Nevsky prospekt

PL. VOSSTANIYA

Ligovsky prospekt

Ploshchad Vosstaniya

N

Nevsky prospekt

MAYAKOVSKAYA M

Vladimirsky prospekt

Rubinshteyna ul.

Stremyannaya ul.

ul. Marata

Pushkinskaya ul.

Goncharnaya ul.

Poltavsky

Poltavskaya ul.

3

Teatr im. Lensoveta

Dimitrovsky pereulok

Povarskoy pereulok

Nevskie Bani

PL. VOSSTANIYA

M Moskovsky vokzal

Maly dramaticheshy teatr

Kolokolnaya ul.

Muzey Arktiki i Antarktiki

Ligovsky prospekt

Kharkovskaya Telezhnaya

Vladimirskaya ploshchad

M DOSTOEVSKAYA

Vladimirskaya sobor

Kuznechny rynok

VLADIMIRSKAYA

Muzey Dostoevskovo

Kuznechny pereulok

Kolomenskaya ul.

Mirgorodskaya

Kremenchugskaya ul.

Bolsh. Moskovskaya ul.

Dostoyevskogo ul.

ul. Marata

pereulok Svechnoy

4

Razyezzhaya ul.

Dostoevskovo ul.

Kolomenskaya ul.

Ligovsky prospekt

0   400 m

0   400 yards

LIGOVSKY PROSPEKT

M

A   B

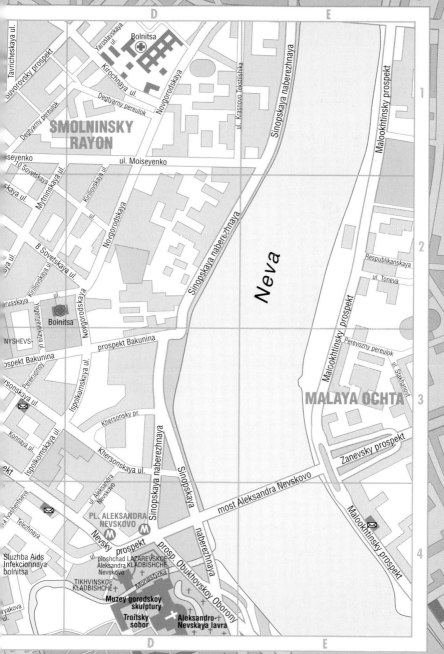

D

E

Tavricheskaya ul.

Suvorovsky prospekt

Yaroslavskaya ul.

Bolnitsa

Kirochnaya ul.

Novgorodskaya

ul. Krasnovo Tekstilshika

Sinopskaya naberezhnaya

Malookhtinsky prospekt

Degtyarny pereulok

1

Degtyarny pereulok

SMOLNINSKY RAYON

-seyenko

10 Sovetskaya ul.

ul. Moiseyenko

Krilovskaya ul.

Mytninskaya ul.

-skaya ul.

8 Sovetskaya ul.

Novgorodskaya

Sinopskaya naberezhnaya

Neva

Respublikanskaya

ul. Toneva

2

ul.

Krilovskaya ul.

-russkaya

Bolnitsa

Yegorovskaya ul.

Novgorodskaya

Malookhtinsky prospekt

Perevozny pereulok

ul. Stakhanovi

NYSHEVS-

prospekt Bakunina

MALAYA OCHTA

3

-spekt Bakunina

Ispolkomskaya ul.

Pereulor

Khersonsky pr.

-sonskaya ul.

Khersonskaya ul.

Zanevsky prospekt

Konnaya ul.

Ispolkomskaya ul.

Khersonskaya ul.

-ekt

Sinopskaya naberezhnaya

Sinopskaya

most Aleksandra Nevskovo

Malookhtinsky prospekt

ul. Aleksandra Nevskovo

d Kvasheniseva

Telezhnaya

PL. ALEKSANDRA NEVSKOVO

Ⓜ

Ⓜ

Nevsky prospekt

naberezhnaya

4

Sluzhba Aids Infekcionnaya bolnitsa

ul.

ploshchad Aleksandra Nevskovo

prosp. Obukhovskoy Oborony

LAZAREVSKOE KLADBISHCHE

TIKHVINSKOE KLADBISHCHE

Monastyrka

-yakova ul.

Muzey gorodskoy skulptury

Troitsky sobor

Aleksandro-Nevskaya lavra

D

E

STREET INDEX

ART & PHOTO CREDITS

PICTURE SPREADS

Map Production: James Macdonald, Maria Randell, Laura Morris and Stephen Ramsay
©2006 Apa Publications GmbH & Co. Verlag KG, Singapore Branch

GENERAL INDEX

St Petersburg Metro

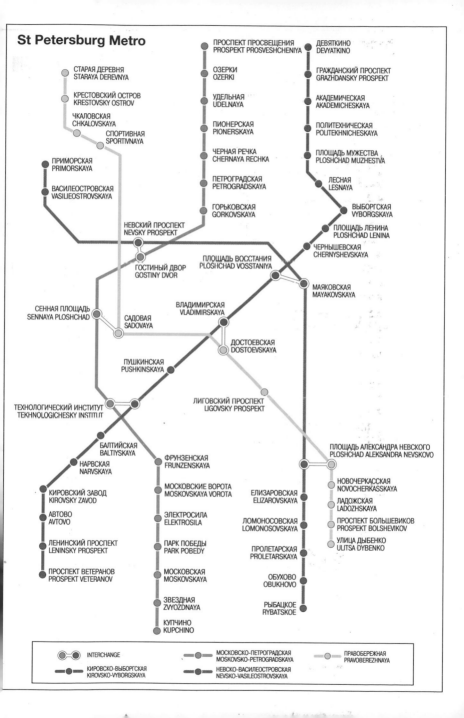

ПРОСПЕКТ ПРОСВЕЩЕНИЯ
PROSPECT PROSVESHCHENIYA

ДЕВЯТКИНО
DEVYATKINO

СТАРАЯ ДЕРЕВНЯ
STARAYA DEREVNYA

ОЗЕРКИ
OZERKI

ГРАЖДАНСКИЙ ПРОСПЕКТ
GRAZHDANSKY PROSPEKT

КРЕСТОВСКИЙ ОСТРОВ
KRESTOVSKY OSTROV

УДЕЛЬНАЯ
UDELNAYA

АКАДЕМИЧЕСКАЯ
AKADEMICHESKAYA

ЧКАЛОВСКАЯ
CHKALOVSKAYA

ПИОНЕРСКАЯ
PIONERSKAYA

ПОЛИТЕХНИЧЕСКАЯ
POLITEKHNICHESKAYA

СПОРТИВНАЯ
SPORTIVNAYA

ЧЕРНАЯ РЕЧКА
CHERNAYA RECHKA

ПЛОЩАДЬ МУЖЕСТВА
PLOSHCHAD MUZHESTVA

ПРИМОРСКАЯ
PRIMORSKAYA

ПЕТРОГРАДСКАЯ
PETROGRADSKAYA

ЛЕСНАЯ
LESNAYA

ВАСИЛЕОСТРОВСКАЯ
VASILIEOSTROVSKAYA

ГОРЬКОВСКАЯ
GORKOVSKAYA

ВЫБОРГСКАЯ
VYBORGSKAYA

НЕВСКИЙ ПРОСПЕКТ
NEVSKY PROSPEKT

ПЛОЩАДЬ ЛЕНИНА
PLOSHCHAD LENINA

ЧЕРНЫШЕВСКАЯ
CHERNYSHEVSKAYA

ГОСТИНЫЙ ДВОР
GOSTINY DVOR

ПЛОЩАДЬ ВОССТАНИЯ
PLOSHCHAD VOSSTANIYA

МАЯКОВСКАЯ
MAYAKOVSKAYA

СЕННАЯ ПЛОЩАДЬ
SENNAYA PLOSHCHAD

ВЛАДИМИРСКАЯ
VLADIMIRSKAYA

САДОВАЯ
SADOVAYA

ДОСТОЕВСКАЯ
DOSTOEVSKAYA

ПУШКИНСКАЯ
PUSHKINSKAYA

ЛИГОВСКИЙ ПРОСПЕКТ
LIGOVSKY PROSPEKT

ТЕХНОЛОГИЧЕСКИЙ ИНСТИТУТ
TEKHNOLOGICHESKY INSTITUT

ПЛОЩАДЬ АЛЕКСАНДРА НЕВСКОГО
PLOSHCHAD ALEKSANDRA NEVSKOVO

БАЛТИЙСКАЯ
BALTIYSKAYA

ФРУНЗЕНСКАЯ
FRUNZENSKAYA

НОВОЧЕРКАССКАЯ
NOVOCHERKASSKAYA

НАРВСКАЯ
NARVSKAYA

МОСКОВСКИЕ ВОРОТА
MOSKOVSKAYA VOROTA

ЕЛИЗАРОВСКАЯ
ELIZAROVSKAYA

ЛАДОЖСКАЯ
LADOZHSKAYA

КИРОВСКИЙ ЗАВОД
KIROVSKY ZAVOD

ЭЛЕКТРОСИЛА
ELEKTROSILA

ЛОМОНОСОВСКАЯ
LOMONOSOVSKAYA

ПРОСПЕКТ БОЛЬШЕВИКОВ
PROSPEKT BOLSHEVIKOV

АВТОВО
AVTOVO

ПАРК ПОБЕДЫ
PARK POBEDY

ПРОЛЕТАРСКАЯ
PROLETARSKAYA

УЛИЦА ДЫБЕНКО
ULTSA DYBENKO

ЛЕНИНСКИЙ ПРОСПЕКТ
LENINSKY PROSPEKT

МОСКОВСКАЯ
MOSKOVSKAYA

ПРОСПЕКТ ВЕТЕРАНОВ
PROSPEKT VETERANOV

ОБУХОВО
OBUKHOVO

ЗВЕЗДНАЯ
ZVYOZDNAYA

РЫБАЦКОЕ
RYBATSKOE

КУПЧИНО
KUPCHINO

INTERCHANGE

МОСКОВСКО-ПЕТРОГРАДСКАЯ
MOSKOVSKO-PETROGRADSKAYA

ПРАВОБЕРЕЖНАЯ
PRAVOBEREZHNAYA

КИРОВСКО-ВЫБОРГСКАЯ
KIROVSKO-VYBORGSKAYA

НЕВСКО-ВАСИЛЕОСТРОВСКАЯ
NEVSKO-VASILEOSTROVSKAYA

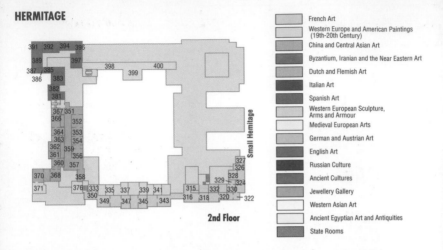
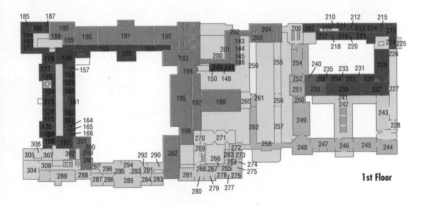
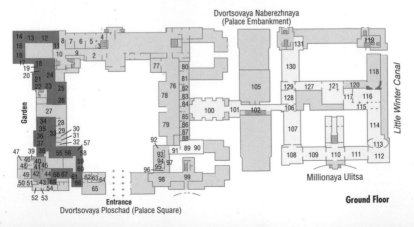